Clarence Streit and Twentieth-Century American Internationalism

In this illuminating and comprehensive account, Talbot C. Imlay chronicles the life of Clarence Streit and his Atlantic federal union movement in the United States during and following World War II. The first book to detail Streit's life, work, and significance, it reveals the importance of public political cultures in shaping US foreign relations. In 1939, Streit published *Union Now*, which proposed a federation of the North Atlantic democracies modeled on the US Constitution. The buzz created led Streit to leave his position at *The New York Times* and devote himself to promoting the union. Over the next quarter of a century, Streit worked to promote a new public political culture, employing a variety of strategies to gain visibility and political legitimacy for his project and for federalist frameworks. In doing so, Streit helped to shape wartime debates on the nature of the postwar international order and of transatlantic relations.

Talbot C. Imlay is Professor of History at Université Laval in Québec, specializing in modern European and international history. He is the author of several books, including *The Practice of Socialist Internationalism: European Socialists and International Politics, 1914–1960* and, with Martin Horn, *The Politics of Industrial Collaboration during World War II: Ford France, Vichy and Nazi Germany*.

Cambridge Studies in US Foreign Relations

Edited by

Paul Thomas Chamberlin,
Columbia University

Lien-Hang T. Nguyen,
Columbia University

This series showcases cutting-edge scholarship in US foreign relations that employs dynamic new methodological approaches and archives from the colonial era to the present. The series will be guided by the ethos of transnationalism, focusing on the history of American foreign relations in a global context rather than privileging the US as the dominant actor on the world stage.

Clarence Streit and Twentieth-Century American Internationalism

TALBOT C. IMLAY

Laval University

CAMBRIDGE
UNIVERSITY PRESS

Shaftesbury Road, Cambridge CB2 8EA, United Kingdom

One Liberty Plaza, 20th Floor, New York, NY 10006, USA

477 Williamstown Road, Port Melbourne, VIC 3207, Australia

314–321, 3rd Floor, Plot 3, Splendor Forum, Jasola District Centre,
New Delhi – 110025, India

103 Penang Road, #05–06/07, Visioncrest Commercial, Singapore 238467

Cambridge University Press is part of Cambridge University Press & Assessment,
a department of the University of Cambridge.

We share the University's mission to contribute to society through the pursuit of
education, learning and research at the highest international levels of excellence.

www.cambridge.org
Information on this title: www.cambridge.org/9781009298988

DOI: 10.1017/9781009299022

First published 2023

A catalogue record for this publication is available from the British Library.

Library of Congress Cataloging-in-Publication Data
NAMES: Imlay, Talbot C., author.
TITLE: Clarence Streit and twentieth-century American internationalism / Talbot C. Imlay.
DESCRIPTION: Cambridge, United Kingdom ; New York : Cambridge University Press,
2023. | Series: Cambridge studies in US foreign relations | Includes index.
IDENTIFIERS: LCCN 2022045599 (print) | LCCN 2022045600 (ebook) |
ISBN 9781009298988 (hardback) | ISBN 9781009298971 (paperback) |
ISBN 9781009299022 (epub)
SUBJECTS: LCSH: International organization. | Streit, Clarence K. (Clarence Kirshman),
1896–1986–Influence. | United States–Foreign relations–20th century. |
Internationalism–History–20th century.
CLASSIFICATION: LCC JX1954 .I45 2023 (print) | LCC JX1954 (ebook) |
DDC 327.1/7–dc23/eng/20221122
LC record available at https://lccn.loc.gov/2022045599
LC ebook record available at https://lccn.loc.gov/2022045600

ISBN 978-1-009-29898-8 Hardback

Contents

Acknowledgments

This book began many years ago as a paper for a graduate student workshop. After the presentation, Zara Steiner gently scolded me for not taking more seriously Streit and his project for an Atlantic federal union. As an undergraduate in the United States at the time, Steiner had been a Streit enthusiast, as were many of her fellow students. She convinced me that there was more to Streit than I thought. After finishing my PhD, I considered working on Streit but ended up pursuing other projects. But Streit lurked in the back of my mind and, when working in an archive or library, I would look to see if there was any relevant material. Over the years, I've accumulated an odd collection of tidbits and potential lines of research, which in time began to feel like a reproach. And so I finally decided to write a book on Streit.

An Insight Development grant from the Social Sciences and Humanities Research Council of Canada provided indispensable financial support. An earlier grant from the Association to Unite the Democracies funded an exploratory research trip to Washington, DC. In addition to financial support, I am extremely grateful to the many archivists and librarians for their help and their helpfulness. A special thanks is due to the Université Laval's interuniversity library loan staff, who speedily and efficiently processed my numerous requests. As university library budgets come under increasing strain, they provide a precious service.

As an outsider to US history, I sometimes felt very much alone in researching and writing this book, a sense of isolation reinforced by the realities of the COVID-19 pandemic. For this reason, I am all the more thankful for the support of friends and colleagues in Québec and beyond. At the risk of omitting someone, they are Andrew Barros, Peter Carroll,

Aline Charles, Christel Freu, Donald Fyson, Martin Horn, Andrew Johnstone, Paul Miller-Melamed, Arthur Ripoll, Jennifer Siegel, Eva Struhal, and Jean-Michel Turcotte. Two friends merit special mention for their willingness to discuss my project: Peter Jackson, whom I have known since our Paris days as research students and who regularly offers much-needed confidence; and Pierre-Yves Saunier, who, since his arrival at the Université Laval in 2013, has contributed so much to enlivening our department and whose departure is a personal as well as professional loss. Feedback from Charles Maier and Anne Sa'adah proved especially helpful at the beginning of the project. I would like to thank Cecelia Cancellaro for her enthusiastic interest in the book project, as well as the anonymous reviewers for Cambridge University Press, whose comments and suggestions allowed me to strengthen the manuscript.

Last but certainly not least, I would like to thank my family. My parents, Camille and Robert Imlay, have been unfailingly supportive, as have my two brothers, Pierre and Patrick, and their families. My own children, Alicia Kate and Julian, have provided immeasurable joy and wonder, as well as occasional bewilderment. As always, my greatest debt is to Alexandra who makes possible so much of what I do and who I am. I dedicate this book to her.

Abbreviations

ALPL	Abraham Lincoln Presidential Library
AP	Associated Press
ASIL	American Society of International Law
AUC	Atlantic Union Committee
AUWG	Americans United for World Government
AUWO	Americans United for World Organization
BHLUM	University of Michigan, Bentley Historical Library
BLCU	Columbia University, Butler Library
BLPES	British Library of Political and Economic Science
BSHU	Harvard Business School, Special Collections
CEIP	Carnegie Endowment for International Peace
CEIP (NY and Wash)	Carnegie Endowment for International Peace. New York and Washington Office Records, 1910–54
CFWG (CO)	Campaign for World Government. Records of the Chicago Office
CFWG (NY)	Campaign for World Government. Records of the New York Office
CKS	Clarence Kirschman Streit Papers
CLA	Center for Legislative Archives
CSOP	Commission to Study the Organization of the Peace
DUAM	Dartmouth University, Archives and Manuscripts
EDC	European Defense Community
EPL	Eisenhower Presidential Library
FLPU	Princeton University, Firestone Library
FPA	Foreign Policy Association
FU	Federal Union

HLSL	Harvard Law School Library, Historical and Special Collections
HTPL	Harry S. Truman Presidential Library
HUHL	Harvard University, Houghton Library
IMAU	International Movement for Atlantic Union
LAC	Library and Archives Canada
LLUI	University of Indiana, Lilly Library
LNA	League of Nations Association
LOC	Library of Congress
LONA	League of Nations Archive
NATO	North Atlantic Treaty Organization
NYHS	New York Historical Society
NYPL	New York Public Library
NYT	*New York Times*
NYTCR	New York Times Company Records
PUFL	Princeton University, Firestone Library
RAC	Rockefeller Archive Center
SCFHL	Swarthmore College, Friends Historical Library
SCRCGWU	George Washington University, Special Collections Research Center
SMLPU	Seely G. Mudd Manuscript Library, Princeton University
UCASC	University of Connecticut, Archives and Special Collections
UIL	University of Iowa Libraries
UM	University of Montana, Mansfield Library, Archives and Special Collections
UNO	United Nations Organization
UOC	University of Chicago, Hanno Holborn Gray Special Collections Research Center
UOO	University of Oregon, University Archives
UOP	University of Pennsylvania, University Archives and Records Center
UOT	University of Tennessee, Betsey B. Creekmore Special Collections and University Archives
UP	United Press
UPITT	Adolph William Schmidt Collection
UWF	United World Federalists
WCASC	Williams College, Archives and Special Collections
YUL	Yale University Library, Manuscripts and Archives

Introduction

On a warm Washington, DC evening in mid-May 1979, a reception got underway in the speakers' dining room in the Capitol building. Cohosted by Paul Findley, a Republican representative from Illinois, and Jim Wright, a Texas Democrat and the House Majority leader, and chaired by Tip O'Neill, the House speaker from Massachusetts, the reception celebrated Clarence Streit, described as the "founder of the Atlantic Union movement and author of 'Union Now.'" Successive speakers affectionately recalled Streit's four decades of dedication, in Findley's words, to the cause of "greater unity among the nations which prize individual liberty." Wright bestowed on the guest of honor an award named after Estes Kefauver, the deceased senator from Tennessee, former vice-presidential candidate, and Streit's political ally during the 1950s. Other tokens of admiration included a card signed by almost 200 well-wishers, as well as a book of "congratulatory messages" with entries from former presidents Nixon and Ford, among other political luminaries. Accompanied by Jeanne, his wife and collaborator of over five decades, Streit characteristically urged the attendees to continue the couple's work. His appeal, though, did little to dent the pervasive sense of nostalgia, of bygone times, and vanishing possibilities. Afterward, Streit quickly faded from view, his death in 1986 at the age of ninety marked by perfunctory obituaries.[1] Today, he is all but forgotten.

---

[1] *Congressional Record*, House, May 21, 1979, 12032. For obituaries, see C. K. Streit, "Advocate of Democracies Union," *New York Times*, July 9, 1986, 27; and Clarence Streit, "Advocate of Global Union, Dies," *Washington Post*, July 8, 1986.

Yet not so long ago, as the reception in the speakers' dining room indicates, Streit was a well-known political figure in the United States. The *New York Times*' correspondent in Geneva covering the League of Nations during the 1930s, Streit shot to prominence in 1939 with the publication of *Union Now: A Proposal for a Federal Union of the Democracies of the North Atlantic*. The book contained a remarkable proposition: that the United States seize the initiative in creating a federation of the Atlantic democracies modeled on the US Constitution. The American federal system, devised in the 1780s for a union of the former thirteen colonies, would now be super-imposed on the transatlantic world, encompassing the United States, Canada, the countries of Western and Northern Europe, and Great Britain (and possibly the British Commonwealth). Against all expectations, except Streit's, *Union Now* attracted considerable attention, going through multiple editions and inspiring reams of commentary. Henry Luce's now-iconic 1941 editorial in *Life* magazine, "The American Century," provides one sign of its visibility. "[N]o thoughtful American has done his duty to the United States of America," the media mogul asserted, "until he has read and pondered Clarence Streit's book ..."[2]

The publication of *Union Now* was just the beginning. Convinced that Atlantic federal union held the key to US foreign relations, Streit quit the *New York Times* to devote himself to promoting the project, a crusade he would doggedly pursue over the next four decades. In the process, Streit became a recognizable presence not only in Washington political circles but also among a larger public. In March 1950, he featured on the cover of *Time* magazine, another piece of Luce's media empire, and the accompanying article likened him to the abolitionist William Lloyd Garrison, the suffragette Susan B. Anthony, and the socialist Eugene Debs, among others – "the reformers, the crusaders, sometimes the bores or the screwballs, sometimes ineffectual, sometimes movers of the world."[3] The same year Streit was one of six Americans nominated for the Nobel peace prize; the others included Harry Truman; George Marshall, the former secretary of state; James Shotwell, the longtime internationalist; Raphael Lemkin, the principal drafter of the United Nations' genocide convention, and

---

[2] Henry R. Luce, "The American Century," March 1941, reproduced in *Diplomatic History* 23 (1999), 16. Luce's editorial was subsequently published in book form with commentaries, several of which mentioned Streit's proposal. See Henry R. Luce, *The American Century* (New York: Farrar & Reinhart, 1941), 50, 55, 78–79.

[3] "Elijah from Missoula," *Time*, March 27, 1950, 24–29.

Robert Hutchins, the educational philosopher and Chancellor of the University of Chicago.[4]

This visibility notwithstanding, Streit is almost entirely absent from twentieth-century US history. Occasionally, he receives passing mention in a book or article, most often in reference to *Union Now*'s publication, leaving an impression of fleetingness. Similarly, his project has been cited as evidence of an upsurge in "globalist ideologies" in the United States (and Britain) during the 1940s, a phenomenon with limited staying power.[5] To be sure, the scholarship on world government constitutes an exception to the neglect of Streit. Often melding analysis with advocacy, students of the world government movement present Streit as a pioneer and *Union Now* as a founding text. This twinning of Streit with world government lends his project a decidedly quixotic flavor, helping no doubt to explain the larger scholarly disinterest.[6] There is an irony here, for Streit persistently labored to distance himself from world government. Throughout his lengthy career, he promoted Atlantic federal union – a significantly different though still hugely ambitious project.

Drawing on an array of published and unpublished sources, *Clarence Streit and Twentieth-Century American Internationalism* provides the first study of Streit's promotional activities during the wartime years

[4] "28 Are Nominated for Nobel Peace Prize, Including Truman, Churchill and Marshall," *New York Times*, February 28, 1950, 21. Two years later, Streit once again was one of six US nominees.

[5] For passing mentions, see Quinn Slobodian, *Globalists: The End of Empire and the Birth of Neoliberalism* (Cambridge, MA: Harvard University Press, 2018), 100; Andrew Williams, *Failed Imagination?: The Anglo-American New World Order from Wilson to Bush* (Manchester: Manchester University Press, 2007), 85–86; Lawrence S. Wittner, *One World or None: A History of the World Disarmament Movement through 1953* (Stanford, CA: Stanford University Press, 1993), 44–45; Robert A. Divine, *Second Chance: The Triumph of Internationalism in America during World War II* (New York: Atheneum, 1971), 39–40; and Mark Lincoln Chadwin, *The Hawks of World War II* (Chapel Hill: University of North Carolina Press, 1968), 19–20. For globalist ideologies, see Or Rosenboim, *The Emergence of Globalism: Visions of World Order in Britain and the United States, 1939–1950* (Princeton, NJ: Princeton University Press, 2017), 114–21.

[6] For Streit and world government, see James A. Yunker, *The Idea of World Government: From Ancient Times to the Twenty-First Century* (London: Routledge, 2011), 50–53; and Joseph Preston Baratta, *The Politics of World Federation: United Nations, UN Reform, Atomic Control*, vol. I (Westport, CT: Praeger, 2004), 49–72. But also see Wesley T. Wooley, *Alternatives to Anarchy: American Supranationalism since World War II* (Bloomington: University of Indiana Press, 1988), 85–134. Invoking Streit, Daniel Deudney has sought to recover federalism for International Relations theory. See his "The Philadelphia System: Sovereignty, Arms Control, and Balance of Power in the American States-Union, circa 1787–1861," *International Organization* 49 (1995), 191–228.

and postwar decades. In so doing, it writes Streit and his Atlantic federal union project back into US history. The purpose is not to identify a missed historical opportunity – a task familiar to historians in general and often accompanied by bows to the importance of contingency. Truth be told, Streit's project had little chance of being realized, requiring, as it did, the United States (as well as several other countries) to agree to transform their political-constitutional structures. Instead of excavating a now-imperceptible but once-plausible "might-have-been," the book uses Streit's activities to address a question of enduring pertinence: How or why do some policy ideas gain public and political traction? In Streit's case, the search for answers leads to an exploration of the "public politics" of foreign relations during a critical time when the United States metamorphosed from a major but still mostly regional power into a superpower with global pretensions and reach. Streit's experience as a foreign policy entrepreneur shadowed this metamorphosis, and a study of his career highlights the vital yet hitherto neglected influence of federalist and Atlanticist ideas in the efforts of mid-century Americans to rethink international politics and their country's role in them.

In promoting Atlantic federal union during and after World War II, Streit mixed and matched several strategies. One involved the courting of a fairly select group of people, those whom Elmo Roper, the prominent pollster and Streit collaborator, termed the "Great Disseminators": National figures, such as Luce, whose status, position, or wealth gave them a say in ongoing debates on the United States' place in the world.[7] A second strategy aimed at mobilizing grass-roots support, principally in the form of a national movement organized into local chapters. A standard practice among political movements at the time, the creation of chapters proved fraught with difficulties for Streit. As a case study, it suggests the need to nuance claims of a collective boom of "civic voluntarism" in the United States across the wartime and postwar years.[8]

[7] Elmo Roper, *You and Your Leaders: Their Actions and Your Reactions, 1936–1956* (New York: William Morrow, 1957), 18–21; and Roper's foreword to Elihu Katz and Paul F. Lazarsfeld, *Personal Influence: The Part Played by People in the Flow of Mass Communications* (New York: Free Press, 1955), xv–xx.

[8] Robert D. Putnam, *Bowling Alone: The Collapse and Renewal of American Community* (New York: Simon & Schuster, 2000); and Theda Skocpol, Zias Munson, Andrew Karch, and Bayliss Camp, "Patriotic Partnerships: Why Great Wars Nourished American Civic Voluntarism," in Ira Katznelson and Martin Shefter, eds., *Shaped by War and Trade: International Influences on American Political Development* (Princeton, NJ: Princeton University Press, 2002), 134–80.

At the grass-roots level, Streit hoped to recruit the "Lesser Disseminators," local versions of Roper's "Great Disseminators"; in practice, he relied on coteries of devotees, often women (such as his wife Jeanne) performing the gendered part of under-paid or unpaid seconds.[9] A third strategy consisted of political lobbying, primarily of Congress, an institution that not only clamored for a more active role in foreign relations but also functioned as a valuable platform for policy entrepreneurs such as Streit.[10]

Taken together, Streit's promotional strategies illuminate the public dimension of politics in the foreign relations realm. A good deal of scholarship on wartime and postwar US foreign relations examines the politics of policymaking, much of it occurring in the corridors of the country's burgeoning national security state, largely beyond public view.[11] Yet there was another, parallel and more accessible, dimension to politics. In some ways, this dimension resembles what Daniel Drezner, borrowing from political economy, refers to as the "modern marketplace of ideas" in the United States.[12] Although Drezner studies the contemporary period, Streit during the mid-twentieth century operated in a vibrant marketplace of foreign policy ideas in which a variety of participants – foundations, think tanks, interest groups and movements, newspaper and magazine editors and journalists, as well as clusters of politicians, experts (academic and nonacademic), public commentators, and activists – all vied for public attention. As with all markets, the participants in this marketplace were not equally competitive. Better positioned and endowed with more resources, some possessed greater market power and thus greater visibility.

---

[9] In his study of the Foreign Policy Association, David John Allen emphasizes the indispensable role played by women in elite foreign policy organizations in the United States. See his "Every Citizen a Statesman: Building Democracy for Foreign Policy in the American Century," PhD, Columbia University, 2019, 16, 53.

[10] Robert David Johnson, *Congress and the Cold War* (New York: Cambridge University Press, 2006). As two political scientists affirm, "Congress is the most accessible federal government institution." See Ralph G. Carter and James M. Scott, *Choosing to Lead: Understanding Congressional Foreign Policy Entrepreneurs* (Durham, NC: Duke University Press, 2009), 12.

[11] For a now classic study, see Melvyn P. Leffler, *A Preponderance of Power: National Security, the Truman Administration, and the Cold War* (Stanford, CA: Stanford University Press, 1992).

[12] Daniel W. Drezner, *The Ideas Industry* (New York: Oxford University Press, 2017), ix. On the political-economic side, see R. H. Coarse, "The Market for Goods and the Market for Ideas," *Economic History Review* 64 (1974), 384–91.

But if the marketplace of ideas usefully highlights the competitive environment in which Streit operated, the concept risks downplaying another and crucial element of his activities – their political nature. In the early modern Republic of Letters, probably the best-known example of a marketplace of ideas, success was defined in terms of money (finding a wealthy patron) and reputation.[13] Streit's priority, however, was to shape US foreign relations. And this is why the marketplace of ideas needs to be enfolded into another concept, that of the public dimension of politics. Its contours were (and are) fluid and its component parts shifting, frustrating attempts to define this dimension in abstract terms. One scholar, for example, talks vaguely of an "intricate midcentury matrix."[14] Accordingly, it is more useful to conceive of this dimension as a function of the porous nature of policymaking in the United States. A number of factors (multiple branches of government, a popular suspicion of centralized authority, a dynamic mediascape, overlapping public, semi-public and private spheres) combined to open the making of foreign (and domestic) policy to public participation, to entangle policymaking in public politics.[15] More precisely, this porousness offered diverse entry points for outsiders – those who, such as Streit, lacked the institutional base or proximity to power of the influential insiders whose impact on US foreign and defense policies has become the subject of a thriving scholarship.[16]

Determined and resourceful, Streit embraced the public dimension of politics, capitalizing on its possibilities and openings to gain visibility and even legitimacy for a project involving a far-reaching reconceptualization

---

[13] Joel Mokyr, *A Culture of Growth: The Origins of the Modern Economy* (Princeton, NJ: Princeton University Press, 2017); and Robert Darnton, *The Business of Enlightenment: A Publishing History of the Encyclopédie 1775–1800* (Cambridge, MA: Belknap Press, 1979).

[14] See Samuel Zipp's comments in the H-Diplo roundtable on his book, *The Idealist: Wendell Willkie's Wartime Quest to Build One World* (Cambridge, MA: Belknap Press, 2020): https://networks.h-net.org/node/28443/discussions/8235082/h-diplo-roundtable-xxiii-2-zipp-idealist-wendell-willkie%E2%80%99s.

[15] Pierre Melandri and Justin Vaïsse argue this porousness is particularly marked in the case of the United States, though a more comparative perspective would be interesting. See their *L'Empire du milieu: les États-Unis et le monde depuis la fin de la Guerre froide* (Paris: Odile Jacob, 2001).

[16] For insiders, see the overview by Daniel Bessner, "Thinking about the U.S. in the World," *Diplomatic History* 41 (2017), 1018–25. Also see Daniel Bessner, *Democracy in Exile: Hans Speier and the Rise of the Defense Intellectual* (Ithaca, NY: Cornell University Press, 2018); and Ron Robin, *The Cold War They Made: The Strategic Legacy of Roberta and Albert Wohlstetter* (Cambridge, MA: Harvard University Press, 2016); A classic study is Walter Isaacson and Evan Thomas, *The Wise Men: Six Friends and the World They Made* (New York: Simon & Schuster, 1986).

of US foreign relations. A study of his extensive promotional activities thus provides a practical and intimate perspective on this public dimension, highlighting its functioning as well as the opportunities and frustrations it engendered. Such a study, moreover, presents something of a mid-range option in relation to two other approaches to public politics. One approach centers on Congress and on the political calculations and maneuverings of its members, while the other explores the production and reproduction of an ambient Cold War culture and consensus. If the political realm in the first approach is arguably construed too narrowly, excluding actors such as Streit, in the second it risks becoming all-embracing, leaving little room for alternative policy visions and projects.[17]

Streit operated in this public dimension of politics for well over four decades, gaining public visibility and political legitimacy in the process. This achievement, in turn, allowed Streit to insert his Atlantic federal union project into two major debates on US foreign policy at the time: the nature of the postwar international order and the nature of transatlantic relations.

World War II witnessed a pivotal domestic debate on the postwar international order and the United States' role in it. More recent studies of this debate have undermined the older binary view of a straightforward struggle between isolationists and internationalists, convincingly demonstrating that so-called isolationists were an eclectic bunch, interested not so much in preventing US interactions with the wider world as in placing

---

[17] For Congress and the Cold War, see Johnson, *Congress and the Cold War*; Hendrik Meijer, *Arthur Vandenberg: The Man in the Middle of the American Century* (Chicago: University of Chicago Press, 2017); Robert A. Caro, *The Years of Lyndon Johnson: Master of the Senate* (New York: Alfred A. Knopf, 2002); and Michael J. Hogan, *A Cross of Iron: Harry S. Truman and the Origins of the National Security State, 1945–1954* (New York: Cambridge University Press, 1998). For a focus on Congress more generally, see Julian E. Zelizer, *Arsenal of Democracy: The Politics of National Security from World War II to the War of Terrorism* (New York: Basic Books, 2010). For Cold War culture and consensus, see Jennifer A. Delton, *Rethinking the 1950s: How Anticommunism and the Cold War Made Liberal America* (New York: Cambridge University Press, 2013); Laura Mcenaney, "Cold War Mobilization and Domestic Politics: The United States" in Melvyn P. Leffler and Odd Arne Westad, eds., *The Cambridge History of the Cold War*, vol. I (Cambridge: Cambridge University Press, 2010), 420–41; John Fousek, *To Lead the Free World: American Nationalism and the Cultural Roots of the Cold War* (Chapel Hill: University of North Carolina Press, 2000); Wendy Wall, *Inventing the "American Way": The Politics of Consensus from the New Deal to the Civil Rights Movement* (New York: Oxford University Press, 2008); and Michael S. Sherry, *In the Shadow of War: The United States since the 1930s* (New Haven, CT: Yale University Press, 1995).

limits on them.[18] Similarly, internationalists now appear as a diverse group, resulting in divergent assessments of wartime internationalism. While many scholars continue to see the wartime years as foundational in the US-led construction of a liberal international order based on multilateral cooperation rooted in democracy, liberalized exchanges, international organizations, and human rights, this generally positive viewpoint has been challenged. For Stephen Wertheim, the origins of Washington's outsized, ongoing, and disastrous quest for global suprem-acy are to be found in the early wartime years when US planners responded to the prospects of a Nazi victory in Europe. An emerging third current, meanwhile, identifies the war as a time of rising global awareness among the informed public, though the policy implications of this globalism appear more elusive.[19]

Absent from this buoyant scholarship are other possibilities for inter-national order circulating during the war, conspicuous among them federalist frameworks. Thanks in good measure to Streit's tireless promo-tional efforts, federalism imposed itself in wartime debates as a way of understanding international order and, more particularly, the issue of national sovereignty – an issue that had so vexed interwar thinking on international politics in the United States. Presented by Streit as a

---

[18] Andrew Johnstone, *Against Immediate Evil: American Internationalists and the Four Freedoms on the Eve of World War II* (Ithaca, NY: Cornell University Press, 2014); Christopher McKnight Nichols, *Promise and Peril: America at the Dawn of a Global Age* (Cambridge, MA: Harvard University Press, 2011); Brooke L. Blower, "From Isolationism to Neutrality: A New Framework for Understanding American Political Culture, 1919–1941," *Diplomatic History* 38, no. 2 (2014), 345–76; and Justus D. Doenecke, *Storm on the Horizon: The Challenge to American Intervention, 1939–1941* (Lanham, MD: Rowman & Littlefield, 2000).

[19] For liberal internationalism, see G. John Ikenberry, *A World Safe for Democracy: Liberal Internationalism and the Crisis of Global Order* (New Haven, CT: Yale University Press, 2020), 141–211; and Elizabeth Borgwardt, *A New Deal for the World: America's Vision of Human Rights* (Cambridge, MA: Belknap Press, 2005). For global supremacy, see Stephen Wertheim, *Tomorrow the World: The Birth of U.S. Global Supremacy* (Cambridge, MA: Belknap Press, 2020); Jenifer Van Vleck, *Empire of the Air: Aviation and the American Ascendency* (Cambridge, MA: Harvard University Press, 2013); and Patrick J. Hearden, *Architects of Globalism: Building a New World Order during World War II* (Fayetteville: University of Arkansas Press, 2002). For globalism, see Rosenboim, *The Emergence of Globalism*; Zipp, *The Idealist*; and Andrew Buchanan, "Domesticating Hegemony: Creating a Globalist Public, 1941–1943," *Diplomatic History* 45 (2021), 301–29. Geographers have also detected this global awareness. See Neil Smith, *American Empire: Roosevelt's Geographer and the Prelude to Globalization* (Berkeley: University of California Press, 2003); and Susan Schulten, *The Geographical Imagination in America, 1880–1950* (Chicago: University of Chicago Press, 2001).

quintessentially American method, one sanctified by the country's own history, federalism shifted the locus from an either-or proposition (retention or loss of sovereignty) to the practical issue of apportioning jurisdiction. In a version of what political scientists call the domestic political analogy, in which the internal becomes the archetype for the external, federalist frameworks worked to domesticate international relations for a US audience. In the wartime debate on postwar international order, they assumed a structuring function, quickly emerging as an alternative to the interwar order centered on the League of Nations, widely judged to be a failure. At the same time, federalism proved to be a plastic concept, facilitating not only its detachment from Streit's project of Atlantic federal union but also its appropriation by advocates of a revamped League of Nations. These advocates would deftly employ federalist language to promote what became the United Nations Organization (UNO) and, more generally, to rehabilitate international organizations as a pillar of postwar international order. In a bitter irony for Streit, the wartime visibility of federalist frameworks facilitated the very outcome his project was designed to avoid.

The second major foreign policy debate influenced by Streit's Atlantic federal union project involved transatlantic relations. Two distinct approaches dominate the scholarship on the subject. An older and still venerable one focuses on interstate relations, and is well represented, for example, in recent studies of NATO. The principal actors are presidential administrations and their high-ranking members. The second approach explores the cross-ocean activities of a variety of non-state actors: the bankers, philanthropists, academics, businesses, foundations, and think tanks among others who collectively constituted what one scholar calls the "transnational transatlantic."[20] Together, these two approaches go far in explaining how the Atlantic and especially the North Atlantic came to be widely perceived as a distinct region whose member countries were

---

[20] For the first approach, see Timothy Andrews Sayle, *Enduring Alliance: A History of NATO and the Postwar Global Order* (Ithaca, NY: Cornell University Press, 2019); and Jeffrey Glen Giauque, *Grand Designs and Visions of Unity: The Atlantic Powers and the Reorganization of Europe, 1955–1963* (Chapel Hill: University of North Carolina Press, 2002). For the second, see Giles Scott-Smith, "The Transnational Transatlantic: Private Organizations and Govermentality" in Charlotte A. Lerg, Susanne Lachenicht, and Michael Kimmage, eds., *The TransAtlantic Reconsidered: The Atlantic World in Crisis* (Manchester: Manchester University Press, 2018), 76–97. For an attempt to combine the two approaches, see Mary Nolan, *The Transatlantic Century: Europe and America, 1890–2010* (Cambridge: Cambridge University Press, 2012).

tied together by multiple and crisscrossing ties, forming what the journalist Walter Lippmann imagined as early as 1917 as a "community."[21]

A study of Streit's activities encompasses both state and non-state actors. And it does so by drawing attention to an issue that was much discussed at the time – that of the appropriate political configuration for transatlantic relations. During the 1950s and into the 1960s, an emerging consensus developed in Washington political circles that transatlantic relations required a political structure, something more elaborated than NATO as a military alliance could furnish. A prolific advocate of this position was Henry Kissinger, at the time an ambitious Harvard lecturer. Positioning himself as a critic of current policy, Kissinger contended in a series of highly visible publications that the moment had arrived "to examine carefully the possibility of creating federal institutions comprising the entire North Atlantic community ..."[22] The Streitian language was not fortuitous, for Streit, principally through the Atlantic Union Committee (AUC), a political lobby group created in 1949, had contributed as much – and probably more – than anyone to foster the idea of NATO's political inadequacy. Indeed, from the outset, Streit threw himself into the AUC's lobbying campaign, seeking to direct it toward his ends.

With a hyper-active Streit as member, the AUC pressed Congress to call for a convention of NATO countries to explore proposals for greater political unity. A focus on Congress offered a means to bypass the hesitations of the Eisenhower Administration and the State Department, while also ensnaring both in a bargaining process between the executive and legislative branches. An extensive lobbying campaign resulted in the passage of a congressional resolution in 1960, followed by a convention in January 1962. Yet in another bitter irony for Streit, the upshot proved disappointing. His forceful advocacy of Atlantic federal union motivated a prominent group of Atlanticists, many of them AUC members or supporters, to articulate an alternative "community" vision of transatlantic relations (or Atlanticism). Explicitly rejecting formal structures such as federal union, these Atlanticists countered that the Atlantic community's political framework should be left to develop organically

---

[21] Anonymous (Lippmann), "The Defense of the Atlantic World," *The New Republic* 120 (February 17, 1917), 59–63.

[22] Henry Kissinger, *The Necessity for Choice: Prospects of American Foreign Policy* (Garden City, NY: Doubleday Anchor, 1961), 172; and "The Search for Stability," *Foreign Affairs* (37), July 1959, 537–60.

(or functionally). More concretely, they envisaged a political community guided by networks of like-minded transatlantic elites centered in and on Washington. The Atlantic Council, the AUC's institutional successor, quickly became the leading voice of this Atlanticism. Today, it is a high-powered and well-funded Washington organization.

Several points are worth emphasizing in regard to Streit's influence on US foreign relations. First, this influence stemmed from his ability to operate within the public dimension of politics and to exploit the opportunities and openings it provided. Second, influence did not necessarily translate into success: After all, Streit's Atlantic federal union remained unrealized. But if this failure was arguably predictable, it makes the public visibility and political legitimacy Streit attained for his project all the more remarkable – and deserving of study. It is worth adding that, along the way, Streit did succeed in influencing two major foreign policy debates, just not in the way he envisioned. In the end, his project functioned as a foil, facilitating the articulation of alternatives which would mark US foreign relations after 1945, whether in terms of an international order centered on international organizations such as the UNO or of a community-oriented Atlanticism. Streit's ultimate disappointment, in short, should not obscure his influence.

Still another point involves the role of federalist frameworks. While scholars have highlighted the importance of federalism to the lively constitutional debates taking place on several continents during the eighteenth and nineteenth centuries, its salience for twentieth-century history is largely confined to studies of the European Union or, most recently, of decolonization in which federalist frameworks appear as a promising if unrealized third way between empire and nation-state.[23] A study of

---

[23] For federalism and constitution-making, see Linda Colley, *The Gun, the Ship, and the Pen: Warfare, Constitutions, and the Making of the Modern World* (New York: Liveright, 2021), 105–54. Also see Thomas Bender, *A Nation among Nations: America's Place in World History* (New York: Hill & Wang, 2006), 133–50; Daniel Ziblatt, *Structuring the State: The Formation of Italy and Germany and the Puzzle of Federalism* (Princeton, NJ: Princeton University Press, 2006); and Michael Dreyer, *Föderalismus als ordnungspolitisches und normatives Prinzip: Das föderative Denken der Deutschen im 19. Jahrhundert* (Frankfurt am Main: Peter Lang, 1987). For decolonization, see Merve Fejzula, "The Cosmopolitan Historiography of Twentieth-Century Federalism," *Historical Journal* 64 (2021), 477–500; Adom Getachew, *Worldmaking after Empire: The Rise and Fall of Self-Determination* (Princeton, NJ: Princeton University Press, 2019); and Frederick Cooper, *Citizenship between Empire and Nation: Remaking France and French Africa, 1945–1960* (Princeton, NJ: Princeton University Press, 2014).

Streit's promotional activities suggests the need to incorporate the United States into the scholarship on twentieth-century federalism. It was not simply that the US federal system continued to offer a potential model for nation-makers in various parts of the world. Federalist frameworks also intrigued many Americans. Indeed, a veritable political cult of the federal system flourished in the United States during the interwar years, furnishing a receptive audience for Streit's argument that federalism offered a home-grown and time-tested conceptual tool and even blueprint for international politics.

Two additional points are worth making, one regarding the book's American-centrism and the other the Western-centrism of Streit's Atlantic federal union. Although Streit's project encompassed several countries, *Clarence Streit and Twentieth Century American Internationalism* concentrates almost entirely on Streit's promotional activities at home. The focus is explained by Streit's belief in the indispensability of the United States to Atlantic federal union: He presumed other countries would follow Washington's lead, a presumption that reflected considerable complacency toward the outside world in general. This complacency, which was hardly unique to Streit, is pertinent to ongoing debates among historians of US foreign relations on the question of perspective. While some favor an international perspective, encouraging efforts to integrate their field into a more expansive international history, others argue for a national perspective that would root or re-root the field more firmly in US history.[24] There is much to be said for both perspectives, and there is certainly considerable middle ground between them.

That said, a study of Streit's promotional activities does highlight the insular and parochial aspects of the public dimension of politics in the United States. Non-American voices were rare and knowledge of Europe and its politics often superficial. What mattered most was what the various (US) participants told one another and what they could convince one another was going on. The impression sometimes is that of a game of mirrors in which cascading perceptions of an object define reality. In a happy irony for Streit, the insularity and parochialism of the public dimension of politics likely helped more than harmed his efforts, allowing

---

[24] For a recent contribution to this debate, see Daniel Bessner and Fredrik Logevall, "Recentering the United States in the Historiography of American Foreign Relations," *Texas National Security Review* 3 (2020), 38–55. Also see the H-Diplo roundtable on the article: https://networks.h-net.org/node/28443/discussions/6165504/h-diplo-roundtable-xxi-42-bessner-and-logevall-%E2%80%9Crecentering.

him to claim that Atlantic federal union enjoyed significant support both abroad and at home.

As for Streit's Atlantic federal union, it was indisputably Western and even white-centric. The historian Gary Gerstle has diagnosed a pervasive "racialized nationalism" during the Roosevelt years manifest in the belief in the superiority of white and especially "Nordic" peoples.[25] Although Streit was no doctrinaire racist, and genuinely disapproved of the treatment of African Americans under Jim Crow, he shared popular assumptions about the geographic, racial, and ethnic hierarchies embedded in international politics. For Streit, the Atlantic countries formed a distinct region construed along broadly civilizational lines – with a common history and culture, as well as a shared political development culminating in democracy, a regime type he came to fetishize. Like so many others, Streit readily accepted that the Atlantic or Western world constituted a higher and more advanced civilizational form than other regions, a proposition that conveniently justified their exclusion from his project.[26] Similarly, he treated empire largely as an afterthought despite the reality that several member countries of his projected Atlantic federal union possessed overseas empires, not least the United States.[27]

The omission of vast swathes of the globe's regions and peoples constituted a major weakness, especially in the context after 1945 of a Cold War rivalry assuming global proportions. Eminent anti-imperialists, such as George Orwell, Jawaharlal Nehru, and W. E. B. Du Bois, certainly criticized Streit's project on these grounds. Yet however merited their criticism, the public visibility and political legitimacy Streit's project garnered underscores another consideration: Even at a time when international relations were becoming more global in scope, when other regions were vying for attention, the West, and the Atlantic world in particular, continued to occupy a prominent and even preeminent place

---

[25] Gary Gerstle, *American Crucible: Race and Nation in the Twentieth Century* (Princeton, NJ: Princeton University Press, 2001), 166–83. And more generally, John M. Hobson, *The Eurocentric Conception of the World: Western International Theory, 1769–2010* (Cambridge: Cambridge University Press, 2012), 169–73.

[26] Michael Kimmage, *The Abandonment of the West: The History of an Idea in American Foreign Policy* (New York: Basic Books, 2020). Also see Jasper M. Trautsch, "Was ist 'der Westen'? Zur Semantik eines politischen Grundbegriffs der Moderne," *Forum Interdisziplinäre Begriffsgeschichte* 6 (2017), 58–66.

[27] For recent studies of the United States as an imperial power, see Daniel Immerwahr, *How to Hide an Empire: A History of the Greater United States* (New York: Farrar, Straus & Giroux, 2019); and Steven Hahn, *A Nation without Borders: The United States and the World in the Age of Civil Wars, 1830–1910* (New York: Penguin, 2017).

in US foreign relations. One reason they did so certainly had to do with widespread ethnic/racial assumptions, but another and related reason is that Streit and other Atlanticists worked long and hard to promote the Atlantic world. The regional hierarchies underpinning US foreign relations (just as the definitions of regions themselves) are never permanently fixed but rather are the sometimes fragile and always contingent result of political contest.[28] And as *Clarence Sreit and Twentieth-Century American Internationalism* shows, the public dimension of politics was a vital element of this contest.

BOOK OUTLINE

The book comprises five chapters together with an Introduction and Conclusion. Chapter 1 considers Streit's career as a foreign correspondent, particularly his lengthy posting in Geneva with the *New York Times*. It frames his growing interest in Atlantic federal union as a response, not simply to first-hand experience of the League's (mal)functioning during the 1930s but also to tensions within the profession of foreign correspondent arising from the imperative of objectivity. Chapter 2 focuses on *Union Now*, Streit's first and best-known book, published in 1939, spotlighting the interaction of two factors to explain its visibility: Streit's energetic promotional campaign and federalism's prominent place in interwar US political culture. Chapter 3 examines Streit's wartime activities on behalf of federal union, which included the creation of a national movement with local chapters as well as direct political action. Significant in this second category of activities was his involvement in the Commission to Study the Organization of the Peace (CSOP), a semi-official grouping that played a key role in designing and championing the UNO as a pillar of postwar US internationalism. Streit's unwillingness to collaborate meaningfully with the CSOP left him with inadequate means either to promote his own project or to counter the appropriation of federalism for other ends.

---

[28] For the constructed nature of regions, see Christina Klein, *Cold War Orientalism: Asia in the Middlebrow Imagination, 1945–1961* (Berkeley: University of California Press, 2003); Schulten, *The Geographical Imagination in America*; and Martin W. Lewis and Kären Wigen, *The Myth of Continents: A Critique of Metageography* (Berkeley: University of California Press, 1997). For the constructed nature of the Atlantic world, see Patrick J. Cohrs, *The New Atlantic Order: The Transformation of International Politics, 1860–1933* (Cambridge: Cambridge University Press, 2022).

The final two chapters investigate Streit's postwar activities. Chapter 4 centers on his educational activism, whose principal vehicle was Federal Union, an organization founded during the war, and which in 1946 launched a monthly magazine, *Freedom & Union*, to stimulate discussion of Atlantic federal union and of federalist frameworks more generally. Political and financial considerations prodded Streit to champion abstract principles of democracy, freedom, and liberty, which further Americanized his project by rooting it in dominant Cold War ideological paradigms while also eliding differences between the United States and Western European countries. Chapter 5 concentrates on Streit's efforts as a political lobbyist, primarily with the AUC, a vocal proponent of Atlanticism during the 1950s and into the 1960s. If Streit's federal union project represented one version of Atlanticism, the AUC's extended give-and-take with Congress acted as a midwife to the emergence in the early 1960s of an opposing version. Imagined as a community of transatlantic elites, this Atlanticism continues to dominate Washington politics today. The Conclusion briefly recapitulates the book's principal arguments.

I

The Making of an Atlantic Federalist, 1914–1939

In May 1956, in response to yet another request for support from Clarence Streit, Arthur Hays Sulzberger, the longtime editor of the *New York Times*, confided to a staff member that Streit "has been a problem for me ever since he left The Times on which he was a good correspondent but he's awfully noble."[1] In addition to Sulzberger's obvious exasperation, the comment directs attention to Streit's initial – and successful – career as a foreign correspondent. This chapter, accordingly, considers Streit's activities before the publication of *Union Now* in 1939. The first section examines his path from an ambitious high school and university student in Montana to Europe: as soldier in World War I, as a low-level member of the US delegation to the Paris peace conference in 1919, as a Rhodes scholar, and finally as a budding journalist. Curious, ambitious, and notably progressive in his politics, Streit profited from the international upheavals of the time to escape what he perceived as the straitened confines of life in the United States.

The next section is devoted to Streit's emergence as a well-regarded foreign correspondent during the 1920s, a period often presented as the profession's golden age. Although Streit lacked the glamor of better-known celebrity colleagues, such as Vincent Sheean and Dorothy Thompson, his experiences offer another perspective on the work of interwar foreign correspondents. More precisely, they highlight the significant gap between professional ideals and practical realities. The resulting frustrations prompted foreign correspondents to redefine their

[1] NYPL, NYTCR, Arthur Hays Sulzberger Papers, Box 171, file 9, Sulzberger to O. E. Dryfoos, May 3, 1956.

profession during the 1930s in the context of mounting international tensions, a response Streit would pursue to the limits and beyond of journalism. The final section focuses on Streit's tenure as the *New York Time*'s correspondent in Geneva for much of the 1930s covering the League of Nations. This extended posting, which proved crucial to his embrace of Atlantic federal union, provides an intriguing vantage point for reconsidering the League's place in US foreign relations at the time. Perhaps no group contributed more to fostering the view of the League as a failure than did foreign correspondents. Although initially a League enthusiast, Streit soon came to share this assessment, inspiring him to plunge into the developing debate in the 1930s about the nature of the international order and the United States' role in it.

FROM MONTANA TO EUROPE

Clarence Streit was born in January 1896 on a farm in California, Missouri, one of five children of Louis Streit, a salesman of farm machinery, and Emma Kirschman. At age fifteen, Streit moved with his family to Missoula, Montana. Entering high school, he threw himself into extra-curricular activities, founding and editing the school newspaper, winning a local championship with the debate team, and earning third-place honors in a state-wide speaking contest. Following graduation, Streit, in 1914, entered the State University of Montana to study journalism. Established the same year, the university's journalism school was part of a nation-wide development that saw journalism emerge as a field of professional study. In addition to playing intercollegiate football, Streit edited the university newspaper (*Montana Kamin*) and participated on the debate team.[2]

At the state university, Streit also distinguished himself as a critic of the Wilson administration. In 1917, he stood alone among students in refusing to sign a supportive telegram to Wilson, who had just taken the United States into the raging war in Europe. In a further act of protest against the administration's clampdown on political dissent, he rejected the first-place medal won at the annual state intercollegiate oratorical contest for a speech entitled "The Hope of Democracy." Going further, Streit publicly requested the prize money be given to the defense fund of Thomas J. Mooney, a socialist and trade union activist tried and

---

[2] The Rhodes Trust, Clarence Streit file, untitled biographical notes; and LOC, CKS, Box I: 40, file: Biographical articles, "Achievers."

convicted for his alleged part in detonating a bomb at a pro-war parade in San Francisco in July 1916.[3] His gesture attracted some attention outside of Montana. "Such a spirit in the new generation that is coming upon the stage of the world's affairs is indeed hopeful," a Kansas newspaper admiringly editorialized. "Would that there were more young men with this honest devotion to justice!"[4]

To be sure, Streit was far from alone in his support of Mooney. The case received wide publicity in the United States and abroad, with numerous observers denouncing what they judged a miscarriage of justice.[5] Streit's criticism of the Wilson administration, though, extended well beyond the Mooney case. In a letter/article written for a local Missoula newspaper in April 1917, he defended Senator Robert La Follette's vote against US entry into the war, deploring the "war hysteria" overtaking the country while also questioning the patriotism of "war-bloated industries." Pointing to US policies at home and abroad, he dismissed as hypocrisy Wilson's claim to be waging a "war for democracy":

> when the liberal thinker, the believer of democracy at home in times of peace, looks at the men in this country who are most anxious to go to war to "protect democracy" he is entitled to his doubts of their sincerity. He finds that the men who would defend the rights of the little nations in Europe are men who in the past have paid no attention to the rights of the little nations of the Caribbean. The men who are feverish to overthrow autocracy in Germany are the most reactionary Tories when the question involves democracy in this country. The newspapers which are loud in praise of revolution in Russia are most bitter in their denunciation of any symptoms of revolt in our own industrial feudalism.

At the same time, Streit expressed faith in Wilson's declared goal of forging a new and better postwar international order. While regretting the president's failure to make US entry into the war "conditional upon the promise of the Allies to form a league to prevent the world from becoming involved in such a catastrophe as this again," he remained confident that "the influence of America may still do some good when the slaughtering part of the war is over."[6]

---

[3] "Medal Is Declined by Clarence Streit," *The Daily Missoulian*, May 13, 1917, 2.
[4] Untitled, *Appeal to Reason* (Girard, Kansas), May 26, 1917, 4.
[5] For a detailed study of the case, see Richard H. Frost, *The Mooney Case* (Stanford, CA: Stanford University Press, 1968). For wartime repression and violence, see Christopher Capozzola, *Uncle Sam Wants You: World War I and the Making of the Modern American Citizen* (New York: Oxford University Press, 2008).
[6] LOC, CKS, Box I: 130, file: CKS – Articles – General, Untitled text, April 1917.

Streit's doubts about the war's purpose did not prevent him from volunteering for military service. In June 1917, he left Missoula to begin training with an army engineer regiment, an assignment likely influenced by his earlier summer employment as a government surveyor in Alaska. By November 1917, Streit was in France, happy to have escaped the stifling political climate at home. "I cannot understand the wave of intolerance, with its determination to suppress the least expression of nonconformity, which seems to have spread over the country which has always acclaimed its freedom of speech and press," he wrote in December. Americans, he added hopefully, would soon "realize that in a country fighting to make the world safe for democracy, intolerance, hate and forced conformity are among the enemies of the cause."[7] As an engineer, Streit worked behind the lines, well away from the murderous trench warfare on the Western front. Most days were spent overseeing an assorted collection of construction workers, which included black Americans, Scandinavians, German and Austrian POWs, and Chinese. Reflecting the casual prejudices of the time, Streit appeared mildly surprised that "the negroes" counted among the best workers.[8]

When not on military duty, Streit penned articles on life in France for a Missoula newspaper. One hallmark of his observations were clichéd contrasts between French and Americans. Thus, while discomfited by the sight of French men kissing each other in greeting instead of using the more American (and manly) handshake, Streit admired the open-minded moral "code" he observed among the French, opposing it to the "Puritan mentality ... entrenched in Americans." Similarly, he marveled at the can-do energy and efficiency of Americans yet also suspected that the "French know how to live better than we do." "It rarely if ever dawns on them [Americans] that there may be a better way of living than the mechanical, commercial existence we follow." However conventional his views, Streit clearly nourished a Francophilia that set him apart from the widespread anti-French sentiments scholars have detected among US soldiers at the time.[9]

---

[7] "Talk of the Town," *The Missoulian*, December 6, 1917, 6.

[8] "Writes of Life with Engineers," *The Daily Missoulian*, February 21, 1918, 3; and LOC, CKS, Box III: 3, file 5, diary, December 1917.

[9] "Talk of the Town" and "American Speed Amazes French," *The Missoulian*, March 19, 1918, 4, and April 1, 1918, 3. For anti-French sentiment among American soldiers, see Jennifer D. Keene, *Doughboys, the Great War, and the Remaking of America* (Baltimore: Johns Hopkins University Press, 2001), 118–25.

Streit's experiences in France also fed a swelling interest in European and international politics, which he observed through his left-leaning politics. Writing home in early 1918, Streit declared himself "a Socialist, a believer in the common man." And as a socialist he itched to be sent to Russia, where he "could have seen and could be seeing the revolution there at first hand ... I have been deeply interested and sympathetic with the Russian revolution since it broke. But it is impossible to get any true idea of conditions in Russia from the outside – of that I am positive."[10] That Streit could contemplate being posted to Russia also reflected his new duties: Sometime in 1918, he transferred from the engineers to military intelligence. Following the armistice in November, he was one of ten army intelligence members assigned to the US delegation to the peace conference. Years later, Streit joked that he served on Woodrow Wilson's security detail, smelling flowers to make sure they were not poisonous. In reality, his job was more prosaic but also more interesting: to oversee the delegation's burgeoning library of material on subjects of potential pertinence to the peace negotiations. Streit relished his duties for the privileged access to information it offered as well as for the vistas on international politics it opened. "It is enough to give one an idea of the immensity of the problems confronting the coming conference," he commented on the size and variety of the documentation.[11]

Even as a junior member of the US delegation, Streit found himself in early 1919 at the center of European and international politics. The peace conference that opened in Paris in January acted as a magnet, drawing to the French capital monarchs, statesmen, diplomats, politicians, advisors, revolutionaries, activists, artists, and even gawkers from across the globe. With much of Europe and beyond roiling from the seismic effects of four years of warfare, the stakes in Paris appeared to be of world-deciding importance. The sense of expectation and possibility was palpable. "I feel that it is an opportunity of a life-time," he wrote his mother, "especially at this particular time when all the world is gathering in Paris for the Peace conference."[12]

---

[10] LOC, CKS, Box III: 6, file 7, Streit to Mother and Folks, June 8, 1918; and "Sergeant Streit Gets Letter from Secretary," *The Missoulian*, October 20, 1918, 1–2.

[11] LOC, CKS, Box I: 1, file: Notebooks and Notes, 1917–1918, entries for December 22 and 23, 1918.

[12] LOC, CKS, Box III: 7, file 3, Streit to Mother, December 22, 1918. For Paris in 1919, see Tyler Stovall, *Paris and the Spirit of 1919: Consumer Struggles, Transnationalism, and Revolution* (Cambridge: Cambridge University Press, 2012).

His security duties left Streit plenty of time to immerse himself in this heady atmosphere – to read up on current issues, to write about them, to take courses at the Sorbonne, and to socialize with the small army of foreign correspondents gathered in Paris. All of this further stoked his interest in politics. As might be expected, Streit sympathized with French trade unionists who called a general strike in May 1919, arguing the "French working class" had been driven to despair by "the stupidity, the brutality of the Clemenceau government and of the ruling class in general."[13] Streit's leftist politics are even more evident in his first book, published in 1920. The book stemmed from his interest in the Briey Basin, an iron-rich region on the Franco-German frontier. In the early months of 1919, a controversy erupted in French newspapers and parliament over allegations, made by an odd coalition of leftists and nationalists, that the region had escaped wartime damage due to a tacit alliance between French and German heavy industry. In endorsing unconditionally the allegations, Streit mimicked notable features of prewar progressive journalism in the United States: its exposé-style, its anti-corruption and anti-business thrust, and its moral fervor. Accusing the *Comité des forges*, the French industry organization, of privileging its business interests over the nation's, he castigated the "'Yellow International of the financial and mineral interests'" for which "[t]he wholesale slaughter of men, it cannot be denied, means good business to those who furnish the instruments of death."[14]

Journalists in the Progressive mold sought to mobilize journalism in the service of reform. The aim was not simply to report on events but also to use reporting to galvanize change. His duties in Paris, though, offered

---

[13] LOC, CKS, Box I: 130, file: CKS – Articles – General, Streit, "May Day in Paris. By an American," *The Liberator*, August 1919, 41–46. Also see Jean-Louis Robert, *Les Ouvriers, la patrie et la révolution. Paris 1914–1919* (Paris: Les Belles lettres, 1995), 291–403.

[14] Clarence K. Streit, *"Where Iron Is, There Is the Fatherland!" A Note on the Relation of Privilege and Monopoly to War* (New York: B. W. Huebsch, 1920), 50–51. For more on the controversy, see Jean-Noël Jeanneney, *François de Wendel en République: L'argent et le pouvoir, 1914–1940* (Paris: Seuil, 1976), 67–107, 121–22. The classic study of Progressive journalism is Richard Hofstadter, *The Age of Reform: From Bryan to F.D.R.* (New York: Vintage, 1956), 185–96. Also see J. Michael Sproule, *Propaganda and Democracy: The American Experience of Media and Mass Persuasion* (New York: Cambridge University Press, 1997), 22–52; and Joseph R. Hayden, *Negotiating in the Press: American Journalism and Diplomacy, 1918–1919* (Baton Rouge: Louisiana State University Press, 2010), 58.

Streit a first opportunity to dabble more directly in policy. In January 1919, he drafted a memorandum for the US delegation on "Bolshevism," an issue lurking menacingly over the peace conference despite (or because of) the absence of the Bolsheviks.[15] Consistent with his sympathy for the revolutionary events in Russia, Streit argued against Allied military intervention on the grounds that it would be counter-productive even if successful as the defeat of the Bolshevik regime would saddle the Allies with the thankless task of imposing order on chaos. Nor did Streit favor a policy of isolating the regime through economic blockade, as this would alienate the Russian people and reinforce their reliance on the Bolsheviks. Instead, he recommended the Allies formally recognize the Bolsheviks and allow normal economic relations to develop with Russia on the principle that "a government tends always to become conservative." In what in retrospect might serve as an epitaph for his own political evolution, Streit declared it "axiomatic that the radicals of today are the conservatives of tomorrow."[16]

There is no evidence the memorandum was read by anyone on the US delegation, let alone that it influenced US or Allied policy. But this hardly mattered, as Streit quickly grew disillusioned with the proceedings in Paris, commenting in March 1919 "that this isn't a Peace Congress but an Inter-Allied Victory meeting, with indignation as the guiding general force and Individual Economic Interest as the chief counselor of each nation."[17] To judge from his activities in Paris, which included writing for *Stars and Stripes*, the US army's newspaper, Streit was becoming far more interested in journalism than in policy. In any case, the signing of the peace treaties in the summer of 1919 put an abrupt end to his twenty-two-month adventure in Europe. Now demobilized, Streit returned to Missoula to complete his journalism degree and to take up a staff position with the *Daily Missoulian*. But not for long. Soon afterward, Streit learned he had been awarded a Rhodes scholarship. In January 1920, he was back in Europe, this time at the University of Oxford to study international relations, modern history, and economics.[18]

---

[15] Arno Mayer, *Politics and Diplomacy of Peacemaking: Containment and Counterrevolution at Versailles, 1918–1919* (New York: Alfred A. Knopf, 1967).

[16] LOC, CKS, Box I: 36, file: Biographical material 1939–86 & undated, "Bolshevism," January 21, 1919.

[17] LOC, CKS, Box III: 7, file 4, Streit to Mother and Folks, March 2, 1919.

[18] The Rhodes Trust, Clarence Streit file, untitled biographical notes.

BECOMING A FOREIGN CORRESPONDENT

Streit's commitment to his studies as a Rhodes scholar is open to question. In 1920, he took a summer job as an assistant in the Paris bureau of the *Philadelphia Public Ledger*'s newly established international news service. Although Cyrus Curtis, the *Ledger*'s owner, preferred to focus on domestic news, he decided his newspaper had to respond to the growing demand for foreign news, partly a by-product of the recent world war. The *Ledger* might have subscribed to an international press service, the three principal American ones being the Associated Press, United Press, and Hearst services. But Curtis sniffed a business opportunity. "What I want," he explained in July 1920, "is a <u>superior</u> news service" that could be sold "to every [sic] worth while newspaper in the United States."[19] Accordingly, he set out to build his own service, tapping Carl Ackerman, a former *Saturday Evening Post*, and then United Press correspondent, to direct the European service.

Ackerman was an interesting choice. A veteran correspondent with considerable experience in Europe, Ackerman had supplemented his wartime journalism with covert reporting for the State Department and for Colonel House, President Wilson's closest confidant. Ackermann's principal task was to keep both informed of the complex and evolving political situation in Russia in 1917–18. It is tempting to imagine Ackerman came across Streit's memorandum on Bolshevism, effectively talent-spotting the fledgling journalist, but Ackermann's virulent anti-communism suggests otherwise. Ackerman, in fact, acted less as a reporter than as a propagandist, writing anti-Bolshevik reports as well as a doctored version of the infamous anti-Semitic *Protocols of the Elders of Zion* (itself a forgery by the prewar Tsarist secret police) in which Bolsheviks replaced Jews as the malevolent actors in a conspiracy for world domination. With the war and his clandestine activities behind him, Ackerman established a central office in London for the *Ledger*'s international news service with branch offices in Paris and Berlin.[20]

---

[19] LOC, Carl A. Ackerman Papers, Box 130, Curtis to Ackerman, July 12, 1920.

[20] Meghan Mernard McCune and John Maxwell Hamilton, "'My Object Is to Be of Service to You': Carl Ackerman and the Wilson Administration during World War I," *Intelligence and National Security* 32 (2017), 744–49; Morrell Heald, *Transatlantic Vistas: American Journalists in Europe, 1900–1940* (Kent, OH: Kent State University Press, 1988), 45, 105–6; and Wythe Williams, *Dusk of Empire: The Decline of Europe and the Rise of the United States, as Observed by a Foreign Correspondent in a Quarter-Century of Service* (New York: Charles Scribner's Sons, 1937), 208.

Having worked during the summer for Ackerman's European service in Paris, Streit returned to Oxford for the autumn term of 1920. Soon afterward, he received permission to interrupt his Rhodes scholarship during the first half of 1921 in order to serve as Ackerman's special correspondent in the "Near East" based in Constantinople. The highlight of his five-month posting was a roundabout voyage to Ankara to interview Turkey's reclusive leader, Mustafa Kemal Atatürk. Streit kept a travelogue that he sought unsuccessfully to publish, pitching it as an antidote to "the prejudice which has so long distorted our [Western] views of the Turk ..."[21] At the end of his posting, Streit resumed the Rhodes scholarship in the summer of 1921 only to abandon it in September. That month, he married Jeanne Defrance, a Parisian whom he had met in the summer of 1920. Although information on her is scarce, Defrance appears to have come from an educated, middle-class milieu – her excellent English being one indication. Prior to the marriage, Streit had requested an exemption to the rule that only bachelors could be Rhodes scholars but was refused.

Unable to stay at Oxford, Streit took up an offer from the *Ledger*. Backed by Curtis's "open purse," its international service, in the words of its Paris bureau chief, Wythe Williams, was engaged in a buying spree, "purchasing news features, sending men on far distant assignments, and hiring writers with big names to give their impressions on the international situation." Among the big names recruited was Colonel House. Less ostentatiously, the service also hired a stable of young talent in what Williams described as a "gold rush from America" – talent that included Dorothy Thompson and Clarence Streit. Toward the end of 1921, Streit accepted a regular position with the *Ledger*, becoming its correspondent in Rome at a starting salary of $5,000 (about $75,000 today).[22]

In Rome, Streit witnessed the death of the liberal political regime and its replacement by Mussolini and his fascist movement. As the historian Mauro Canali notes, unlike most foreign correspondents, who tended to report admiringly on *Il Duce*, Streit maintained a critical attitude toward the new regime, emphasizing the minority and even seditious nature of the

---

[21] It would eventually be published as Heath W. Lowry, ed., *Clarence K. Streit's The Unknown Turks: Mustafa Kemal Paşa, Nationalist Anakara & Daily Life in Anatolia, January–March 1921* (Istanbul: Bahçeşehir University Press, 2011). See p. xv for the citation. Also see The Rhodes Trust, Clarence Streit file, Streit to Mr. Wylie, December 18, 1920.

[22] Williams, *Dusk of Empire*, 207–8; and Joseph C. Goulden, *The Curtis Caper* (New York: G. P. Putnam's Sons, 1965), 37.

march on Rome while working to puncture the myth of Fascist popularity. Passivity not enthusiasm struck Streit as the dominant response of Italians to fascism.[23] In early 1923, the *Ledger* made Streit its Balkan correspondent based in Constantinople and Athens. The newspaper, he boasted, has "doubled my salary, making me the highest paid man in the foreign service" apart from the bureau chiefs. The *Ledger*, he added, "spends a good deal of money advertising its foreign correspondents." The salary increase notwithstanding, Streit found the new posting difficult, admitting at the end of the year "I am getting tired of jumping about from one crisis to another in the Balkans." The birth of his first child in January no doubt added to the burden of frequent travel.[24]

Streit would remain in the Balkans for almost two years, during which time his frustrations mounted. One problem came from John Spurgeon, the newspaper's editor, who pressed Ackerman to report less political news and more human-interest stories. "*Please*, for the love of Mike," he scolded Ackerman, "try to think of news in the human sense. Give use something with people. We are fed up on Russia, Bolshevism, Czechoslovakia, Poland and what the various Prime Ministers are doing or saying to one another." Streit became a point of contention, with Spurgeon judging his Turkish assignment an unnecessary luxury and Ackerman defending his protégé as a "live wire" with immense promise.[25] Mounting tensions between the two men soon prompted Ackerman to resign, leaving Streit alone to face Spurgeon's pressure exercised through Williams, his immediate superior. From Paris, Williams unleashed a steady barrage of criticism, beseeching Streit to reduce his expenses, to shorten his reports, to write more "human-interest stuff" and, perhaps most of all, to set aside any illusions about his task as a journalist. "Please remember," he admonished, "that the newspaper business is a daily affair. We have no time to do things as they should be done. It is often a case of snap judgment and speeding up, and no one knows

[23] Mauro Canali, *La scoperta dell'Italia: Il fascismo raccontato dai corrispondenti americani* (Venezia: Marsilio, 2017), 10, 106–7, 168–70. Streit soon nuanced his position, describing Mussolini in private as a "moderate" who "has much more brains than his followers." See LOC, CKS, Box III: 8, file 4, Streit to Dad, November 4, 1922.

[24] The Rhodes Trust, Clarence Streit file, Streit to Mr. Wiley, March 14 and December 29, 1923.

[25] For Spurgeon, see Gerald L. Feltner, "Modern Foreign Correspondents after World War I: The *New York Evening Post*'s David Lawrence and Simeon Stunsky," *American Journalism* 34 (2017), 328–31. Also see LOC, Carl W. Ackerman Papers, Box 131, Spurgeon to Ackerman, May 25, 1920; and Ackerman to Spurgeon, December 12, 1930.

better than I do how wrong often it all is. So I decline to take it too seriously." As early as 1921, Streit privately complained that "its [sic] sometimes a bit difficult to know what to send."[26]

In early 1924, Williams resigned from the Paris bureau. By then the *Ledger*'s international service was in fatal decline, its revenues and Curtis's interest both shrinking. Recognizing the obvious, Streit began moonlighting for other US newspapers before accepting a position in 1925 with the *New York Times*. With a daily circulation of well over 400,000 copies (and almost double on Sunday) in 1930, the *Times* not only enjoyed a wide readership but also was the newspaper of choice for much of the US political elite. The *Times*, one knowledgeable observer noted in 1935, "will remain America's greatest newspaper because it is rich enough to employ men who write well, rich enough to operate the largest foreign news service, to print documents in full, to give the public a far greater quantity of news than any other paper."[27] Its foreign news service was unrivaled in its geographic scope and content. A position with the *Times* thus promised Streit secure employment, greater prestige, and a wider readership. It also entailed considerable travel: Posted initially to Vienna, he moved around a great deal over the next several years, working not only in Europe but also in North Africa and the Caribbean.

Among Streit's assignments was a stint in Haiti in 1928 to study the "ways of the American intervention," which had begun in 1915 and was scheduled to end (as it did) in 1934.[28] In addition to reports for the *Times*, Streit penned an article for *Foreign Affairs*, a journal published by the Council on Foreign Relations, the elitist club of US internationalists. The article criticized the military occupation regime for its counter-productive results. Despite their declared aim of building an independent Haiti, the occupation authorities were doing almost nothing to train Haitians to run their own affairs while pursuing development policies privileging US-owned plantations at the expense of a growing "landless proletariat," effectively reproducing dependence. Writing to his wife, Streit castigated occupation officials for their ignorance of Haiti, of its history and

---

[26] LOC, CKS, Box III: 13, file 3, Williams to Streit, July 23 and August 7, 1923; and Box III: 8, file 3, Streit to Dad, October 27, 1921.

[27] George Seldes, *Freedom of the Press* (Indianapolis, IN: Bobbs-Merrill, 1935), 214. On the newspaper more generally, see Yves-Mair Péreon, *L'Image de la France dans la presse américaine, 1937–1947* (Bruxelles: Peter Lang, 2011), 33–43; and Laura Leff, *Buried by the Times: The Holocaust and America's Most Important Newspaper* (Cambridge: Cambridge University Press, 2005), 9–19.

[28] The Rhodes Trust, Clarence Streit file, Streit to Mr. Wylie, March 26, 1929.

languages, as well as for their "enormous self-complacency" and lack "of the spirit of sympathetic understanding." In the article, though, he identified the principal problem as the "system," defined obscurely as "circumstance and drift," rather than the occupation itself or its US personnel, whose good intentions he never questioned. The solution, accordingly, was not to change the system but to reinforce it through greater political oversight by Washington.[29]

If Streit's somewhat critical position points to the continued relevance of his left-leaning politics, it also suggests a blind spot when it came to issues of empire and race in US policies. Like many well-meaning people, Streit, while recognizing "race prejudice" as a factor on US occupation policies, could be serenely unaware of his own racism. For instance, he recounted to his wife a party at the presidential palace, describing as "amusing and pathetic" the attempts of Haitians to imitate their more civilized betters. But arguably even more telling was the assumption that Haiti desperately needed to be developed (civilized) and that only the United States could do so, notwithstanding the occupation's patent problems, among them its exploitative nature. Rather than structural elements of US occupation, Streit viewed its shortcomings as an inherent function of "backward and weak" countries. The result was a convenient alibi not only for the regrettable aspects of US policies but also for what Streit discerned as the predictable failure of the occupation to match US ideals.[30]

Shortly after the article's publication in *Foreign Affairs*, the *Times* posted Streit to Geneva, where he would remain as its foreign correspondent until 1938. Never again would he venture beyond the north Atlantic world.

THE FRUSTRATIONS OF A FOREIGN CORRESPONDENT

Streit's thriving career as a foreign correspondent paralleled the development of the profession in general. Indeed, the interwar years have been

---

[29] Streit, "Haiti: Intervention in Operation," *Foreign Affairs* 6 (July 1928), 615–32, 619, 627–29; and LOC, CKS, Box III: 4, file 7, Streit to Wife, January 25, 1928.

[30] LOC, CKS, Box III: 4, file 7, Streit to Wife, January 20, 1928. For the occupation, see Mary A. Renda, *Taking Haiti: Military Occupation and the Culture of U.S. Imperialism* (Chapel Hill: University of North Carolina Press, 2001). Even after the end of the military occupation, the United States continued to control Haitian finances until 1947. See Emily S. Rosenberg, *Financial Missionaries to the World: The Politics and Culture of Dollar Diplomacy, 1900–1930* (Durham, NC: Duke University Press, 2003), 250.

called the "golden age" for US foreign correspondents.[31] The boom in newspaper readership, which began in the mid-nineteenth century and was fueled by the expansion of education, falling prices, and various marketing techniques, carried over after 1918. At the start of the 1920s, the United States could boast of some 2,500 daily newspapers published in 11,000 towns for a combined circulation of 32 million. By one estimate, 95 percent of adult Americans read at least one newspaper on a regular basis.[32] Over the next decade, circulation figures continued to grow, though at a reduced rate even if some newspapers showed remarkable gains. The *New York Times*, for example, increased its circulation by 60 percent between 1920 and 1930.[33]

Accompanying the overall growth of newspaper readership was an expanding market for foreign news, a development that can also be traced back to the nineteenth century. If the Spanish-American War and, more generally, the United States' emergence as an imperial power, stimulated this expansion, US involvement in World War I and in the peacemaking in Paris 1918–19 added a potent spur. "The war has developed a new sort of Washington correspondent," one journalist commented in 1920. "Five years ago it helped a Washington correspondent very little to be familiar with European politics. To-day such knowledge enhances his value beyond measure."[34] Newspaper content reflected the change. In the case of the *New York Times*, by one estimate 19 percent of front-page articles dealt with foreign news between 1900 and 1905; the corresponding figure for 1920 to 1925 was 32 percent.[35]

More foreign news required more foreign correspondents, and the early postwar years witnessed a notable increase in their numbers. As recently as the end of the nineteenth century, most newspapers had relied

---

[31] John Maxwell Hamilton, *Journalism's Roving Eye: A History of American Foreign Reporting* (Baton Rouge: Louisiana State University Press, 2009), 2; and Nancy C. Cott, "Revisiting the Transatlantic 1920s: Vincent Sheean vs. Malcolm Cowly," *American Historical Review* 118 (2013), 46–75, 68.

[32] Nancy F. Cott, *Fighting Worlds: The Bold American Journalists Who Brought the World Home between the Wars* (New York: Basic Books, 2020), 11; and Thomas C. Leonard, *New for All: America's Coming-of-Age with the Press* (New York: Oxford University Press, 1995), 69, 91, 179.

[33] Robert W. Desmond, *Crisis and Conflict: World News Reporting Between Two World Wars, 1920–1940* (Iowa City: University of Iowa Press, 1982), 291–303.

[34] Cited in Feltner, "Modern Foreign Correspondents after World War I," 327.

[35] Christine Ogan, Ida Plymale, D. Lynn Smith, William H. Turpin, and Donald Lewis Shaw, "The Changing Front Page of the New York Times, 1900–1970," *Journalism Quarterly* 52 (1975), 343.

for foreign content on local reporters who were paid by the story (stringers). At the beginning of the twentieth century, the *Chicago Daily News* was the first newspaper to develop an extensive news service with its own full-time US correspondents, but before the Great War it remained modest in size and reach. In the wake of the war, several major news-papers scrambled either to follow the *Chicago Daily News*' example in creating a service or, as in the case of the *New York Times*, in enlarging their existing structures. In the early 1920s, Adolph Ochs, the *Times*' owner, resolved to build "the widest and most comprehensive newspaper coverage in the world," notwithstanding the estimated annual costs of $500,000.[36] Unlike Curtis and the *Ledger*, Ochs and the *Times* would enjoy sustained success in the endeavor.

Newspapers appeared ideally placed to meet the demand for foreign news. After all, they faced few competitors in the field. Television had yet to be invented while radio remained in its infancy; only toward the end of the 1930s would it seriously challenge the predominance of newspapers. As for other printed media, such as magazines and reviews (most of which were published on a weekly or monthly basis), they complemented more than rivaled newspapers' often quotidian reporting. This prominence has led one historian to declare "[p]rint journalists created the public sphere during the interwar years." While this assessment is perhaps exaggerated, it is nevertheless true that newspapers and the correspondents who worked for them functioned as a leading source of information about the outside world – about its people, places, and events – for much of the US public. Foreign correspondents at the time, another historian remarks, served "as antennae, as interpreters and expositors" for Americans back home.[37]

For all these reasons, the job of foreign correspondent appealed to ambitious, curious, and intrepid Americans in the early postwar years. The urge to escape the geographical limits as well as the social and moral

---

[36] Meyer Berger, *The History of the New York Times: The First 100 Years, 1851–1951* (New York: Simon & Schuster, 1970), 249. Also see Jaci Cole and John Maxwell Hamilton, "A Natural History of Foreign Correspondence: A Study of the *Chicago Daily News*, 1900–1921," *Journalism & Mass Communication Quarterly* 84 (2007), 151–65.

[37] Cott, *Fighting Worlds*, 324; and Heald, *Transatlantic Vistas*, xiii. Giovanna Dell'Orto argues that "it is through the ecology of discourses created, circulated and maintained through the press that foreign realities are understood and acted on." See her *American Journalism and International Relations: Foreign Correspondence from the Early Republic to the Digital Age* (Cambridge: Cambridge University Press, 2013), 18.

constraints of living in the United States clearly activated Streit, but, as Nancy Cott and Deborah Cohen show, the quest for personal freedom and novel experiences spurred others whose careers began in the 1920s.[38] Admittedly, not all these early-career correspondents found their way to Europe: The number of US journalists working in China rose steadily after 1918, one sign of the globalizing scope of public interest in the world beyond the United States.[39] Still, Europe continued to draw a disproportionate share of US journalists. If the strong dollar offered important advantages, a far more important reason was the strength of overlapping transatlantic bonds – political, economic, cultural, and ethnic – that had made Europe the seemingly obvious destination for students, tourists, and other travelers from the end of the nineteenth century.[40] The recent world war, which for the US public was fought preponderantly on the Western front, strengthened this focus on Europe. Reflecting this bias, Europe and especially Western Europe accounted for upwards of 80 percent of foreign coverage in US newspapers during the interwar years.[41]

The 1920s, then, were an auspicious time to become a foreign correspondent in Europe – a time when personal and professional opportunities seemingly abounded. This is certainly the impression foreign correspondents themselves cultivated in their first-hand accounts of perilous journeys, intrigue-laced politics, and encounters with the good and the great. Streit's travelogue of his 1921 expedition to interview Atatürk offers an early example, even if it was published long afterward. But the paragon is Vincent Sheean's 1935 best-selling memoir, *Personal History*, which became the basis for Alfred Hitchcock's 1940 thriller, *Foreign Correspondent*.[42] Although few correspondents possessed Sheean's literary skills, growing numbers, responding to a burgeoning market, penned memoirs, which grafted personal histories onto dramatic narratives of international politics. Summing up his career in 1936, Webb Miller, a United Press (UP) correspondent, recounted:

---

[38] Cott, *Fighting Words*; and Deborah Cohen, *Last Call at the Hotel Imperial: Reporters Who Took on a World at War* (New York: Random House, 2022).

[39] Yong Volz and Lei Guo, "Making China Their 'Beat': A Collective Biography of U.S. Correspondents in China, 1900–1949," *American Journalism* 36 (2019), 473–96.

[40] See Whitney Walton, *Internationalism, National Identities, and Study Abroad: France and the United States, 1890–1970* (Stanford, CA: Stanford University Press, 2010).

[41] Cleo Joffrion Allen, "Foreign News Coverage in Selected U.S. Newspaper 1927–1997: A Content Analysis." PhD, Louisiana State University, 2005, 71; and W. James Potter, "News from Three Worlds in Prestige U.S. Newspapers," *Journalism Quarterly* 64 (1987), 77.

[42] For Sheean, see Cott, "Revisiting the Transatlantic 1920s," 46–75.

During twenty-four years I have had a grandstand seat at the momentous show in history. From there I have witnessed the decline and fall of empires, the birth of new nations, the rise of new philosophies of government and the disappearance of old ones. I have seen the map of the world redrawn and come to known men and women of fifty-one nationalities and a dozen creeds and religions. I have made friends with presidents, premiers, dictators, generals, soldiers, common workers, murderers, thieves, pimps, panders, and prostitutes.[43]

In placing themselves at the center of events, foreign correspondents imbued their profession – and themselves – with a sense of importance and purpose. "We made it a point to be casual and nonchalant about kings and dictators and premiers," Eugene Lyon, a UP correspondent, remarked. But "[u]nderneath it [nonchalance] we were thoroughly impressed with the importance of our calling and our privileged vantage point on History in the Making."[44]

All told, descriptions of the interwar years as the golden age of the foreign correspondent are readily understandable: In this formative period for the profession, talented and determined individuals enjoyed considerable freedom to forge careers whose rewards included not only travel and adventure but also attractive salaries, prestige, and relevance. Yet this description, now something of a cliché, neglects an important element: the professionalization of journalism. During the opening decades of the twentieth century, journalism became a well-defined profession with its own educational requirements, skills-set, norms, rules, and expectations. And one unintended consequence of this process was the emergence of a palpable gap between professional ideals and realities.

Historians of journalism have identified an emerging norm and even ideology of "objectivity" centered on an ideal of factual, disinterested, apolitical, and in-depth reporting.[45] The initial impulse dated to the late

---

[43] Webb Miller, *I Found No Peace: The Journal of a Foreign Correspondent* (New York: The Literary Guild, 1936), 317.

[44] Eugene Lyons, *Assignment in Utopia* (New York: Harcourt, Brace, 1937), 394.

[45] Michael Schudson, "The Objectivity Norm in American Journalism," *Journalism* 2 (2001), 149–70. Also see Richard L. Kaplan, *Politics of the American Press: The Rise of Objectivity, 1865–1920* (Cambridge: Cambridge University Press, 2002); David T. Z. Mindich, *Just the Facts: How "Objectivity" Came to Define American Journalism* (New York: New York University Press, 1998); and Hazel Dicken-Garcia, *Journalistic Standards in Nineteenth-Century America* (Madison: University of Wisconsin Press, 1989). Schudson' claim that the "objectivity norm" distinguished American from European journalism is questionable. See Michael Homberg, *Reporter-Streifzüge: Metropolitaine Nachrichtenkultur und die Wahrnehmung der Welt 1870–1918* (Göttingen: Vandenhoeck & Ruprecht, 2017); and Christian Delporte, "Les journalistes dans l'entre-deux-guerres. Une identité en crise," *Vingtième siècle* 47 (1995), 158–75.

nineteenth century and was the product of several factors, including a reaction to the sensationalism, luridness, and distortions if not outright fabrications of the "yellow press." The World War I experience of government control and censorship, together with patriotic self-censorship on the part of newspapers and journalists, generated a reaction, reinforcing the appeal of objectivity as an ideal. Journalists should be independent seekers, not simply of the facts but also of a deeper and truer understanding of events, a type of reporting requiring them to dig beneath and beyond the propaganda and censorship of various kinds.[46]

The most prominent contemporary proponent of objectivity in journalism was Walter Lippmann, the prolific journalist and political commentator. In a series of articles for the *Atlantic Monthly* in 1919, subsequently issued as a short book, he warned of the dangers of government efforts to influence, if not control, the news. But Lippmann reserved his sharpest criticism for the self-censorship practiced by newspapers, warning "the most destructive form of untruth is sophistry and propaganda by those whose profession is to report the news." The following year, the *New Republic* published a much-commented-upon study by Lippmann, cowritten with Charles Merz, of the *New York Times*' coverage of events in Russia in 1917, pointedly demonstrating the newspaper's invasive anti-Bolshevism, a bias in which the editorial staff and journalists were equally complicit. Incidentally, Streit, back in 1918, had privately railed at the Press' "bourgeois prejudice" against Russia. Lippmann and Merz were no less scathing, judging the *Times*' coverage as "nothing short of a disaster. On the essential questions the net effect was almost always misleading, and misleading news is worse than none at all."[47]

For Lippmann and Merz, one solution was to raise the "professional standards of journalism" as "the discipline by which standards are maintained are not strong enough." To do so, they recommended codes of ethics, greater accountability, and transparency in the operations of

---

[46] David R. Spencer, *The Yellow Journalism: The Press and America's Emergence as a World Power* (Evanston, IL: Northwestern University Press, 2007); and Hayden, *Negotiating in the Press*. Journalism was not alone in undergoing a process of professionalization associated with the ideal of objectivity. For another case, see Peter Novick, *That Noble Dream: The "Objectivity Question" and the American Historical Profession* (Cambridge: Cambridge University Press, 1988).

[47] Walter Lippmann, *Liberty and the News* (New York: Harcourt, Brace & Howe, 1920), 10; and Walter Lippmann and Charles Merz, "A Test of the News," supplement to *The New Republic*, August 4, 1920, 3. For Streit, see LOC, CKS, Box III: 7, file 3, Streit to Mother, October 30, 1918.

newspapers, and better training of staff and of journalists in particular. Invoking public concern about the shortage of objective reporting, an alarmed Lippmann cautioned that if the profession did not take measures to regulate itself then "some day Congress, in a fit of temper, egged on by an outraged public opinion, will operate on the press with an ax."[48]

If Lippmann's alarmism expressed a general malaise at the time, it was also overblown, for journalism was undergoing an accelerating process of professionalization – one centered on the ideal of objectivity. One element of this process, illustrated by Streit's own educational path, was the rapid multiplication of journalism schools and programs in the United States. The University of Missouri created the country's first journalism school in 1908; 20 years later there were some 430 instructors teaching 5,500 students in over 50 institutions. In 1913, Columbia University's school opened its doors, signaling that journalism now belonged among the professions taught at elite universities. Ackermann, Streit's first boss, would graduate from Columbia's school in 1913 and later become its dean. Although curricula varied from school to school, typical programs lasted from two to four years and emphasized professional ethics as well as practical skills. Journalists, these schools taught, served not a particular country, interest, or political cause but the greater or public good.[49] Other elements of professionalization included the creation of prizes, most notably the Pulitzer first awarded in 1917, and the elaboration of codes of conduct – as Lippmann himself had recommended. In 1914, the National Press Club adopted the "Journalist's Creed" written by Walter Williams, the founder of the University of Missouri's journalism school. Identifying the profession as a "public trust," it insisted "clear thinking and clear statement, accuracy and fairness are fundamental to good journalism."[50]

Thus, Streit became a journalist at the very moment the profession was assuming a corporate identity, which esteemed the ideal of objectivity, defined as a responsibility to strive for accurate, value-free, and thorough reporting. More than a mere inspiration, the idea of objectivity was intended to be a practical guide for journalists in their day-to-day

---

[48] Lippmann and Merz, "A Test of the News," 41; and Lippmann, *Liberty and the News*, 76, 74–103.

[49] Jean Folkerts, "History of Journalism Education," *Journalism & Communication Monographs* 16 (2014), 231–40.

[50] Ronald T. Farrar, *A Creed to My Profession: Walter Williams, Journalist to the World* (Columbia: University of Missouri Press, 1998), 192–206.

activities. One result, as Streit's experience suggests, was a frustrating gap between the ideal and reality.

Foreign correspondents faced practical difficulties that all the talk of a golden age easily elides. As Lippmann recognized, there was government censorship, which became an especially visible problem during the 1930s when several European regimes, and most notably Nazi Germany, placed tight controls on information. Webb Miller thus lamented in 1937 that "[f]ollowing the rise of dictatorial governments ... censorship became a fundamental rule ..." But even in the 1920s government censorship appeared ominous. A conference of press experts, convened in 1927 under the auspices of the League Nations, called on governments to end various measures of censorship, including the banning of foreign correspondents.[51] The year before, Streit, working as the *New York Times*' correspondent in Rumania, had been expelled from the country for articles judged hostile to the monarchical regime.[52]

Journalists in the 1930s were even more troubled by what the League's conference of press experts labeled "tendentious news" – that is, news provided by governments. The 1920s saw the proliferation of national news agencies across Europe, which increasingly exercised a guiding hand on (and sometimes a monopoly of) national news, a significant source for foreign correspondents and an absolutely vital source for US news services. By 1934, the Associated Press received the majority of its European news from state-controlled national agencies. John Gunther recognized the obvious problem with such news, remarking "handouts" by their very nature constituted propaganda; he nevertheless expressed confidence that the knowing correspondent would be able to filter out biases. Gunther's confidence, though, was questionable at a time when national services increasingly served, in the words of one historian, as "gatekeepers" not only for the larger US news services such as AP and UP but also for correspondents working directly for newspapers.[53]

Less direct, but not necessarily less irksome, forms of censorship occurred on the US side. If individual correspondents had their preferences and prejudices, so too did the newspapers they worked for. The editorial biases of some, such as the isolationist and arch anti-Democrat

---

[51] Miller, *I Found No Peace*, 318; and Christopher A. Casey, "Deglobalization and the Disintegration of the European News System, 1918–34," *Journal of Contemporary History* 53 (2017), 281.

[52] "Rumania Expels Times Reporter," *New York Times*, May 25, 1926, 3.

[53] Casey, "Deglobalization and the Disintegration," 278–79. On the role of the larger American news services, see Desmond, *Crisis and Conflict*, 225–34.

Chicago Tribune, were self-evident. Those of others, such as the *New York Times*, were more or less explicit – and also a matter of political perspective. In the 1930s, George Seldes, a former foreign correspondent in Europe turned fierce critic of the Press, accused the *New York Times* of being "the organ of the men of the *status quo*, the friend of those in power, the conservative spokesmen of a system which dreads change and which fears every reform or radical plan …"[54] In terms of international politics, though, the newspaper was not so much pro-status quo as it was staunchly internationalist in a broadly Wilsonian sense, which translated into general support for greater US engagement in the world as well as sympathy for the League of Nations, while also shying away from specific commitments. If this orientation left room for maneuvre, the possibilities were not unlimited as Streit himself would discover when his editors, deeming he had strayed too far from the *Times*' line, questioned his "reputation for objective reporting."[55]

Commercial imperatives, broadly construed, probably had a more practical impact on journalists than political censorship. In principle, a division of labor existed between the larger US news services and foreign correspondents working directly for newspapers: While the former concentrated on "facts" (deaths, elections, disasters, etc.), the latter provided the context – or what Gunther termed "the significance behind the facts." In reality, correspondents were less free than Gunther maintained to "explore, elucidate, and editorialize."[56] One reason, mentioned earlier, is that newspaper owners and editors perceived the growing demand for foreign news through the lens of an imagined everyday American. Correspondents came under pressure to Americanize foreign news, and, as Seldes explained, this entailed approaching foreign news as one would domestic news. And the dominant approach to the latter was that of the local beat reporter, whose copy combined basic information with an emphasis on immediacy and personalities. Tellingly, Seldes deemed this reporting and not journalism.[57]

Financial considerations reinforced the constraints on journalism. Maintaining an adequate foreign news service proved expensive, spurring

[54] Seldes, *Freedom of the Press*, 214. For Seldes in general, see Helen Fordham, *George Seldes' War for the Public Good: Weaponising a Free Press* (London: Palgrave, 2019).

[55] LOC, CKS, Box I: 13, file: Press: General, 1932, Streit to Carl Ackermann, October 31, 1934.

[56] John Gunther, "Funneling the European News," *Harper's Magazine*, April 1, 1930, 638.

[57] George Seldes, *Lords of the Press* (New York, 1938), 283–91. Also see Fordham, *George Seldes' War for the Public Good*, 27–28.

an ever-greater reliance on the larger news services such as AP and UP, whose limits were increasingly evident. Even the handful of newspapers, the *New York Times* among them, willing and able to incur the costs involved, sought to curb spending. Streit's editors, indeed, repeatedly pressed him to keep costs down. One way to do so, given the high costs of telegraph communication at the time, was to reduce the length (word count) of stories sent by wire. As with social media today, the incentives to be succinct produced a distinct and even abstruse vocabulary among correspondents. But they also pushed correspondents to sacrifice context in favor of "facts." Clearly chafing under such constraints, Streit during the 1920s toyed with several ideas: to create an expatriate daily to provide the in-depth reporting for the "thinking intelligent man," or even to establish a syndicated service offering higher quality international news.[58]

Additional constraints involved newsgathering. Contrary to a popular portrait of journalists dashing from one adventure to another in pursuit of their stories, the reality was far more routine – and frustrating. For most correspondents, the principal sources of information consisted of national news agencies, newspapers, government handouts, and the larger news services, all of which were problematic. The ambitious correspondent who endeavored to expand this source base quickly encountered obstacles. Most US correspondents possessed limited language skills at a time when English was less omnipresent than now. Streit spoke French, which proved handy in Romania but less so in Vienna, his first regular job with the *Times*.[59] And, like many correspondents, Streit moved from one posting to another in rapid order (four times between 1922 and 1927). In addition to the disrupting effects on family life, this frequent movement hindered the ability to develop in-country expertise and contacts. To be sure, foreign correspondents formed a relatively tight-knit fraternity in interwar Europe, often sharing information with one another. But however useful, this cooperation offered no real solution to the limits of inadequate sources. Foreign correspondents could do little more than scratch the surface.

The overriding result was a frustrating gap – indeed gulf – between what foreign correspondents were enjoined to do (and many sought to do) and what they did. Journalism's ongoing professionalization,

---

[58] LOC, CKS, Box I: 12, file: Daily Why Project, untitled note, August 1, 1924; and Box III: 8, file 6, Streit to Dad, September 23, 1924.
[59] For one correspondent's emphasis on the importance of linguistic capabilities, see J. C. Oestreicher, *The World Is Their Beat* (New York: Duell, Sloan & Pearce, 1945), 72.

epitomized in the ideal of objectivity, held out a tantalizing promise: Correspondents could produce the factual, sourced-based, and in-depth reporting needed for the public to grasp the stakes of international politics. Yet multiple practical factors – editorial politics, commercial imperatives, inadequate sources – rendered this promise all-too elusive. If the resulting gulf between the promise and the realities of the job has probably become a permanent feature of the profession, it was particularly palpable during the interwar period because the process of professionalization was so recent.

The frustration generated by this gap is evident in a lengthy report Streit wrote in 1932 in his function as president of the association of journalists accredited to the League of Nations. The occasion was a League inquiry into the relationship between the Press and the promotion of peace, which included the subject of "false news," defined as information that was deliberately distorting. Streit sought to expand the scope of the inquiry to encompass the practical difficulties facing foreign correspondents. "Always," he opened, "we journalists have had to fight for accuracy against heavy odds." A key problem lay in the gulf between professional ideals and reality. While the demand for, and need of, "accurate news" was ever more apparent, the ability of correspondents to respond fell woefully short. One handicap was the need to simplify complex issues requiring 25,000 words into "500 words." Another was the shortage of time, support, and sources. Rather than "do work of the standard he would like to do," a correspondent is forced "to dash off two or three reports ... for newspapers in different places, and then write reports on several other different things, and they have to grind away like this every day." Streit understood that "accurate news" – reporting approaching more closely the ideal of objectivity – could be prohibitively expensive as the "*newspaper cannot live on what people will pay directly for the news.*" Accordingly, he recommended international subsidies to defray the costs involved in the production and dissemination of news. The recommendation proved controversial, earning Streit a reprimand from his editor who viewed it as veiled criticism of the *Times.*[60]

---

[60] LONA, Association internationale des journalistes accrédités auprès de la S.D.N., Box P 14, file: Correspondance, etc 1932, "The Problem of False News. Reply to the Council of the League of Nations by the Committee of the International Association of Journalists Accredited to the League of Nations," Streit, July 26, 1932. Emphasis in original. For the enquiry, see Carolyn N. Biltoft, *A Violent Peace: Media, Truth, and Power at the League of Nations* (Chicago: University of Chicago Press, 2021), 105–10. For the reprimand, see

Streit was far from alone in his frustration. As is well-known, several of the most prominent US correspondents at the time – John Gunther, Vincent Sheean, H. R. Knickerbocker – voiced dissatisfaction at the constraints operating on them. Having observed first-hand the aggressive nature of the fascist states, they urgently sought to warn Americans back home of the looming threat.[61] Finding foreign reporting too constraining, too limited in its influence, these correspondents responded by re-defining journalism. Most often they donned the mantle of opinion-maker as reporting gave way to commentary. Here, Lippmann had blazed a path with his column in the *New York Herald Tribune*, which others would follow, for example, Dorothy Thompson.

The frustration felt by Thompson and others, however, did not date from the 1930s. Its roots can be traced back to the postwar years and to the ongoing professionalization of journalism, encapsulated in the ideal of objectivity, which created a gulf between ideal and reality. It was not that this ideal excluded the role of Cassandra; if anything, it encouraged it. And the ideal of objectivity did so by inculcating a strong sense of purpose and self-importance among foreign correspondents. "We felt that what we wrote was important, that it could not only interest people, but influence them – and through them events" recollected Geoffrey Cox of his American (and British) colleagues.[62] In the context of mounting international tensions during the 1930s, correspondents believed they had a duty, indeed a responsibility, to influence policies. If journalism and its objectivity ideal could not accommodate this imperative, then it would need to be reformed – or abandoned.

Streit, too, was tempted by the idea of the journalist as commentator/opinion-maker – hence his interest in founding his own expatriate newspaper in the mid-1920s. Ultimately, though, he went further. Rather than issuing general calls for opposition to the dictator states, Streit began to devise proposals for specific international issues. At the end of 1920s, he concocted a plan to reduce the dangers of international conflict by having nations pledge themselves to hold plebiscites before declaring war. Thanks largely to his status as a *New York Times*' correspondent, Streit received numerous comments on his plan, including one from Franklin

---

NYPL, NYTCR, Arthur Hays Sulzberger, Box 72, file 72.17, E. L. J. to Sulzberger, October 12, 1932.

[61] Cohen, *Last Call at the Hotel Imperial*, 136–66; and Cott, *Fighting Worlds*, 4–5, 321.

[62] Geoffrey Cox, *Eyewitness: A Memoir of Europe in the 1930s* (Dunedin, NZ: University of Otago Press, 1999), 249.

D. Roosevelt, soon to become governor of New York, who remarked that the US Congress would certainly reject the idea, and from Lippmann, who pointed out that, if all countries were sincerely willing to adopt the plan, the problem (war) would no longer exist.[63] A few years later, Streit returned to the charge, this time with a plan to solve the war debts/reparations issue that had so bedeviled international politics in the 1920s. Although managing to get a lengthy article published in the *Times* on the plan, few seemed interested. As Lippmann gently counseled Streit, the issue had lost much of its pertinence by the early 1930s.[64]

In the face of discouraging responses, Streit dropped both plans. The urge to find solutions to pressing international problems, however, remained.

IN GENEVA COVERING THE LEAGUE OF NATIONS

In early 1929, *the New York Times* assigned Streit to Geneva to cover the League of Nations, where he would remain until the end of 1938. The lengthy stay in one place testifies to the value the *Times* placed in him, for Streit successfully resisted pressure to be reassigned, including to the newspaper's head office in New York, presumably to be groomed for its editorial staff. To be sure, Streit confronted familiar pressures, not least that of adapting his reporting to the demands of objectivity. Unhappy with "Streit's discursive articles," the *Times*' managing editor reminded its European editor in 1932 that "[w]hat we want from Geneva, as you know, is news." While "[t]here is room for a certain amount of interpretation," too many of Streit's despatches "have been edited or omitted."[65]

But for all the constraints, Geneva was an exciting place to work for a foreign correspondent during the 1930s. During the sessions of the League's General Assembly or during periods of crisis, the city became the focal point of international politics, bringing together national

[63] See LOC, CKS, Box I: 12, file: Peace Plan, "Checking War by Reciprocal Pledge," Streit, May 23, 1929; for Roosevelt, see CKS, Box I: 4, file: Chronological correspondence, Roosevelt to Streit, July 27, 1928; and for Lippmann, see SMLPU, Hamilton Fish Armstrong Papers, Box 60, file: Streit, Clarence, Fish to Streit, January 23, 1929.

[64] YUL, Walter Lippmann Papers, Box 104, file 2021, Lippmann to Streit, November 10, 1933; and Streit, "A Plan for World Recovery Based on Use of War Debts," *New York Times*, September 24, 1933, 4.

[65] NYPL, NYTCR, Arthur Hays Sulzberger Papers, Box 72, file 72.17, Sulzberger to E. L. J., December 13, 1933; and LOC, CKS, Box III: 8, file 7, E. L. James to Birchall, October 31, 1932.

leaders, foreign ministers, and diplomats from several continents. Upward of 100 foreign correspondents were accredited to the League, with another 200 or so passing through on a regular basis, making Geneva a hub of international journalism. The League, an English correspondent commented in 1938, "possesses a curious fascination for the world's newspapers and their correspondents. Geneva is the first laboratory to be created for the manufacture of world opinion."[66] It was also a congenial place to work, thanks to the League, whose information section, headed by a former US journalist, Arthur Sweetser, cultivated foreign correspondents, providing them with ample documentation and comfortable facilities.[67]

Streit thrived in Geneva. Colleagues referred to him as "the able and popular Clarence Streit" and as the "most distinguished among the residents." In addition to such praise, Streit, in 1932, was nominated for a Pulitzer Prize for his reporting on the world economic conference.[68] In the process, he became a recognized expert on the League of Nations, writing articles for magazines as well as giving lectures and radio addresses in Europe and the United States on the organization.

In his public appearances, Streit addressed the fraught subject of the United States' relations with the League – a subject on which scholarly views diverge. An older view emphasizes the United States' absence from the League following the Senate's rejection of the peace treaty in 1919 and again in 1920, an absence supposedly emblematic of the country's isolationist orientation during the interwar years. Organized groups such as the League of Nations Association (LNA), founded in 1923, labored to persuade the public and Congress of the League's merits, though ultimately with little success. After the Senate's 1935 rejection of membership in the World Court, a tribunal attached to the League, support for US participation in the latter rapidly faded.[69] A newer view, by contrast,

---

[66] George Slocombe, *A Mirror to Geneva: Its Growth, Grandeur and Decay* (Freeport, NY: Books for Libraries Press, 1970), 315.

[67] For Sweetser, see Isabella Löhr and Madeleine Herren, "Gipfeltreffen im Schatten der Weltpolitik: Arthur Sweetser und die Mediendiplomatie des Völkerbunds," *Zeitschrift für Geschichtswissenshaft* 62 (2014), 411–24; and Heidi J. S. Tworek, "Peace Through Truth?: The Press and Moral Disarmament through the League of Nations," *Medien & Zeit* 4 (2010), 22–28.

[68] Slocombe, *A Mirror to Geneva*, 317; and John T. Whitaker, *And Fear Came* (New York: Macmillan, 1936), 88.

[69] Warren F. Kuehl and Lynne K. Dunn, *Keeping the Covenant: American Internationalists and the League of Nations, 1920–1939* (Kent, OH: Kent State University Press, 1997); Robert D. Accinelli, "Militant Internationalists: The League of Nations Association, the

underscores the country's involvement in the League, particularly in its diverse "technical" activities (health, education, finance and economics, labor). If the principal actors were nongovernmental organizations such as private banks and foundations, many enjoyed the State Department's blessing and sometimes active if discreet backing. This second view, moreover, belongs to a larger effort to rehabilitate the League's historical reputation: Rather than a failed security institution, it now appears as a dynamic and innovative participant in efforts to devise new forms of international governance – forms that would mark international relations after 1945.[70]

Foreign correspondents in Geneva during the 1930s would have been surprised by subsequent efforts to rehabilitee the League's record. By the second half of the decade, their collective assessment of the institution was markedly negative. "It was, unfortunately, impossible to follow the proceedings of the League at Geneva without becoming cynical about it," Robert Dell, a well-known journalist, remarked in an account tellingly entitled *The Geneva Racket* and published in 1940. Dell was British but well before then US correspondents in Geneva had issued harsh assessments of the League. It had "failed lamentably," Webb Miller bemoaned in 1936, making another European war unavoidable, a prediction echoed by John Whitaker, a *New York Herald Tribune* journalist, who deemed the League to have "failed, and failed miserably."[71] Wythe Williams, who had been Streit's immediate boss at the *Ledger* before also joining the *New York Times*, denounced the League as a "colossal failure – of which it furnished almost daily proof." Looking back from 1940, Frederick Birchall, another *Times*' correspondent, dismissed the institution as the "Futile League."[72]

Peace Movement, and U.S. Foreign Policy, 1934–28," *Diplomatic History* 4 (1980), 19–38; and Gary B. Ostrower, *Collective Insecurity: The United States and the League of Nations during the Early Thirties* (Lewisburg, PA: Bucknell University Press, 1979).

[70] For the United States' involvement, see Ludovic Tournès, *Les États-Unis et la Société des Nations (1914–1946): Le système international face à l'émergence d'une superpuissance* (Bern: Peter Lang, 2016). For the more general rehabilitation of the League, see Patricia Clavin, *Securing the World Economy: The Reinvention of the League of Nations, 1920–1946* (Oxford: Oxford University Press, 2013); and Susan Pedersen, "Back to the League of Nations," *American Historical Review* 112 (2007), 1091–117.

[71] Robert Dell, *The Geneva Racket 1930–1939* (London: Robert Hale, 1940), 7; Miller, *I Found No Peace*, 322; and Whitaker, *And Fear Came*, 98.

[72] Williams, *Dusk of Empire*, 227; and Frederick T. Birchall, *The Storm Breaks: A Panorama of Europe and the Forces that Have Wrecked Its Peace* (New York: Viking, 1940), 89–101.

As prominent purveyors of foreign news, correspondents were well placed to influence opinion at home. Perhaps unsurprisingly, then, the image of the League as a failure became common currency among US commentators by the second half of the 1930s. Speaking at a conference on foreign policy in the autumn of 1938, Samuel Flagg Bemis, a distinguished Yale historian, recognized the events of the last few years had demonstrated "that no world peace is possible through the League of Nations." Shortly afterward, John Foster Dulles, a Republican foreign policy heavyweight and future secretary of state who would soon collaborate with Streit, concluded the League had "failed to become an instrument qualified to preserve the peace."[73] This generalized sense of failure is worth underscoring, for it prompted an extended debate on the reasons for the League's failure as well as on what could and should be done. Streit would become a prominent participant in this debate with the publication of *Union Now* in 1939. But even before then Streit's evolving views of the League from his perch in Geneva provide an interesting perspective on this developing debate.

Reflecting his confidence in Wilson's vision of internationalism, Streit initially exhibited considerable enthusiasm for the League as an instrument for building peaceful relations between states. One fellow correspondent remembered him as "the self-appointed voice of the League's Wilsonian conscience," while an Italian observer described him less charitably as an "infatuated fanatic of the LoN."[74] Streit's Wilsonian internationalism can be seen in his tenure as president of the professional association of foreign correspondents in Geneva in the early 1930s, during which he aggressively lobbied League officials to open all deliberations to the public. The "rule of secrecy," he insisted to one of them, undermined the open diplomacy essential "to peace and good understanding among peoples."[75]

Streit's early reporting also evinced a strong faith in the League. During the first half of the 1930s, he strove to counter the "anti-League dogma at

---

[73] Samuel Flagg Bemis, "Main Trends of American Foreign Policy" in Frank P. Davidson and George S. Viereck, Jr., eds., *Before America Decides: Foresight in Foreign Affairs* (Cambridge, MA: Harvard University Press, 1938), 99; and John Foster Dulles, *War, Peace and Change* (New York: Harper & Brothers, 1939), 84.

[74] Edmond Taylor, *Awakening from History* (Boston: Gambit, 1969), 164; and Canali, *La scoperta dell'Italia*, 342.

[75] LONA, Association internationale des journalistes accrédités auprès de la S.D.N., Box P 13, file: sujets divers, 1928–1938, Streit to Paul Hymans, March 9, 1932; and the file in LONA, League of Nations, R2442/7B/29034/3071.

home," urging US membership in radio addresses to American listeners while highlighting the institution's positive contributions to international politics in his articles.[76] More fundamentally, Streit portrayed the League less as an institution than as a method whose effect was to foster peaceful relations between states. Although delegates were sent to Geneva to defend their countries' narrow and selfish policies, once there they found themselves enmeshed in extended exchanges with one another from which emerged a shared understanding of collective interests:

> Nowhere else are men subjected constantly to this . . . pressure to see the world as a whole and their own country in perspective as a part of it. Nowhere else is the suicidal character of the war relationship brought home so repeatedly to them in its various phrases. Nowhere else is the imagination so stimulated to see what peace would really mean and to understand the advantages it would bring to everyone. And nowhere else does practice so monotonously remind one that the way to peace is discouragingly long and hard.

The League, as Streit endeavored to explain to a US public, offered a microcosm of a cooperative and therefore peaceful practice of international relations. It "is a fact," he proclaimed, "that few men can come to know the League at first hand without becoming converted to Wilson's basic idea."[77]

Streit by no means presented the League as an unqualified success in his articles. In reporting on the world disarmament conference, which ran from 1932 to 1934, he pointed to the difficulties of convincing sovereign nations to cooperate with one another – a difficulty that would increasingly preoccupy him. Nevertheless, during the first half of the 1930s Streit's confidence in the League appeared resilient. He framed the League as a bold and even revolutionary experiment in international relations as well as a work in progress. The main task, accordingly, was to strengthen the League's "new peace machinery" by persuading the United States to join but also by developing its provisions for collective action. Critics of the League must be patient, he counseled readers, as its development would take time, reminding them "that no better alternative has been proposed."[78]

---

[76] For example, see in the *New York Times*, "Streit, on Radio, Urges League Aid," February 6, 1932, 9; and "Big Advance Made by League in Year," January 4, 1931, 79.

[77] "The Coldest Audience in all the World," *New York Times*, May 14, 1933, 119, 130.

[78] "The World's Efforts to Attain Peace," August 12, 1934, 114, 125; and "League Prestige Falls and Rises," February 23, 1936, 74, both in *New York Times*. Also see Streit, "The League's Defenders Make Answer," *International Conciliation* 16 (1934), 83–90.

In calling for a strengthened League, Streit implicitly took sides in a debate among internationalists in the United States at the time. Almost all internationalists judged the League's present state as inadequate, and almost all of them supported US membership. They disagreed, however, on what needed to be done. One group advocated reform of the League to make it more acceptable to the US public, which effectively meant weakening the institution. Writing in 1936, A. Lawrence Lowell, a former president of Harvard and longtime pro-League Republican, thus suggested transforming it into a "purely consultative body, shorn of teeth and claws." Such a League, Lowell conjectured, might persuade Congress that membership posed no threat to the country's freedom-of-action.[79]

Another group of internationalists expressed interest in reinvigorating rather than weakening the League. Many of them gravitated to the LNA, the principal pro-League organization in the United States. During the second half of the 1930s, the LNA suffered from deepening divisions between pacifists, who advocated American neutrality in a future war, and the advocates of a League-centered collective security. Prominent among the latter was James Shotwell, a Columbia University professor and LNA president from 1935, best known today for his part in the 1928 Kellogg-Briand pact, an international agreement seeking to outlaw recourse to war as a tool of state policy.[80] Like all internationalists, Shotwell lobbied for US membership in the League, deeming it an essential condition for an effective international organization. But he did not support participation at any price, and certainly not that of further weakening the League. Instead, in a book published in 1937, Shotwell discussed how to strengthen the League's "machinery of peace enforcement," floating the idea of reorganizing collective security on a regional basis. Rather than defining collective security in terms of a "uniform, world-wide obligation to take military action in the case of aggression anywhere in the world," a definition imposing unrealistic burdens on members, Shotwell proposed a system of "concentric circles of graded responsibility" in which the states most immediately concerned would cooperate under the League's aegis to preserve and enforce peace, if necessary by military means. Elsewhere, Shotwell even spoke of reviving

[79] A. Lawrence Lowell, "Alternatives before the League," *Foreign Affairs* 15 (January 1936), 102–11.
[80] For Shotwell, see Harold Josephson, *James T. Shotwell and the Rise of Internationalism in America* (Rutherford, NJ: Fairleigh Dickinson University Press, 1975); and Oona A. Hathaway and Scott J. Shapiro, *The Internationalists: How a Radical Plan to Outlaw War Remade the World* (New York: Simon & Schuster, 2017).

the "old diplomacy" with its "secret dealings" in order to facilitate such cooperation. The key point, though, is that Shotwell and his allies were searching for the means to revitalize both the League and collective security.[81]

By the time Shotwell's book appeared, Streit's thinking on the League had considerably evolved, kindled by several overlapping considerations. One was his deepening belief that the foundational divide in international politics was between democracies and authoritarian or dictator states. Although this belief might be ascribed to Wilson's enduring legacy, for Streit it had become a preoccupation by the 1930s. What he called the "militant autocracies" – a bloc comprising Germany, Italy, and Japan but not necessarily the Soviet Union – posed an existential challenge, not only to the League but also to democracy itself, which he associated with the principle of "freedom." "It is democracy that brings not only freedom to man but wealth and power," he asserted as early as November 1934; "it is the peoples who have longest endured autocracy that have been blighted most." If freedom initially encompassed both the collective and the individual, Streit soon defined democracy exclusively in terms of the latter. Unlike the authoritarian states, he lectured in 1936, "Democracy puts its faith in the individual."[82]

Several aspects of this binary vision of international politics deserve mention. First, a focus on democracy, defined in terms of individual freedom as opposed to the collectivism of the autocracies, facilitated Streit's estrangement from the Progressive-reformist political sympathies so evident in his early journalism. A focus on the chasm between democracies and non-democracies ("militant autocracies") obviated a critique of the internal functioning of democratic regimes. Whatever its shortcomings, democracy as a regime type appeared decidedly preferable to its nondemocratic counterparts. Although Streit was certainly not alone in shifting the political reference point from inside to outside democracy, it is striking the extent to which his earlier critical stance toward the United

[81] James T. Shotwell, *On the Rim of the Abyss* (New York: Macmillan, 1937), 18, 28, 333–36; and James T. Shotwell, "Mechanism for Peace in Europe," *Proceedings of the Academy of Political Science* 17 (May 1937), 292–93.

[82] "Democracy versus Absolutism: A Measuring Rod Is Applied to the Two Groups of Nations," *New York Times*, November 25, 1934, 154; and Streit, "World Organization through Democracy," in R. B. Mowat, W. Arnold-Forster, H. Lauterpacht et al., eds., *Problems of Peace. Tenth Series. Anarchy or World Order* (London: George Allen & Unwin, 1936), 236.

States became blunted. During a brief visit home in the midst of the Depression, Streit wrote not of the suffering and misery of millions of people but of the population's general wealth and contentment. The "sum total of individual anguish does not necessarily reflect that condition of the community, viewed as a community, as society," he lectured. If Streit suspended his typical emphasis of the individual, it was to defend the reigning economic system. "Foreclosures of mortgages have never killed the country," he insisted, adding that the solution to the economic crisis "will be not toward discarding private enterprise but toward freeing it from its enemies ..."[83] Absent entirely was the critical fervor of his earlier journalism.

Another notable aspect of Streit's binary vision of international politics is that it placed him at odds with other US correspondents in Geneva. Significantly, many of the latter perceived the principle international divide during the 1930s in terms not so much of regime type but of wealth in what amounted to the internationalization of the Progressive critique of inequalities within the United States. In this schema, there existed the have and have-not powers. The latter category, which included but was not limited to Germany, Italy, and Japan, consisted of states dissatisfied with the status quo and especially with the privileged access to resources which Britain, France, and the United States enjoyed. Probably the best-known exponent of this view was Frank Simonds, whom Hamilton Armstrong Fish, the longtime editor of *Foreign Affairs*, considered one of the "two best Americans" in Geneva (the other being Streit). In a popular study cowritten in 1935, Simonds claimed international politics were determined by the dynamics between two groups of states: "those who possess [the 'static' powers] and those who seek to possess [the 'dynamic' powers]." Continuing, he blasted the League as nothing more than a tool of the static powers to preserve the status quo at the expense of the dynamic powers. Given the unwillingness of the static powers to alter the distribution of resources, "a dynamic power has no other choice but to appeal to force." Similarly, John Whitaker bristled at the League's hypocrisy, denouncing the institution "as an alliance of the 'have gots' against the 'have nots.'" Talk of keeping the world safe for democracy, he

---

[83] Streit, "America Revisited and Revealed Anew," *New York Times*, November 25, 1934, 25, 124; and "An Inquiry into the Nation's Thoughts," *New York Times*, December 2, 1934, 151, 159.

growled, entailed "keeping the world safe for perpetual dividend-clipping in the United States, Great Britain, and France."[84]

But if Streit appeared at odds with his fellow correspondents in Geneva, his more political-ideological as opposed to class-oriented understanding of international politics resonated at home. To be sure, several prominent US internationalists, among them Clark Eichelberger, the LNA's national director, warned against simply dismissing all of Germany, Italy, and Japan's professed grievances, asserting collective security must be accompanied by "peaceful procedures for securing justice."[85] Nevertheless, as scholars have shown, by the second half of the 1930s the drawing of sharp distinctions between democracies and non-democracies (variously labeled totalitarian, authoritarian, dictator, fascist, militarist) had become a notable trait of US political culture.[86] Illustrative, here, is a short book written by Streit's friend, Armstrong Fish, entitled "*We or They*." The "gulf" between democracies and dictators was not only "deep and wide," Fish contended, but also unbridgeable because of their opposing "conceptions of life." Whereas democracies championed "great and precious freedom – freedom to think, to believe, to disbelieve, to speak, to will, to choose," dictatorships offered "nothing but obeisance, body, mind and soul, before the iron will and upstretched arms of a restless, infallible master." War between the two might be averted, Fish added, but only if the democracies cooperated. Their leaders must strive "to minimize minor conflicts between themselves, remembering how much it is in the interests of every democracy that every other democracy be strong and prosperous enough to maintain its existing form of government."[87]

[84] Hamilton Fish Armstrong, *Peace and Counterpeace: From Wilson to Hitler* (New York: Harper & Row, 1971), 488; Frank H. Simonds and Brooks Emeny, *The Great Powers in World Politics: International Relations and Economic Nationalism* (New York: American Book, 1939), 128–29; and Whitaker, *And Fear Came*, 264–69.

[85] William T. Stone and Clark M. Eichelberger, *Peaceful Change: The Alternative to War* (New York: FPA, 1937); and Eichelberger, "Forth to Peace," *The American Scholar* 8 (1938–39), 122.

[86] Benjamin L. Alpers, *Dictators, Democracy, and American Public Culture: Envisioning the Totalitarian Enemy, 1920s–1950s* (Chapel Hill: University of North Carolina Press, 2003); Abbott Gleason, *Totalitarianism: The Inner History of the Cold War* (New York: Oxford University Press, 1995); and Terry A. Cooney, *Balancing Acts: American Thought and Culture in the 1930s* (New York: Twayne Publishers, 1995).

[87] Hamilton Fish Armstrong, *"We or They": Two Worlds in Conflict* (New York: Macmillan, 1937), 3, 46–47.

Looking back, it is tempting to see this distinction between democracies and non-democracies as prefiguring the Cold War, though doing so risks overstating the role of the Soviet Union and of anti-communism in domestic political debates while understating that of the fascist states and Nazi Germany in particular.[88] But the more pertinent point for the time concerns Armstrong Fish's belief in the need for a common front of the democracies against the dictator states – a call that also resonated at home, even if it left the question of the United States' precise role unanswered. Equally important, a flipside of this belief consisted of growing doubts about the strength of the democracies and about their ability to compete successfully with the dictator states. "[S]kepticism," Ira Katznelson writes in his study of the New Deal United States, "was prevalent about whether representative parliamentary democracies could cope within their liberal institutional bounds with capitalism's utter collapse, the manifest military ambitions by the dictatorships, or international politics characterized by ultranationalist territorial demands."[89] Among the skeptics was Leslie Raymond Buell, the president of the Foreign Policy Association and prominent commentator on international affairs. In a lecture series in which Streit participated, Buell wondered "why is it that the democracies of the world, including our own, seem to be going down to defeat, while the dictators are going ahead."[90]

Buell feared the democracies, lacking sufficient internal unity and "concept of purpose," would be tempted to imitate the dictator states in order to compete with them. Streit, though, sought to counter what he believed was the mistaken impression of democratic weakness. Marshaling a bevy of quantitative indices, he insisted that, taken together, the democracies enjoyed an impressive preponderance of power in multiple areas: economic, financial, raw materials, and military. Although these figures might buttress arguments about the unfair global

---

[88] Michaela Hoenicke Moore, *Know Your Enemy: The American Debate on Nazism, 1933–1945* (Cambridge: Cambridge University Press, 2010).

[89] Ira Katznelson, *Fear Itself: The New Deal and the Origins of Our Time* (New York: Liveright, 2014), 114.

[90] Buell, "Where Are the Democracies Going?," in Raymond Leslie Buell, George Gallup, Robert J. Watt, and Clarence K. Streit, eds., *Howard Crawley Memorial Lectures 1939* (Philadelphia: University of Pennsylvania Press, 1939), 1–17. In lectures in Chicago in 1938, William Rappard, a US-born Swiss diplomat and academic, remarked that "the cyclone of the authoritarian reaction that has passed over the world has even shaken the institutions of democracy where they were older." See his *The Crisis of Democracy* (Chicago: University of Chicago Press, 1938), 6.

distribution of resources, Streit's point was the opposite: that the democracies suffered from an unjustified "inferiority complex." As a bloc, they "have such overwhelming power that they have no need to bother whether the autocracies come or go." Rather than seek to appease the autocracies, the democracies were in a position to dictate to them the terms of prolonged peace. Significantly, while in accord with Fish on the need for cooperation among the three leading democracies (Britain, France, and the United States), Streit's vision was more expansive, encompassing in his calculations of resources the fifteen democracies ringing the Atlantic Ocean – a group he called the "Free Fifteen."[91]

For Streit, then, the principal threat to peace – as well as the biggest challenge to overcome – was disunity among the democracies. The solution, though, demanded more than mere cooperation among democracies, regardless of the number involved. It required some form of common political structure – or "world government." "Every year has more convinced me that in all this pother of war, peace, neutrality, depression, recovery, nationalism, internationalism," Streit intimated to Lippmann in early 1936, "the central issue and the only basic problem is the problem of organizing effective world government."[92] Initially, Streit hoped the League, as he explained in a *New York Times* article, might furnish the democracies "with a mechanism for coordinating the action of great and small nations ..." But he soon concluded the League was incapable of doing so, principally because an institution of sovereign nation-states was fatally flawed in conception. "The League method cannot possibly work," he confided to Ackerman in 1935, though adding that he could not say so in his reporting, "for in my cables I give the League view, not my own."[93]

Streit would soon become less cautious. Rather than expending time and effort on "League reform," he lectured a Geneva audience in 1937, "we must start afresh our thinking on our problem of world government." No less importantly, Streit offered the US federal system as a promising source of inspiration for such thinking:

I think the most stimulating field for anyone interested in this great problem [of world government] to study is the history of the Constitution of the United States.

[91] "Democracy versus Absolutism," 154; and Streit, "World Organization through Democracy," 220–51.
[92] YUL, Walter Lippmann Papers, Box 104, file 2012, Streit to Lippmann, January 6, 1936.
[93] Streit, "League Still Gives Democracies Hope," *New York Times*, November 8, 1936, 124; and LOC, Carl W. Ackerman Papers, Box 79, Streit to Ackerman, May 24, 1935.

The United States is the outstanding success in the domain of the rationally constructed, large-scale democratic inter-state government. Since that is precisely the field we are in, the common-sense thing is to study the American experience for guidance.[94]

Or as he told a US audience: "It is high time we Americans returned to our great tradition of constructive pioneering. If we are to win this race [between dictatorship and democracy] we must take the lead ourselves and lead the world the American way."[95]

By the end of 1938, Streit had traveled a long way from Missoula, Montana. Beginning in the aftermath of World War I, he forged a successful career in journalism, becoming the *New York Time*'s correspondent in Geneva, a posting which placed him at the center of international politics. At the same time, the constraints of journalism – constraints rooted in the process of professionalization and encapsulated in the ideal of objectivity – proved frustrating to Streit as it did to other correspondents. Rather than simply observe and report events, Streit wanted to shape policy, to find solutions to pressing issues. Early on, Streit's progressive sympathies directed his activist inclinations more toward domestic policies – hence his protest of the Wilson administration's clampdown on internal dissent. But by the 1930s, Streit's binary understanding of international politics as a contest between democracies and non-democracies had effectively dissolved his critique of US democracy. No less importantly, his experience in Geneva convinced him of the need for unity among the democracies. The pressing question now became how to unify the latter – a question Streit was eager to answer.

---

[94] Streit, "Reform of the Covenant Is Not Enough," in Herbert S. Morrison, Gaston Riou, Stephan Osusky et al., eds., *The League and the Future of the Collective System* (London: George Allen & Unwin, 1937), 230–31.

[95] Streit, "Can We Avert War," in Raymond Leslie Buell, George Gallup, Robert J. Watt, and Clarence K. Streit, eds., *Howard Crawley Memorial Lectures 1939* (Philadelphia: University of Pennsylvania Press, 1939), 50.

2

The Making and Selling of *Union Now*, 1939–1941

In late March 1939, the annual congress of the American Academy of Political and Social Science opened in Philadelphia. Along with academics, the participants included politicians, government officials, Wall Street bankers, and journalists. Prominent among the latter was Clarence Streit, whose *New York Times*' affiliation dominated his biographical blurb. In his talk, Streit ardently promoted *Union Now*, his recently published book proposing a federal union of the Atlantic democracies. Invoking his lengthy experience as a journalist in Geneva, Streit argued that the alternatives to federal union ("neutrality, balance of power, alliance, or League of Nations") had all failed and would continue to fail because none of them addressed the principal ill afflicting international politics: "the heresy of absolute national sovereignty." No less significantly, Streit invoked US history, emphasizing the parallels between the revolutionary period and his own time. Just as the thirteen colonies in 1787 had replaced the interstate confederation (or league of nations) created a decade earlier with a federal union, so too must the Atlantic democracies "establish that 'more perfect Union' to which we Americans are dedicated in our Constitution." Rather than something quixotic or alien, Streit insisted, federal union was quintessentially American. Indeed, it was the "answer America was born to champion."[1]

This emphasis on federal union is worth underscoring in light of the scholarship on Streit. Although long overlooked, Streit's project has resurfaced in recent years, most notably as evidence of the lingering

[1] Streit, "The Atlantic Union Plan and the Americas," *Annals of the American Academy of Political and Social Science* 204 (July 1939), 93–101.

appeal of visions of an Anglo-American or Anglo-Saxon grouping popular on both sides of the Atlantic around 1900 – visions, moreover, whose racial and imperial inflections are all too apparent.[2] Streit provided grist to this mill in 1941 with the publication of *Union Now with Britain*, a short book proposing an immediate federation of the United States, Britain, and the (white) Dominions.[3] For Or Rosenboim, who situates Streit in a larger Anglo-American discussion on globalism during the 1940s, the latter's "conceptual attachment to the legacy of [the British] empire" constituted a fundamental and even fatal weakness of his project.[4]

This chapter redirects attention on Streit's project toward federalism, rather than empire. The argument is not that Atlantic federal union was free of bias: Its preoccupation with the Atlantic world and its Western- and even white-centeredness reflected what Gary Gerstle has described as the "racialized nationalism" of the Roosevelt years manifested in the presumed superiority of white or "Nordic" peoples.[5] Rather, the argument is that Streit's project is best understood less as a legacy of Anglo-Saxonism and more as part of a transition in US political culture from the appeal of an Anglo-American or larger Anglo-world to a growing interest in a more expansive but still ethnically/racially infused white (Western) world.

At the same time, an emphasis on empire risks downplaying what lay at the heart of Streit's project – its federalist framework. As Chapter 3 will discuss, Streit presented *Union Now with Britain* not as an end in itself

---

[2] Or Rosenboim, *The Emergence of Globalism: Visions of World Order in Britain and the United States, 1939–1950* (Princeton, NJ: Princeton University Press, 2017), 114–21; Duncan Bell, "The Project for a New Anglo-Century: Race, Space, and Global Order," in Duncan Bell, ed., *Reordering the World: Essays on Liberalism and Empire* (Princeton, NJ: Princeton University Press, 2016), 196–203; Srdjan Vucetic, *The Anglosphere: A Genealogy of a Racialized Identity in International Relations* (Stanford, CA: Stanford University Press, 2011), 22–53; Daniel H. Deudney, *Bounding Power: Republican Security Theory from the Polis to the Global Village* (Princeton, NJ: Princeton University Press, 2007), 236–41; and Warren F. Kuehl and Lynne K. Dunn, *Keeping the Covenant: American Internationalists and the League of Nations, 1920–1939* (Kent, OH: Kent State University Press, 1997), 102–3. Quinn Slobodian enfolds Streit's federal union project in neoliberal stratagems to weaken the nation-state. See his *Globalists: The End of Empire and the Birth of Neoliberalism* (Cambridge, MA: Harvard University Press, 2018), 91–120.

[3] Streit, *Union Now with Britain* (New York: Harper & Brothers, 1941).

[4] Rosenboim, *The Emergence of Globalism*, 102.

[5] Gary Gerstle, *American Crucible: Race and Nation in the Twentieth Century* (Princeton, NJ: Princeton University Press, 2001), 166–83.

but as a response to the emergency created by Nazi Germany's stunning military victories in the summer of 1940. More pertinent to this chapter, federalism provides a key to understanding the considerable attention Streit's *Union Now* attracted at the time, itself the product of two interacting factors. One factor was Streit's tireless publicity activities during 1939 and 1940: He succeeded in creating a public buzz around the book while also interesting leading members of the foreign policy elite. The second factor concerned the place of federalism in interwar US political culture. In publicizing his book, Streit drew both on a popular cult of the constitution, which developed after the Civil War and reached its climax with the 150th-anniversary celebrations in the 1930s, and on the attraction of federalism among international lawyers as a framework for thinking about international organization. Together, these two factors allowed Streit to become a prominent participant in an emerging debate on the US role in a postwar international order.

FINDING A PUBLISHER

Streit's prolonged experience in Geneva covering the League of Nations left him increasingly frustrated with the constraints of journalism. As he later recounted to a fellow journalist, "I got fed up merely telling us [sic] news stories what the facts of the situation are. I wanted to say what we could do about it."[6] Streit's restlessness manifested itself in a desire to find solutions to current international problems, a desire rooted in a sense of mission and of self-importance that his time in Geneva hobnobbing with leading statesmen and officials did much to reinforce.

To recall from Chapter 1, Streit concocted at least two international plans: one to reduce the risks of war (through national plebiscites) and another to solve the vexed issue of reparations and war debts. Neither plan gained political traction and Streit quickly dropped both – but not the ambition to shape politics. "I've plenty of other ideas," he confessed to William Bullitt in the mid-1930s, "and think that I'm a fool for not working on them instead of wasting my time on things of less interest to me – but do nothing."[7]

---

[6] Robert Root, "Streit Sees New Order. Wants World Union," *Des Moines Tribune*, April 3, 1939, 13.

[7] YUL, William C. Bullitt Papers, Box 79, file 2033, Streit to Bullitt undated but sometime in late 1933 – early 1934.

Far from doing nothing, Streit by then was hard at work on a new idea: a federal union of the Atlantic democracies. Its first articulation took the form of a *New York Times* article in November 1934, in which he adduced thirty measures of power to demonstrate the combined superiority of the democracies over the autocracies.[8] By then Streit had completed a book manuscript, variously entitled "Thy Freedom" or "For Man's Vast Future." The manuscript, he explained to Carl Ackerman, dean of Columbia University's school of journalism,

attempts to do something very big: nothing less than to demolish the dominant political theory (national sovereignty) and to offer in its place a practical proposal for solution of the world's war, economic, monetary and other troubles – a solution that is based mainly on American principles, practice and experience. It is a plan for uniting the fifteen leading democracies on the great lines that proved so successful in 1787 in uniting the thirteen American democracies.

Streit could hardly conceal his enthusiasm or ambition. "I am sure you will understand my feeling that this book must be extraordinary if it is to get anywhere with the extraordinary task it attempts."[9]

In writing Ackerman, Streit sought his help in finding a commercial publisher. At the time, the major presses were few in number and concentrated on the East Coast, particularly in New York. Streit first tried with Harpers, profiting from his friendship with Hamilton Fish Armstrong to get a hearing with its editor, Cass Canfield. Though judging the manuscript "readable," Canfield turned it down, remarking "that we have already too large a proportion of books dealing with current affairs."[10] Other publishers proved less generous. Viking thought the manuscript "too large and elaborate"; Alfred A. Knopf deemed the writing "simply atrocious" and the thesis "interesting and logical" but bearing "absolutely no relation to the economic and political realities of the world today"; and Macmillan questioned Streit's "grasp of current political situations." Simon and Schuster expressed disappointment, given Streit's reputation as the *New York Times*' correspondent in Geneva. "I could explain at some length why it [the manuscript] seems to me wordy,

---

[8] Streit, "Democracy versus Absolutism: A Measuring Rod Is Applied to the Two Groups of Nations," *New York Times*, November 25, 1934, 154.

[9] LOC, Carl W. Ackerman Papers, Box 79, Streit to Ackerman, April 12, 1935.

[10] SMLPU, Hamilton Fish Armstrong Papers, Box 60, file: Streit, Clarence, Canfield to Streit, July 5, 1934.

confused, journalistic, legalistic," the editor wrote Streit's agent, "but the real point is that I'm afraid it's pretty dull."[11]

Streit's agent grew discouraged, expressing doubts in 1936 as to whether the "book of the general nature you propose will have a market." Streit characteristically remained undeterred, convinced he had discovered the answer to mounting international tensions. When the *New York Times*' editor declined to publish parts of the manuscript in article form, he decided to rework the text. But the results were the same: In early 1938 Houghton Mifflin and Doubleday both turned down the manuscript on the grounds that it "is unsaleable to the public as a book."[12] Unable to find a British editor, Streit decided to publish several hundred copies of the book at his own expense, having identified a printer in southern France. The goal, he later recounted, was to produce several hundred copies to give "to leaders in the N. Atlantic democracies, hoping to get enough support to get a publisher, and at least to get the plan before policymakers."[13]

Soon after the decision to publish the book at his own expense, Streit achieved a breakthrough. Through the intermediary once again of Fish, Canfield agreed in the summer of 1938 to reconsider the manuscript for Harper's. And this time Canfield gave a positive response, reassured perhaps by Streit's offer to assume some of the financial risk in the event of disappointing sales. Canfield also agreed to buy several hundred copies of the book being printed in France and sell them in the United States under Harper's imprint. By the beginning of January 1939, Streit finally had a signed contract.[14]

That it was Canfield who chose to publish the manuscript was not fortuitous. In his memoirs, Canfield, who became a "legendary figure" in the publishing industry, defined the publisher's role as reflecting rather than seeking to influence public opinion. So viewed, Canfield's offer of a contract made sense: The gathering war clouds in Europe in 1938–39

[11] LOC, CKS, Box I: 137, file: CKS-Books-*Union Now*, "Streit's Pre-publication Correspondence on <u>Union Now</u> – Excerpts, 1934–1938."

[12] Ibid.

[13] LOC, CKS, Box I: 129, file: Harper & Brothers Publishers, 1938–39, Les Presses Zoniennes to Streit, September 5, 1938; and BLCU, Harper & Row Collection, series II, Box 164, file: Streit, Clarence, untitled and undated MS note.

[14] SMLPU, Hamilton Fish Armstrong Papers, Box 60, file: Streit, Clarence, Fish to Streit, July 1, 1938. For the details of the contract, see LOC, CKS, Box I: 129, file: Harper & Brothers Publishers, 1938–39, Canfield (Harper) to Willis Kingsley Wing, November 14, 1938.

heightened public interest in international politics. Over the next few years, moreover, Canfield would expand Harper's list on the subject, recruiting prominent figures such as John Foster Dulles and Sumner Welles.[15] But he also appears to have been genuinely intrigued by federalist frameworks for international relations. During World War II, Canfield would become a proponent of international federalism, and after 1945 would be active in the United World Federalists, an organization advocating the development of the United Nations into a world government along federalist lines.[16]

UNION NOW: THE BOOK

In February 1939, Streit's book, *Union Now*, appeared in the United States.[17] Although the final version had been significantly reworked over several years, the core proposal remained unchanged: to create a federal union between the eleven "North Atlantic" democracies (the United States, Canada, France, Belgium, Holland, Switzerland, Denmark, Norway, Sweden, Finland, Great Britain) or fifteen if one added other British Dominions (Australia, New Zealand, Ireland, and South Africa). Echoing his 1934 *New York Times*' article, Streit maintained that the combined wealth and power of these countries, together with their "strong natural bonds" (geographical, political, cultural, and economic), made them a coherent bloc, if not a distinct civilization. And as he had explained to Ackerman, Streit presented the US federal system as the model. "[W]hen we study carefully ... the subject," he affirmed in the book, "I believe that we should turn particularly to the American constitution and experience for guidance."[18] Accordingly, there would be a Union (federal) government responsible for several areas (citizenship, defense, money, trade, and communications) and national governments responsible for everything else. There would be two legislative assemblies: an upper house (resembling the Senate), in which nations would be

---

[15] Cass Canfield, *The Publishing Experience* (Philadelphia: University of Pennsylvania Press, 1969), 6, 11. For his legendary status, see John Tebbel, *Between Covers: The Rise and Transformation of Book Publishing in America* (New York: Oxford University Press, 1987), 203–4.

[16] See the file: Cass Canfield, in LLUI, United World Federalist Papers, Box 45.

[17] Streit, *Union Now: A Proposal for a Federal Union of the Democracies of the North Atlantic* (New York: Harper & Brothers, 1939). The book appeared simultaneously in Britain with Jonathan Cape.

[18] Ibid., 184.

represented on an equal basis, and a lower house (resembling the House of Representatives), with the number of delegates proportionate to national populations, which not incidentally would accord the United States major if not decisive influence; and there would be a federal executive, as well as judiciary, to ensure respect for federal and state competencies.

Streit's argument for Atlantic federal union combined several basic elements. One was a suspicion of national sovereignty. "[A]ll my experience," he wrote, had demonstrated that nations must abandon "the heresy of absolute national sovereignty and its vain alternatives, neutrality, balance of power alliance or League of Nations." Unconditional attachment to national sovereignty was dangerous because it promoted the primacy of the state over the individual, a primacy fostering interstate rivalry and conflict. International organizations such as the League of Nations could not preserve peace because they were bodies of states. Throughout the book, Streit contrasted the League of Nations with a federal union in which the individual and not the state constituted the foundational element. No less importantly, he equated the primacy of the individual with democracy, another basic element of his proposal. The "nucleus" of a union, Streit insisted, "must be composed exclusively of democracies," for it "is no accident that the desire for world law and order is strongest among the democratic peoples." It was axiomatic for Streit that the collective will of people was peaceful and law-abiding, and that only democracies, reflecting this will, could be trusted to use the federal powers of the union for the general good.[19]

Together, his understanding of national sovereignty and democracy provided Streit with an answer to the anticipated criticism that his proposal entailed a loss of national sovereignty for the United States – a charge critics had lobbed at the League of Nations after World War I. Because in a democracy sovereignty resided in the individual and not the state, transferring areas of national governance to the union involved no loss of sovereignty. No less significantly, this claim permitted Streit to underline the value of the United States, not simply as a model but also as a historical precedent. In the book, Streit repeatedly emphasized the parallels between the US revolutionary period and his own time, likening the League of Nations, an organization of nation-states, to the United States formed by the articles of confederation in 1777. The inability of

---

[19] Ibid., 4, 89–90.

this confederation to provide for a minimum of common purpose among its member states led directly to the Constitution of 1787, which created a genuine federal union among the thirteen states. In exercising sovereignty on behalf of the people whom they represented, the founding fathers gathered in Philadelphia in 1787 and devised a political system whose supposed genius lay in its ability to reconcile the collective and particular needs of member states. The urgent task now was to convoke a similar constitutional convention of the North Atlantic democracies in order to forge a *"great federal republic"* on a transatlantic scale.[20]

For Streit, the United States alone could take the initiative. Its immense resources, its relative distance from the boiling cauldron of European politics, and even more its pioneering role "on the frontiers of self-government and Union" bestowed the mantle of leadership on the country. More generally, a sense of US exceptionalism infused the proposal. Streit embraced a popular understanding of the United States as a providential global force – as the proverbial "city on a hill."[21] This exceptionalism came with a strong dose of ethnocentrism. As mentioned earlier, Streit's proposal was markedly Western and even white-centric in conception, placing the North Atlantic region at the heart of US foreign relations while downplaying the rest of the world, both colonial and non-colonial. No less importantly, it was also notably US-centered, never really considering, for example, why other countries would find Atlantic union attractive.

If Streit's project was US-centered, it was also expansionist, though perhaps not in the sense in which the term is typically understood. As so much scholarship on the United States' deepening political, economic, cultural, and other imprints across the globe in the nineteenth and twentieth centuries has shown, exceptionalism fostered far more than hampered what Emily Rosenberg called the "spreading [of] the American dream." The United States exported a way of life – consumer-oriented capitalism, business practices, political and social values, etc. – though with decidedly mixed results depending on the region and society.[22] Streit, however, conceived of expansion of another kind:

---

[20] Ibid., 2, 6–7, 63, 90.

[21] For recent analyses of American exceptionalism, see Abram C. Van Engen, *City on a Hill: A History of American Exceptionalism* (New Haven, CT: Yale University Press, 2020); and Daniel T. Rodgers, *As a City on a Hill: The Story of America's Most Famous Lay Sermon* (Princeton, NJ: Princeton University Press, 2018).

[22] Emily S. Rosenberg, *Spreading the American Dream: American Economic and Cultural Expansion, 1890–1945* (New York: Hill & Wang, 1982). And for an updated and

The idea was not to export the US system of democratic federalism to other countries but to import the Atlantic region into this system. This being so, it is tempting to dismiss the proposal as hopelessly quixotic, if not downright bizarre. And, yet, in championing the US federal system as a framework for international politics, Streit spoke in a conceptual language familiar to many Americans.

FEDERALISM'S FERTILE HISTORICAL TERRAIN

Writing to a supporter after the war, Streit recounted how, while working on a draft of *Union Now* in the mid-1930s, he had read intensely on the history of the 1780s, mentioning in particular John Fiske's *The Critical Moment in American History*.[23] The reference to Fiske, a prolific popularizer of science and history, was no coincidence. First published in 1889, Fiske's political narrative of the 1780s would remain in print until 1970, becoming, in the words of one scholar, "probably the most widely read book ever published on the formation of the U.S. Constitution."[24] It was also an unapologetic paean of praise to the US federal system. In Fiske's telling, the "creation and maintenance of such a political structure as our Federal Union" constituted not merely a decisive moment for the United States but also "a turning point in the development of political society in the western hemisphere." Equally pertinent, Fiske compared unfavorably the federal union of 1787 with the structure created by the articles of confederation creating a "league of friendship" among the thirteen colonies/states rather than an effective federation.

Five years earlier, Fiske had published a collection of three essays on *American Political Ideas, Viewed from the Standpoint of Universal History*, which also appeared in multiple editions. The second essay, dedicated to the "federal union," saluted the US federal system for preserving a perfect balance between national and state authority. The 1787 Constitution, Fiske insisted, "has proved in its workings a masterpiece of

transnational version, see her chapter "Transnational Currents in a Shrinking World," in Emily S. Rosenberg, ed., *A World Connecting, 1870–1945* (Cambridge, MA: Belknap Press, 2012), 813–996. On exporting a way of life, see Victoria de Grazia, *Irresistible Empire: America's Advance through Twentieth-Century Europe* (Cambridge, MA: Belknap Press, 2005).

[23] HTPL, William L. Clayton Papers, Box 96, file: Federal Union folder 1, Streit to Glen A. King, April 7, 1952.

[24] Michael Kammen, *A Machine That Would Go of Itself: The Constitution in American Culture* (New York: Vintage, 1987), 25.

political wisdom."[25] And in so doing, it promised a glorious future, not only for the United States but for all countries. "To have established such a federal system over one great continent," Fisk enthused in a magazine article, "is to have made a very good beginning toward establishing it over the world."[26]

Fiske's studies formed part of a larger phenomenon, what one foreign observer in the 1870s gently derided as the American "worship of the Constitution."[27] While its roots go back to the revolutionary period, this admiration for, and even cult of, the constitution gained renewed strength in the wake of the US Civil War before reaching its full flourishing in the interwar years. Several aspects of the phenomenon are worth underscoring. First, it was dual in nature, possessing a popular strand, evident in widely read historical and political studies as well as in officially sponsored celebrations, and a more policy-oriented strand observable in discussions among international jurists. Second, the two strands increasingly shared a focus on the US federal system. And last but not least, together the two strands provided fertile terrain for the reception of Streit's proposal in 1939.

From early on, the revolutionary period was bathed in an admiring glow. Pauline Maier relates how the Declaration of Independence quickly became a sacred text, what she terms "American scripture," while David Armitage shows how the Declaration's association of independence with statehood spread across various parts of the globe. Biographies of the founding fathers, meanwhile, soon established themselves as an important – an enduring – genre of historical writing.[28] The Civil War, though,

---

[25] John Fiske, *The Critical Period of American History, 1783–1789* (Boston: Houghton, Mifflin, 1889), vi–vii, 55, 92; and John Fiske, *American Political Ideas, Viewed from the Standpoint of Universal History* (Boston: Houghton, Mifflin, 1911), 88.

[26] John Fiske, "Manifest Destiny," *Harper's New Monthly Magazine*, 70, December 1884, 589.

[27] Dr. H. von Holst, *The Constitutional and Political History of the United States: 1750–1833, State Sovereignty and Slavery* (Chicago: Callaghan, 1877), 65–79. Also see Kammen, *A Machine That Would Go of Itself*, 22.

[28] Pauline Maier, *American Scripture: Making the Declaration of Independence* (New York: Vintage, 1997); David Armitage, *The Declaration of Independence: A Global History* (Cambridge, MA: Harvard University Press, 2007); and Wesley Frank Craven, *The Legend of the Founding Fathers* (Ithaca, NY: Cornell University Press, 1956). Recent scholarship underscores the uncertainty surrounding the Constitution's meaning in the early postrevolutionary decades. See Jonathan Gienapp, *The Second Creation: Fixing the American Constitution in the Founding Era* (Cambridge, MA: Belknap Press, 2018); and David Brian Robertson, *The Original Compromise: What the Constitution's Framers Were Really Thinking* (New York: Oxford University Press, 2013).

provoked a shift in focus, one now centered on the country's political system and especially its federal character. The North's decisive victory dampened the rancorous antebellum debate on federalism (and the fraught issue of the location of sovereignty between the state and federal governments); the emphasis shifted to practical questions of divided jurisdiction and authority in particular domains of governmental action.[29]

The federal government contributed to this shift in focus in its celebration of the constitution's centennial. "Under the Constitution," proudly declared the centennial commission created in 1886 to prepare for the event, "this great nation has grown up and prospered, and on the continued success of our system of constitutional government depend, in large measure, the future welfare and happiness, not only of our own people, but of mankind."[30] Less grandiloquently, the focus on the federal system was observable in George Bancroft's popular two-volume *History of the Formation of the Constitution of the United States of America*, first published in 1882, whose second volume described in loving detail the genius of the federal system crafted in 1787. To be sure, Charles Beard attacked head-on Bancroft's uncritical interpretation of the work of the Founding Fathers in his *Economic Interpretation of the Constitution* (1913). But Beard's hard-headed view, while in tune with Progressivist political impulses, did little to dent popular admiration for the federal system. A good example is Philemon Bliss, a politician, high court judge, and prolific commentator, whose 1885 book-length panegyric for the US political system concluded with a plea for its wider pertinence: "What blessings would flow, could the idea of federalism possess the mind, with attendant forbearance and holy love of law, – could contiguous nations unite as friends, could they become one as matters of common interest, still retaining local control as to local concerns!" Woodrow Wilson echoed Bliss two decades later: The federal system, the Princeton president lectured, has "been an incomparable means of sensitive adjustment between popular thought and governmental method, and may yet accord

[29] Rogan Kersh, *Dreams of a More Perfect Union* (Ithaca, NY: Cornell University Press, 2001). For a good example, see C. E. Merriam, *History of the Theory of Sovereignty since Rousseau* (New York: Columbia University Press, 1900).

[30] *Centennial Celebration of the Framing of the Constitution of the United States: Official Programme* (Philadelphia: J. F. Dickson, 1887), 4–5. And R. B. Bernstein, *The Founding Fathers Reconsidered* (Oxford: Oxford University Press, 2009), 125–31.

the world itself the model of federation and liberty it may in God's providence come to seek."[31]

Similar panegyrics would multiply during the interwar years. Writing in 1928, Charles Warren, author of a three-volume history of the Supreme Court awarded a Pulitzer Prize, welcomed the growing attention paid to the "making of the Constitution" as "one of the healthiest signs of the fundamental soundness of American policies." Warren had good reason to be satisfied. A popular history in 1922 by Charles Pierson, citing Fiske, insisted the Constitution's "novelty and greatness" lay in the federal system it created. The same year, Thomas James Norton, in a text meant for students as well as a broad public, acclaimed the constitution's federal system as a model to imitate. To "the extent that other countries failed to follow the Constitution of the United States," Norton contended, "their governmental structures are weak."[32] Two years later, James Beck, at the time the Solicitor-General, identified US federalism as "a unique contribution to the science of politics," adding "[i]t is not too much to say that the success with which the framers of the Constitution reconciled national supremacy and efficiency with local self-government is one of the great achievements in the history of mankind."[33]

Even Robert Livingston Schuyler, a prominent constitutional historian, who sought to offer a more even-handed assessment, could not disguise his admiration. In a 1923 survey aimed at a wide audience, he presented the federal system as an exemplar. "It was reserved for the United States to give the first example of federal government on a large scale, and wherever federalism has been established during the last hundred years there has been indebtedness to the American experiment." No less importantly, Schuyler fused federalism with democracy as a distinctly American project. Since the revolutionary period, he explained, when Americans look abroad they saw "not orderly republics or democratic monarchies, but despotisms, aristocracies, Jacobinical excesses and

---

[31] Philemon Bliss, *Of Sovereignty* (Boston: Little, Brown, 1885), 176–77. For Beard, see Craven, *The Legend of the Founding Fathers*, 196–203. Woodrow Wilson, *Constitutional Government in the United States* (New York: Columbia University Press, 1908), 50.

[32] Charles Warren, *The Making of the Constitution* (Boston: Little, Brown, 1928), iv; Charles Pierson, *Our Changing Constitution* (Garden City, NY: Doubleday, Page, 1922), 3, 7; and Thomas James Norton, *The Constitution of the United States: Its Sources and Its Application* (Boston: Little, Brown, 1922), viii–ix.

[33] James M. Beck, *The Constitution of the United States: Yesterday, Today – and Tomorrow* (New York: George H. Doran, 1924), 210–12.

military imperialism, with its train of ruin." "Small wonder," Schuyler remarked, "that they [Americans] thought the Constitution a light to lighten the world."[34] To mark the 150th anniversary of American independence, Congress authorized the printing of 10,000 copies of a documentary collection on the "formation" of the federal union. "The wide dissemination of these documents, dealing with those momentous and stirring questions associated with the birth of our country, and its subsequent constitutional development," the preface announced, "will do incalculable good and will foster a better understanding of the principles upon which our government is founded."[35]

To be sure, the US federal system came under increasing scrutiny during the 1930s. The principal cause was the constitutional crisis triggered in mid-decade by the Supreme Court's opposition to several of the New Deal's legislative planks and by Roosevelt's threat to pack the Court in response. For some observers, the solution to the crisis lay in a return to the seemingly more balanced federalism of the 1780s – and to a more restrained federal government. Others, such as Henry Wallace, Roosevelt's secretary of agriculture, likewise pleaded for a return to the "spirit" of the Founding Fathers but did so to argue for the more interventionist government the federal system supposedly allowed.[36] In his "biography" of the constitution published in 1937, the journalist and Pulitzer Prize winner, Burton J. Hendrick, sought to reassure readers that US federalism would survive the current crisis just as it had previous ones. Hendrick's confidence, as is well known, proved well-placed: The Supreme Court contributed to defusing the crisis by adopting a more flexible position toward the federal government's regulatory powers.[37] But less well known perhaps is the boost in constitution-mindedness provided by the crisis and its dénouement. Looking back from 1941, Robert H. Jackson, a Supreme Court justice and future chief prosecutor

---

[34] Robert Livingston Schuyler, *The Constitution of the United States: An Historical Survey of Its Formation* (New York: Macmillan, 1923), 1, 203–4.

[35] Charles C. Tansill, *Documents Illustrative of the Formation of the Union of the American States* (Washington, DC: Government Printing Office, 1927), vi–vii.

[36] Henry A. Wallace, *Whose Constitution: An Inquiry into the General Welfare* (New York: Reynal & Hitchcock, 1936), 204–5, 322–27; and Kammen, *A Machine That Would Go of Itself,* 272–75.

[37] Burton J. Hendrick, *Bulwark of the Republic: A Biography of the Constitution* (Boston: Little, Brown, 1937), xxvi–xxviii. For the Supreme Court, see Bruce Ackerman, *We the People,* vol. 2 *Transformations* (Cambridge, MA: Harvard University Press, 1998), 279–312; and William G. Ross, *The Chief Justiceship of Charles Evan Hughes, 1930–1941* (Columbia: University of South Carolina Press, 2007), 58–140.

at the Nuremberg war crimes tribunal, credited the crisis with fostering a "Constitutional Renaissance – a rediscovery of the Constitution." Though perhaps exaggerated, Jackson's claim did reflect a generalized belief that the US federal system had once again demonstrated its unrivaled value.[38]

An ambitious official celebration of the constitution during the second half of the 1930s propagated this belief to a wider public. In August 1935, Congress created a commission to oversee the commemoration of the 150th anniversary of the first Congress in 1789, eventually appropriating over $350,000 for the endeavor. Chaired by Sol Bloom a colorful representative from New York, the Commission focused on the making of the constitution in the 1780s. In addition to organizing countless events at the national, state, and local levels (speeches, exhibits, ceremonies), it oversaw the production of myriad commemorative material (medals, postage stamps, information sheets, broadsides, maps, music, copies of the constitution, cut-out displays, programs for model ceremonies, facsimiles of the constitution's shrine sent to forty-one cities) aimed at inculcating "a proper understanding of the meaning of the constitution and its place in the history and daily life of the country – of the origins and principles of our nation." The material included a "History of the Constitution" written by Bloom, 700,000 copies of which were distributed. Its tone was predictably hagiographic, especially in the descriptions of federalism. "The symmetry of arrangement and beautiful coordination of motion in the several governments constituting the American system," it gushed, "may be compared to the solar system." Overall, Bloom concluded, the federal system "has been found to approach more nearly the symmetry of the Law that rules the universe than any other emanation of the human mind and will."[39]

Marking almost two years of festivities, President Roosevelt in a speech in March 1939 described the 1780s, in an unacknowledged reference to Fiske, as "the critical period in American history" when men of "vision and courage" composed an "immortal document" uniting a "society of thirteen republics" through a "system of representative democracy." And as Roosevelt made clear, in a world witnessing a return of tyranny, the

---

[38] Robert H. Jackson, *The Struggle for Judicial Supremacy: A Study of a Crisis in American Power Politics* (New York: Vintage, 1941), xiv–xv, 316.

[39] Sol Bloom, *History of the Formation of the Union under the Constitution: With Liberty Documents and Report of the Commission* (Washington, DC: Constitution Sesquicentennial Commission, 1941), vii, 1–138, 583–637; and Sol Bloom, *The Autobiography of Saul Bloom* (New York: G. P. Putnam's Sons, 1948), 220–24.

home-grown fusion of federalism and democracy was as pertinent now as it had ever been.[40] The historian Michael Kammen expressed skepticism at the Commission's efforts, suggesting they promoted a "blind adoration" of the constitution rather than true understanding.[41] Yet however superficial the results, the Commission did contribute to a heightened awareness of, and reverence for, the federal system among many Americans – including Streit.

FEDERALISM AND INTERWAR INTERNATIONAL JURISTS

If the "worship of the Constitution" manifested itself in the popular appeal of the US federal system during the interwar years, it was also apparent, albeit in somewhat less adulatory form, in the writings of specialists, particularly international jurists. In the United States, the pre-1914 period witnessed the convergence of two burgeoning movements: one for peace and one for the judicialization of international relations. For the overlapping members of the two movements, the elimination of war could be achieved by the growing practice of arbitration to settle interstate disputes, buttressed by the ongoing development of an international judicial structure. The two Hague conferences in 1899 and 1907, which established a permanent court of arbitration, offered grounds for optimism that a third conference would see international law progress still further as the "gentle civilizer of nations."[42]

Not surprisingly, US jurists took their own Supreme Court as a model for an international court. But comparisons extended well beyond the similarities between two judicial institutions. For many commentators, the US federal system offered a framework for envisaging the functioning of an international relations reconfigured along judicial lines. International relations, whose principal actors were nations as well as the world community embodied in the emerging organized structure of international law, would parallel US politics in which the principal actors were individual states and the federal government. Just as the use of force was excluded in US politics (at least since the Civil War), with the

[40] Bloom, *History of the Formation of the Union*, 667–85.
[41] Kammen, *A Machine That Would Go of Itself*, 282–312.
[42] The classic study is Martti Koskenniemi, *The Gentle Civilizer of Nations: The Rise and Fall of International Law, 1879–1960* (Cambridge: Cambridge University Press, 2001). For the US case, see Benjamin A. Coates, *Legalist Empire: International Law and American Foreign Relations in the Early Twentieth Century* (New York: Oxford University Press, 2016).

Supreme Court peacefully resolving disputes between states and/or between states and the federal government, so too would war disappear from international relations as interstate arbitration progressed as a practice and also, more generally, as a form of international governance. The prominence of the US federalist system as a template for understanding international politics fueled what the historian Roland Marchand described as the "veritable flood of plans for world courts, world federation, and world government (nearly all of them drawing heavily upon the American political experience and American institutions as models) that poured from American authors after the mid-1890s ..."[43]

At the turn of the twentieth century, racially infused visions of Anglo-American commonalities – and even of a shared Anglo-Saxon race or civilization – grafted themselves onto the swirling interest in federalism, leading to talk on both sides of the Atlantic of English-speaking unions and federations.[44] John Fiske figured among the more visible proponents of Anglo-Saxonism, a creed that expressed itself not only in support for some form Anglo-American or English-speaking unity but also, within the United States, in opposition to immigration from outside the Anglo-world.[45] This racist, Anglo-Saxon inflection of federalism points to the well-known hierarchies in so much of the thinking on international politics at the time, which drew sharp distinctions between civilized states,

[43] C. Roland Marchand, *The American Peace Movement and Social Reform, 1898–1918* (Princeton, NJ: Princeton University Press, 1972), 23–24. Also see Brian C. Schmidt, *The Political Discourse of Anarchy: A Disciplinary of International Relations* (Albany: State University of New York Press, 1998), 112–15; Warren F. Kuehl, *Seeking World Order: The United States and International Organization to 1920* (Nashville, TN: Vanderbilt University Press, 1969), 36–54; and Sondra R. Herman, *Eleven Against War: Studies in American Internationalist Thought, 1898–1921* (Stanford, CA: Hoover Institution Press, 1969), 69–73.

[44] In addition to Kuehl, *Seeking World Order*, see Duncan Bell, *Dreamworlds of Race: Empire and the Utopian Destiny of Anglo-America* (Princeton, NJ: Princeton University Press, 2020); Nell Irvin Painter, *The History of White People* (New York: W. W. Norton, 2010), 244–55; Anthony Brundage and Richard A. Cosgrove, *The Great Tradition: Constitutional History and National Identity in Britain and the United States, 1870–1960* (Stanford, CA: Stanford University Press, 2007); and Reginald Horsman, *Race and Manifest Destiny: The Origins of American Racial Anglo-Saxonism* (Cambridge, MA: Harvard University Press, 1981).

[45] On Fiske, see Milton Berman, *John Fiske: The Evolution of a Popularizer* (Cambridge, MA: Harvard University Press, 1961), 136–40. Also see Rogers M. Smith, *Civic Ideals: Conflicting Visions of Citizenship in U.S. History* (New Haven, CT: Yale University Press, 1997), 347–469; and Bluford Adams, "World Conquerors or a Dying People? Racial Theory, Regional Anxiety, and the Brahmin Anglo-Saxonists," *Journal of the Gilded Age and Progressive Era* 8 (2009), 198–215.

the subjects of international law, and other entities ("decaying" empires, non-Western states, colonies, dependencies) conceived more often as the objects of international law. Yet for all its visibility, in the United States at least the appeal of union/federation with Britain waned considerably after 1900, a process spurred by confluent currents of US exceptionalism and of Anglophobia. Increasingly, the most vocal proponents of Anglo-Saxonism would be found in Britain and not in the United States.[46] Just as importantly, within the latter, the interest in federal frameworks would prove enduring.

Federalist frameworks not only lived on but received a powerful fillip from World War I. If the raging conflict in Europe and beyond provoked heated debate about US intervention, it also prompted jurists to consider an eventual postwar international order. Among the most eminent members of this elite group was James Brown Scott. As head of the Carnegie Endowment's division of international law, as well as secretary of the American Society for International Law (ASIL), which he helped to found, vice-president of the American Peace Society, and former State Department consultant, Scott was exceedingly well-placed to influence the developing debate on the postwar order. In 1919, he would be in Paris as a member of the US delegation to the peace conference.

Scott is most often portrayed as a fervent advocate of international law as a vital instrument for the peaceful settlement of interstate conflict. Although its progress might occasionally stall, the ultimate triumph of international law was inscribed in the thickening interdependence of states and in the strengthening influence of world public opinion. This judicial approach underlay Scott's wartime opposition to the proposals, championed by the League to Enforce Peace, for a postwar international organization endowed with some enforcement capabilities. In rejecting a "legalist-sanctionist" League of Nations endowed with powers to punish aggressors, Scott (and ultimately Woodrow Wilson) placed his faith in a gradualist and noncoercive approach in which states would voluntarily commit themselves to the peaceful settlement of disputes, whose binding force would come from the deepening collective internationalization of norms and practices on a global scale. For Scott, the United States

---

[46] Paul A. Kramer, "Empires, Exceptions, and Anglo-Saxons: Race and Rule between the British and United States Empires, 1880–1910," *Journal of American History* 88 (2002), 1315–53; and John E. Moser, *Twisting the Lion's Tale: American Anglophobia between the World Wars* (New York: New York University Press, 1999). Tellingly, three of the four people examined in Bell's *Dreamworlds of Race* were British, the fourth being Andrew Carnegie, a Scottish-born American.

provided an exemplar of law's compelling power, as differences between states and the federal government were resolved not by force but by courts. Given the course of international politics during the interwar period, it is not surprising that an aura of naive optimism surrounds Scott's historical reputation.[47]

A focus on his opposition to a sanctionist League, however, risks overlooking Scott's determined efforts to fashion and refashion the analogy between the US federal system and international organization. Here, the key question for Scott was how, in a world of sovereign nation-states, to persuade the latter to join an international organization in which membership entailed the renunciation of the sovereign right to wage war.[48] His answer was not simply to hold up the US federal system as a model, but even more so to maintain that the making of the constitution provided a roadmap for states to follow. "What thirteen sovereign, free, and independent States have done," he announced in October 1916, "forty-four sovereign, free, and independent States may do, if they only can be made to feel and to see the consequences of this simple step in international development and supervision."[49]

Over the next two years, Scott elaborated on this point, arguing that the 1777 articles of confederation constituted an initial attempt to form a "league of independent states" but that this "very loose union" had proven inadequate. Consequently, delegates from the thirteen states convened in Philadelphia, in what amounted to an "international conference in the sense in which the term is understood in diplomacy," to forge a new league or federation (the United States), which they invested "with the exercise of certain sovereign powers," among them a mechanism

---

[47] On Scott in general, see John Hepp, "James Brown Scott and the Rise of International Law," *Journal of the Gilded and Progressive Age* 7 (2008), 115–79. For his wartime views, see Paolo Amorosa, "The American Project and the Politics of History: James Brown Scott and the Origins of International Law," PhD, University of Helsinki, 2018, 129–39; and Coates, *Legalist Empire*, 153–63. Also see Stephen Wertheim, "The League that Wasn't: American Designs for a Legalist-Sanctionist League of Nations and the Intellectual Origins of International Organization, 1914–1920," *Diplomatic History* 35 (2011), 797–836.

[48] Natasha Wheatley identifies a more general move away from the pre-1914 emphasis on national sovereignty in international law during the interwar period. See her "Spectral Legal Personality in Interwar International Law: On New Ways of Being a State," *Law and History Review* 35 (2017), 753–87.

[49] James Brown Scott, "The Organization of International Justice," *The Advocate of Peace* 79 (January 1917), 10–22; James Brown Scott, ed., *The Declaration of Independence, the Articles of Confederation, the Constitution of the United States* (New York: Oxford University Press, 1917), iii–iv.

(the Supreme Court) for settling disputes.[50] In a text signed on the same day as the armistice came into effect in November 1918, Scott beseeched the victorious powers to do the same:

Will the sovereign States of the Society of Nations obstinately refuse to follow the path beaten out and marked by the sovereign States of the New World, which recognized that between diplomacy and war, which they renounced, there is only war? The question is not what existed before the meeting of the States in conference in Philadelphia, in the year of grace 1787. It is no longer necessary to *originate*, it is only necessary to *follow* ...

Just as the "imperfect union under the Articles gave way to the more perfect union under the constitution," so too should the wartime alliance "give way to more perfection association devised in a conference of nations."[51]

As the debate on the League became increasingly virulent in the immediate postwar years, Scott adjusted his position, associating the path of virtue more with the articles of confederation than with the constitution. Nevertheless, in a study released in 1920 and aptly entitled *The United States of America: A Study in International Organization*, he insisted states today confronted the same challenge as the thirteen American states had in the 1780s: that "of renouncing in the common interest the exercise of certain sovereign rights, while retaining unimpaired the exercise of all sovereign rights not so renounced." And in this sense, for the League's architects "the experience of the framers of the Constitution who traversed the entire path should be as a lamp to their feet." The Senate's rejection of US participation in the League did not terminate Scott's campaign, even if his attention turned increasingly to the Pan-American realm. Over the next fifteen years, Scott would reiterate his understanding of the United States as the product of a federal "compact of States" – and its federal system, accordingly, as a promising approach to international organizations.[52]

---

[50] James Brown Scott, *Judicial Settlement of Controversies between States of the American Union* (New York: Oxford University Press, 1918), 536–42.

[51] James Brown Scott, *James Madison's Notes of Debates in the Federal Convention of 1787, and Their Relation to a More Perfect Society of Nations* (New York: Oxford University Press, 1918), 73–74, 97.

[52] James Brown Scott, *The United States of America: A Study in International Organization* (New York: Oxford University Press, 1920), 467–68; and James Brown Scott, "Government of Laws and Not of Men," *Advocate of Peace Through Justice* 88 (June 1926), 360–68. Interestingly, a recent "International interpretation" of the revolutionary period unknowingly echoes Scott's approach. See Max M. Edling, "Peace Pact and

Scott was not a lone voice. As mentioned, he occupied the heights of his profession; no less importantly, the sizeable resources of the Carnegie Endowment allowed him to diffuse his views widely, for example, through the subsidized publication and dissemination of edited collections of documents from the 1780s.[53] Several of Scott's colleagues, in any case, echoed his perspective. Referring explicitly to the "closer union under the [US] constitution," Raleigh Minor, a law professor at the University of Virginia, called on the "Allied Nations" in 1918 to create a "federal international government" in which member nations agreed "to surrender to the government of all jointly their power to injure or work injustice upon their sister States or agree that they shall not be exercised at all." Similarly, John Clarke, a Supreme Court justice, while recognizing the difficulties involved in creating a postwar "league," insisted nevertheless "they are not greater than were met and solved by our forefathers when they formed the league of the thirteen original states, framed and adopted our Constitution and established this indissoluble union of indestructible states."[54]

Although the Senate's rejection of US membership in the League reduced the immediate relevance of analogies to the revolutionary period, they did not disappear, thanks partly to Scott. In the introductory note to a 1922 study of the 1787 Philadelphia convention as an "international conference" by Arthur Deerin Call, a well-known peace activist, Scott presented the United States as an "international experiment" and "[a]s such it is the New World's chief contribution to the solution of the World World's problems of war and peace."[55] In an address several years later, Scott lauded the federal union created in 1787 as the "outstanding event" of both the eighteenth and twentieth centuries. A decade later, he once

Nation: An International Interpretation of the Constitution of the United States," *Past & Present* 240 (2018), 267–303.

[53] For example, see James Brown Scott and Gaillard Hunt, eds., *The Debates of the Federal Convention of 1787 Which Framed the Constitution of the United States of America* (New York: Oxford University Press, 1920). For the Carnegie Endowment, see Katharina Rietzler, "Fortunes of a Profession: American Foundations and International Law, 1910–1939," *Global Society* 28 (2014), 8–23.

[54] Raleigh C. Minor. *A Republic of Nations: A Study of the Organization of a Federal League of Nations* (New York: Oxford University Press, 1918), vii, xxx; and John H. Clarke, "A Call to Service. The Duty of the Bench and Bar to Aid in Securing a League of Nations to Enforce the Peace of the World," *American Bar Association Journal* 4 (October 1918), 567–82, 573.

[55] Arthur Deerin Call, *The Federal Convention of 1787: An International Conference Adequate to Its Purpose* (Washington, DC: American Peace Society, 1922), 7–8.

again invoked the analogy between the revolutionary period and contemporary international politics. "What thirteen American States could and did establish and 48 States of the expanded American Union accept as a means for the final settlement of controversies that arise between them from time to time," Scott lectured fellow members of the ASIL at its annual meeting in 1936, "the civilized States of the world could likewise establish and accept."[56]

That federalist frameworks remained influential among international jurists during the 1930s is evident from the case of Clyde Eagleton, a New York University law professor and member of the ASIL's executive council. Eagleton belonged to what several scholars identify as rising group of international lawyers who, in the interwar period, promoted a "new international law" as an alternative to the "judicialist legalism" associated with Scott, among others. Rather than confining international law to legal texts and codes, they sought to anchor it more firmly in political realities, drawing on work in disciplines such as sociology and political science.[57] Eagleton's thinking on the League, though, suggests the divide between the "traditionalists" and "reformers" can be overdrawn. In a 1937 study on the "problem of war," Eagleton maintained there "is no alternative to collective action" to preserve peace. And this required "a better League of Nations," one with the ability to impose sanctions on aggressor states, a precondition of which was a willingness on the part of states to "surrender some of their national sovereignty." Significantly, in envisaging this revamped League, Eagleton pointed to the US federal system as a potential model: "the United States set the world the example of combining jealous and separatist nations under a common system of government, and it has been remarkably successful." The leading countries, he elaborated in Scottian fashion, must collaborate to create a more effective League of Nations, just as the Founding Fathers, recognizing that

---

[56] James Brown Scott, "What America Is Doing for Peace," *Advocate of Peace through Justice* 89 (July 1927), 419; and James Brown Scott, "What Does International Law Mean to Us?" *Proceedings of the American Society of International Law at Its Annual Meeting* 30 (April 1936), 12.

[57] Coates, *Legalist Empire*, 167–70; and Hatsue Shinohara, *US International Lawyers in the Interwar Years: A Forgotten Crusade* (Cambridge: Cambridge University Press, 2012). Jonathan Zasloff, by contrast, argues for continuity across the prewar and interwar periods in the attachment of international lawyers to a "classical legal ideology." See his "Law and the Shaping of American Foreign Policy: The Twenty Years' Crisis," *Southern California Law Review* 77 (2004), 583–682.

a "stronger system was needed," had in 1787 replaced the articles of confederation with the constitution.[58]

Given his interest in federalist frameworks, Eagleton was understandably intrigued by Streit's *Union Now*. The two had met earlier in Geneva, and Streit sent him an advanced copy in late 1938. Although deeming it a "strange book, both in form and style," Eagleton judged *Union Now* "most persuasive." When it came to "rebuild[ting] the League," he confided to Streit, "my argument leads necessarily to something such as you propose."[59] During World War II, Eagleton would be active in semi-official efforts to draft proposals for a postwar international organization, eventually serving as a State Department consultant on the United Nations Organization. As we shall see in Chapter 3, he also remained in contact with Streit.

The argument is not that Eagleton embraced Streit's Atlantic federal union. In truth, the two approached federalism differently. Whereas Streit's project entailed, quite literally, superimposing the US federal system onto a larger North Atlantic world, Eagleton, like Scott, employed federalism more as a metaphor, as a means to envisage an effective international organization of nation-states – one equipped with sufficient binding authority on its members. As we shall see, these differences would become significant during the war. But, for now, the more pertinent point is that by the 1930s federalism had become a familiar and even appealing framework for thinking about international politics both for jurists and for a broader public. This was a factor Streit could exploit in publicizing his proposal.

SELLING *UNION NOW*: CREATING A BUZZ

For Streit, getting the book published was only the first step. As he explained to the *New York Time*'s managing editor, *Union Now* "is not a book in the usual sense; it is a great concrete enterprise." Streit, in fact, was convinced the book could become a force of its own with the potential to alter the course of international politics. Writing to his wife Jeanne in November 1938, Streit wondered whether he was up to the

---

[58] Clyde Eagleton, *The Analysis of the Problem of War* (New York: The Ronald Press, 1937), 103–4, 115, 127, 131–32. Also see Eagleton, "Collective Security," in Frank P. Davidson and George S. Viereck, Jr., eds., *Before America Decides: Foresight in Foreign Affairs* (Cambridge, MA: Harvard University Press), 210–11.

[59] LOC, CKS, Box I: 129, file: Harper & Brothers Publishers, 1938–39, Eagleton to Streit, December 27, 1938.

challenge, whether "I can be the instrument of so great a thing as I am trying to do." He feared the book's success would bring fame with its accompanying "loss of privacy, the living in the public eye ... the life where you cant [sic] call your soul your own and you need to think so much before you speak."[60] It is tempting to snicker at Streit's pretensions but they underscore his unshakeable belief in the urgency of *Union Now*'s proposal as well as in its potentially broad appeal. "For what I seek right now," Streit informed Bullitt in December 1938, "is to change public opinion with this book ..."[61]

The first step, then, was to attract attention – to create a buzz around *Union Now*. Streit understood the book alone could not achieve this goal, if only because of the realities of the publishing industry at the time. The industry's biggest problem was the lack of an effective distribution system. Most books were sold through a small number of under-stocked bookstores, which offered little more than a handful of best-sellers. A report on the publishing industry at the end of the 1930s counted a mere 4,000 bookstores in the United States, with most of them concentrated in East coast and West coast cities. Two-thirds of counties and one-half of cities and towns with a population of 100,000 or less did not have even one bookstore. Publishers, meanwhile, did little to spur sales through advertising. Aside from occasional spots in major dailies such as the *New York Times*, advertisement consisted mostly of book lists in literary or industry journals, both of which reached circumscribed audiences. Although the US advertising industry was in full development, selling an American way of life combining free enterprise, individual choice, and mass consumption, many publishers remained reticent: Working with narrow profit margins, they doubted whether greater advertising would generate sufficient sales to offset the costs involved. As a result, publishers generally relied more on free publicity (book reviews, word-of-mouth, prizes, etc.) than on advertising.[62]

---

[60] LOC, CKS, Box I: 4, file: Chronological correspondence 1938–1939, Streit to Edwin L. James (NYT), May 19, 1938; and BLCU, Harper & Row Collection, series II, Box I: 164, file: Streit, Clarence, Streit to Jeanne Streit, November 3, 1938.

[61] YUL, William C. Bullitt Papers, Box 79, file 2034, Streit to Bullitt, December 5, 1938.

[62] Linda M. Scott, "Markets and Audiences," in David Paul Nord, Joan Shelley Rubin and Michael Schudson, eds., *A History of the Book in America*, vol. 5 *The Enduring Book: Print Culture in Postwar America* (Chapel Hill: University of North Carolina Press, 2009), 72–90; James L. W. West III, "The Expansion of the National Book Trade System," 78–89; and Ellen Gruber Garvey, "Ambivalent Advertising: Books, Prestige, and the Circulation of Publicity," both in Carl F. Kaestle and Janice Radway, eds., *A History of the Book in America*, vol. 4 *The Expansion of Publishing in the United*

Streit threw himself into the task of generating a buzz even before *Union Now*'s publication. From the outset, he pestered Canfield to publicize the book, bombarding him with suggestions for posters, flyers, postcards, and endorsements. Canfield repeatedly reassured Streit he "fully realize[d] that you want the message spread as widely as possible," remarking in February 1939 that "we have worked harder in the production of UNION NOW than any book on the spring list." Three months later he added, "[W]e are anxious to promote UNION NOW just as effectively as we can." And Canfield did exceed the normal publicity budget for books, agreeing for example to buy several advertisements in the *New York Times*.[63] But Harper's resources were limited, and Canfield turned down several of Streit's proposals as commercially unviable, including a book of short essays by prominent figures endorsing Atlantic federal union and a simplified version of *Union Now* for high school and college audiences. Frustrated with what he deemed to be Canfield's inadequate efforts, Streit privately grumbled "I have to do all the pushing for it [*Union Now*] – and how wearing it is."[64]

Streit, in any case, had no intention of leaving the task of promoting his book to Harper. In early 1939, he persuaded CBS to broadcast two radio addresses and also arranged to give a lecture series at Swarthmore College, whose president, Frank Aydelotte, oversaw the US Rhodes scholarship program that had chosen Streit as a recipient in 1920. Streit also exploited his ties to the *New York Times*, seeking to convince its editor, Arthur Sulzberger, to serialize the book. Although Sulzberger eventually declined to do so, Streit negotiated a glowing front page review in the *Times*' Sunday book review by James Truslow Adams, a prolific and Pulitzer Prize-winning historian of revolutionary New England.[65] Streit,

States, 1880–1940 (Chapel Hill: University of North Carolina Press, 2009), 78–89, 170–89; and Dwight Garner, *Read Me: A Century of Classic American Book Advertisements* (New York: HarperCollins, 2009), 15–17. For the advertising industry in general, see Jackson Lears, *Fables of Abundance: A Cultural History of Advertising in America* (New York: Basic Books, 1994), 219–35.

[63] LOC, CKS, Box I: 129, file: Harper & Brothers Publishers, 1938–39, Canfield to Streit, February 1939 and May 1, 1939. Also see the CKS, Box I: 138, file: Books – Union Now – Promotion 1939.

[64] BLCU, Harper & Row Collection, series II, Box 164, file: Streit, Clarence, Streit Diary, December 6, 1938.

[65] NYPL, NYTCR, Arthur Hays Sulzberger Papers, Julius Ochs Adler memorandum to Sulzberger, December 28, 1938; and James Truslow Adams, "A Union of the Democracies: Mr. Streit's Plan for a Federation to Safeguard the World's Peace," *New York Times Book Review*, February 19, 1939.

in turn, worked hard to disseminate this and other favorable opinions. When in April 1939 *Fortune* magazine published an enthusiastic two-page review, Streit got it reprinted in *Readers' Digest*, thereby ensuring a larger readership.[66] Through his contacts with Nicholas Murray Butler, who had lectured in Geneva in 1937 on US federalism as a "laboratory experiment in world organization," Streit convinced the Carnegie Endowment to purchase 1,150 copies for libraries and international relations clubs across the country and another 1,100 for newspaper editors and journalists.[67] Streit also courted Harry Scherman, the book-of-the-month club's president. Having initially turned down *Union Now* for its list, Scherman agreed in 1941 to offer the book, along with *Union Now with Britain*, to its 200,000 members as its monthly "book-dividend." Before then, Scherman, who became a life-long supporter of Streit, helped to finance the distribution of *Union Now.*[68]

All this frenetic activity soon confronted Streit with a career dilemma. Streit had expected the *New York Times* to support his "enterprise" which, he contended, constituted a logical extension of the newspaper's internationalist orientation. Although the *Times* granted Streit an unpaid leave in 1939 to promote *Union Now*, Sulzberger worried his journalist was becoming a "fanatic." Their differing views highlight the tensions, discussed in Chapter 1, affecting foreign correspondents at a time of heightening international tensions: Sulzberger insisted a correspondent's job was not to campaign for specific political projects but to report the news, a job description that frustrated Streit. In agreeing to extend his leave until the end of 1939, the *Times* made it conditional on Streit's ability to retain his "objectivity," of which the *Times* would be the "sole judge."[69]

The extended leave from journalism allowed Streit to redouble his promotional activities. Following the release of *Union Now*, he undertook several cross-country speaking tours. In one forty-eight-hour span in February 1939, he visited three mid-western cities (Columbus, Cincinnati,

---

[66] "Union Now," *Readers' Digest*, June 1939, 99–102.
[67] LOC, Norman H. Davis Papers, Box 8, Henry Haskell (CEIP) to Davis, May 3, 1939. For Murray, see "Dr. Butler Applies U.S. Plan to World," *New York Times*, June 15, 1937, 6. My university library's copy of *Union Now* came from Carnegie Endowment funds.
[68] NYHS, Henry Luce Papers, Box 139, Scherman to Luce, July 26, 1941; and BLCU, Harry Scherman Papers, Series IV, Box 10, file: Federal Union, 1948–66.
[69] BLCU, Harper & Row Collection, series II, Box 164, file: Streit, Clarence, Streit to Jeanne Streit, February 21, 1940 (but 1939); and LOC, CKS, Box I: 5, file: Chronological correspondence, 1939, E. L. James (NYT) to Arthur Krock (NYT), April 22, 1939.

and Detroit) giving six talks. "Continue to be so worked," Streit penned his wife in April from a hotel in Des Moines, Iowa, "that I don't know where I'm at ..."[70] Along with lecturing, Streit began to raise money for his cause, which allowed him to expand his publicity efforts in the form of pamphlets, flyers, and newspaper advertisements. In March 1939, a monthly "Union Now Bulletin" appeared whose purpose, Streit announced in the first issue, was to provide "the essence of the book, *Union Now*. It is not meant to replace the book but to help spread more quickly its basic ideas."[71]

Sales of *Union Now*, while not spectacular, rose steadily during 1939, reaching close to 10,000 by November. But for Streit sales counted less than visibility, and newspapers.com offers one means to measure the latter.[72] The graph above traces the mentions of "Clarence Streit" in

[70] LOC, CKS, Box I: 5, file: Chronological correspondence, 1931, Streit to Jeanne Streit, April 6, 1939. And see the list of speaking engagements for April to June 1939 in LOC, CKS, Box III: 8, file 8.

[71] A collection of publicity material is in NYPL, CFWG (NY), Series III, Box 20, file 20.5. For the Bulletin, see LOC, CKS, Box I: 76, file: publications, news bulletins.

[72] LOC, CKS, Box I: 129, file: Harper & Brothers Publishers, 1938–39, Canfield to Streit, November 8, 1939.

newspapers across the United States from October 1938 to December 1941, indicating the fluctuating rise in number beginning in the spring of 1939 with peaks in November 1939 and again in June 1941. Despite its limits, the graph does suggest Streit succeeded in getting himself (and his book) talked about.

Evidence of a more anecdotal nature points to the same conclusion. Writing to a friend in February 1939, Felix Morley, the *Washington Post*'s editor, marveled at Streit's "magnificent propaganda job." Two months earlier, a report by the American Association of University Women credited Streit for having "stirred up discussion and [having] caught the imagination of many people."[73] Streit's visibility was also evident at the local level. An article in a Maryland newspaper in March 1939 remarked Streit's book "is attracting a great deal of attention," while in April an Oregon newspaper, citing Truslow's *New York Times* review and Streit's radio broadcasts, reported *Union Now* "has made quite a sensation"; two months later a newspaper in Santa Cruz, California warned tongue-in-cheek that the book was provoking never-ending discussions.[74] In July 1939 Herbert Agar, a Pulitzer Prize-winning journalist and editor of the *Louisville Courier-Journal*, informed his readers *Union Now* "has aroused such interest that clubs to study and promote Mr. Streit's plan are forming throughout the country." The next day Agar added the plan "is treated as a serious contribution to thought by many of our leading newspapers, college presidents and publicists."[75] Just as importantly, newspapers across the country underscored the federalist thrust of Streit's proposal. "The interesting point about Mr. Streit's book," one Indiana newspaper explained, "is that it suggests little that is new in the way of theory. He simply applies the American form of government to a wider area. He points to the American success and argues that the new union would have the same success because of the principles incorporated."[76]

[73] LOC, Arthur Sweetser Papers, Box 33, Felix Morley to Arthur Sweetser, February 12, 1940; and SPRCGW, Carnegie Peace Pamphlet and Microfilm Collection, Box 3, Esther Caukin Brunauer, *Building the New World Order* (Washington, DC: American Association of University Women, December 1939), 25.

[74] "More Copies of Popular Books Added to Library's Shelves during Current Week," *The Daily Mail* March 29, 1939, 4; "But Internationally Self-Interest Rules!," *Medford Mail Tribune*, April 2, 1939, 8; and "As We See It," *Santa Cruz Sentinel*, June 23, 1939, 1.

[75] Herbert Agar, "Time and Tide", *The Courier-Journal*, July 12 and 13, 1939, 6.

[76] "Advocates Union upon American Plan," *The Daily Clintonian*, March 20, 1939, 4.

In addition to generating a public buzz, Streit sedulously wooed people in a position to influence foreign policy debates in the United States. Although the makeup of this group is fuzzy, limiting the value of terms such as the "power elite" or the "establishment," it encompassed government officials, politicians, academics and university leaders, bankers, and journalists, among others.[77] Even before *Union Now* appeared, Streit began sending versions (page proofs and advanced copies) at his own expense to a lengthening list of people. In early March 1939, Streit estimated he had already distributed some 400 copies.[78] Having sent the book to someone, Streit systematically followed up, badgering the recipient for comments, endorsements, and references, which he then used to underscore the *Union Now*'s significance to still more people. This flurry of networking and name-dropping drew in a diverse array of influential people: journalists such as John Gunther, Robert Dell, and Dorothy Thompson; newspaper editors such as Gardner Cowles and William Allen White; the jurists Manley Hudson and Clyde Eagleton; the diplomat Norman Davis; and activists such as Eleanor Roosevelt and James Shotwell. The result was something of an echo chamber in which more and more influential people appeared to be talking about Streit's book.

Streit believed personal contact to be all-important, convinced he could persuade anyone of Atlantic union's merits if given the chance. "I have seen how I can make women's eyes shine and big men look at me in a fascinated away [sic]," he wrote to his wife in December 1938, "and change and begin to think their impossibles are possibles."[79] To be sure, not everyone proved susceptible to this personal touch. "Streit takes his ideas so seriously that I think he wanted to convert me to the plan then and there," a State Department official sardonically commented after an encounter in November 1938.[80]

---

[77] C. Wright Mills, *The Power Elite* (New York: Oxford University Press, 1956); and Priscilla Roberts, "The Anglo-American Theme: Anglo-American Visions of an Atlantic Alliance, 1914–1933," *Diplomatic History* 21 (1997), 333–64.

[78] LOC, CKS, Box I: 4, file: Chronological correspondence, 1938–1939, Streit to Frank Aydelotte, March 5, 1939.

[79] BLCU, Harper & Row Collection, Series II, Box 164, file: Streit, Clarence, Streit to Jeanne Streit, December 24, 1938.

[80] HUHL, Jay Pierrepont Moffat Papers, Diary 1938, vol. 41, November 21, 1938.

Nevertheless, multiple examples exist of Streit's success in interesting influential people in *Union Now*'s proposal. There is Thomas Lamont, the J. P. Morgan partner and advisor to successive presidents, whom Streit first met in January 1939 in New York at an event hosted by the Council for Foreign Relations, probably the most influential foreign policy think tank at the time. This led to a breakfast meeting at which Lamont expressed interest in federal union and promised to do "what he could" to help. Soon afterward, he donated $1,000 to a "Fund for Union Now of the democracies" dedicated to publicizing the proposal.[81] Although Lamont remained prudent regarding the immediate prospects of federal union, he was struck by the attention it received. Streit, he recounted to a British friend in March 1939, "is making quite a bit of an impression here, not so great of course as to mean that anything will come of the idea for years to come, but it is a good thing to have people discuss formulas that would really mean an end to world war."[82] If Lamont's interest in Atlantic union waned during the war, his wife would become one of Streit's more generous supporters.

Another example is John Foster Dulles, the Republican foreign policy heavyweight. In 1939, Dulles published a book with Harper on international policy, arguing for the need to fuse political and ethical imperatives – an operation involving "changes to human nature" and to the "existing organization of the world." While scholars have emphasized the role of Christian faith in his thinking at the time, Dulles was also attracted to federalist frameworks as a means to tame what he saw as a fundamental problem afflicting international relations: the unbending attachment of nations to the principle of national sovereignty.[83] Dulles, accordingly, responded warmly when sent an advanced copy of *Union Now*. Writing to Streit in January 1939, Dulles, while deeming the proposal too "dramatic" for his "lawyer's natural caution," expressed hope that "a new instrument of union, of the general type you describe" will develop between the United States and other democracies. Ten months later he confided to Streit: "I am becoming more and more impressed with

[81] BSHU, Thomas William Lamont Collection, Box 28, file 9, Lamont to Streit, January 20, 1939; and R. Frazier Potts to Lamont, May 30, 1939.

[82] BSHU, Thomas William Lamont Collection, Box 112, file 11, Lamont to Lord Catto, March 13, 1939.

[83] John Foster Dulles, *War, Peace and Change* (New York: Harper & Brothers, 1939), 167. For a helpful discussion of the scholarship on Dulles, see Bevan Sewell, "Pragmatism, Religion, and John Foster Dulles's Embrace of Christian Internationalism in the 1930s," *Diplomatic History* 41 (2017), 799–823.

some form of federal principle being the only solution of the problem in which the world now finds itself."[84] Although Dulles judged Streit as too attached to the US federal system as a model, he continued to be intrigued by federalism. Not only did Dulles agree to act as an unofficial advisor to Streit, but in late 1940 the two worked closely together to sketch out a draft constitution for a federal union.[85]

Henry Luce, the media mogul, provides still another example of Streit's success in arousing the interest of influential people in his proposal. Fellow journalist Dorothy Thompson provided an introduction to Luce and to Russell Davenport, the editor of the Luce-owned business magazine, *Fortune*. If Luce initially appeared noncommittal, Davenport reacted with enthusiasm, impressed by Lamont's endorsement. "He's [Streit] really got his campaign going," Davenport reported in a note circulated within Luce's media empire, "and it will do us good to be on the band wagon."[86] Having arranged for the publication of a two-page endorsement of Atlantic union in *Fortune* in April 1939, Davenport over the next twelve months threw himself into networking and fund-raising for Streit among his well-connected and wealthy acquaintances. In September 1939, for instance, he urged Nelson Rockefeller to read Streit's book, claiming it possessed "enormous educational value" and that international events were "playing into Mr. Streit's hands." "It seems to me that as pressure upon democracies increases," Davenport asserted, "they will become eager to embrace some such concept as UNION NOW." Although John Rockefeller found the book's proposal "somewhat visionary and idealistic," his brother Nelson did agree to provide rent-free office space for Streit in Manhattan.[87]

In the summer of 1940, Davenport would abandon Streit to help run Wendell Willkie's presidential campaign but not before nudging Luce to take a second look at federal union. In May 1939, Davenport organized a lunch for the three, after which Streit doggedly courted Luce. With the

[84] SMLPU, John Foster Dulles Papers, Box 18, reel 4, Dulles to Streit, January 23 and October 19, 1939.
[85] SMLPU, John Foster Dulles Papers, Box 18, reel 4, Dulles to Marquess Lothian, January 3, 1940.
[86] NYHS, Henry R. Luce Papers, Box 102, file: Streit, Clarence, Streit to Luce, January 14, 1939; Davenport to Luce, May 10, 1939. And LOC, Russell W. Davenport Papers, Box 34, file 5, Davenport to Gratz, Time office memorandum, April 6, 1939.
[87] LOC, Russell W. Davenport Papers, Box 34, file 5, Davenport to Nelson Rockefeller, September 13, 1939; and RAC, Office of the Messrs. Rockefeller records, World Affairs, Series Q, Box 24, file 205, John Rockefeller to Packard, Oct 9, 1939.

advent of war in Europe in September 1939, Luce proved receptive to Streit's efforts, convinced the United States needed not just a "Foreign Policy" but, as he argued in staff memorandum in July 1940, a "Project for the Future" that reflected its global leadership pretentions, fostered democracy at home and abroad, and acknowledged the limits of national sovereignty in an interconnected world. "Practically," he affirmed, "this means giving serious attention to proposals like Union Now."[88] In addition to Davenport, Raymond Buell, perhaps the most visible foreign policy expert of the interwar years and who in 1939 became a paid advisor to Luce, encouraged the latter in this direction. Though uncertain about the political realism of Streit's proposal, Buell was attracted to its federalist framework. "I am trying to make something real out of Clarence Streit's idea which is now utopian," he confided to Lamont in August 1939.[89]

All this provides the background to Luce's famous editorial, "The American Century," published in *Life* in February 1941. The editorial has attained iconic status as an expression of the United States' mid-century claims to global dominance. Yet almost never mentioned is the fact that Streit figured as the sole person named who was not a current or past political leader. Streit's proposal to "create a new and larger federal union of peoples ... may not be the right approach to our problem," Luce's editorial ventured before going on to recommend: "But no thoughtful American as done his duty to the United States of America until he has read and pondered Clarence Streit's book presenting that proposal."[90]

Luce was not an unconditional advocate of Streit's Atlantic federal union. Nor were Davenport, Lamont, and Dulles for that matter. But the more important point is that Streit succeeded in drawing attention to his project, particularly among the select group of people capable of influencing public debate.

---

[88] NYHS, Time Inc. Box 414, file: Edit 1940, "Subject: War," Luce, July 17, 1940. On Luce more generally, see Alan Brinkley, *The Publisher: Henry Luce and His American Century* (New York: Alfred A. Knopf, 2010), 243–48.

[89] LOC, Raymond Leslie Buell Papers, Box 9, file 11, Buell to Thomas Lamont, August 15, 1939. For Buell's interest in federalist frameworks, see LOC, Russell W. Davenport Papers, Box 56, file 13, "Memorandum on Fortune Round Tables and Fortune's Think-Job," Buell, July 18, 1941. For Buell in general, see Robert Vitalis, *White World Order, Black Power Politics: The Birth of American Foreign Relations* (Ithaca, NY: Cornell University Press, 2015), 56–64.

[90] Luce, "The American Century" (1941), reproduced in *Diplomatic History* 23 (1999), 16.

UNION NOW AND THE DEBATE ON THE POSTWAR INTERNATIONAL ORDER

Union Now's growing visibility among the wider as well as expert public, itself the result of the synergy between the publicity efforts surrounding the book and the more general appeal of federalist frameworks, allowed Streit to become a fixture in an emerging debate in the United States on the postwar international order. A Google Ngram for "Clarence Streit" points to the sharp rise of mentions in books beginning in 1938–39 and reaching a peak in 1941:

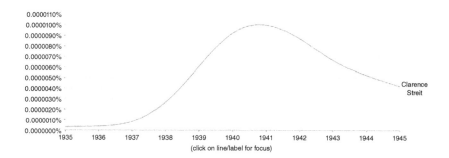

Other sources confirm this impression. A bibliography compiled in December 1940 by the Carnegie Endowment on "The New World Order" listed nine entries for Streit, the most for any author. In 1941 a study issued by the Foreign Policy Association on the "struggle for world order" devoted several pages to Streit's proposal and listed *Union Now* among its suggested readings. Early the following year Percy Corbett, a Yale political scientist, published, under the auspices of the Institute of Pacific Relations, a survey of postwar planning with an entire chapter on the "Ascendency of the Federal Idea."[91]

But Streit did not simply participate in the emerging debate; he also helped to shape its structure, as an analysis of the responses to his proposal indicates. These responses can be divided into three groups: converts, opponents, and sympathizers. The converts, those who fervently embraced the proposal and were often willing to work with Streit in

---

[91] CEIP, "The New World Order" (New York: CEIP, December 12, 1940); Vera Micheles Dean, *The Struggle for World Order* (New York: FPA, November 1941), 71–84, 95–96; and P. E. Corbett, *Post-War Worlds* (New York: Institute of Pacific Relations, 1942), 42–53.

publicizing it, will be examined in the next chapter. The opponents, meanwhile, comprised several groups. Much of the limited scholarly attention accorded to Streit focuses on the anti-imperialists – those who denounced his proposal as a stratagem to perpetuate empire and Western (white) domination. George Orwell wrote a blistering critique in this sense, as did H. G. Wells, who also condemned the book as anti-socialist.[92] From India, Jawaharlal Nehru, a Congress party leader and future prime minister, while praising Streit's "bonafides," expressed his fear that the "imperialist powers will inevitably take advantage of any such development to consolidate their position." Even Lionel Curtis, a longtime proponent of imperial federation who worked to publicize *Union Now* in Britain, urged Streit to "readjust your views about India," which had been excluded on the grounds it counted "too many voters untrained for self-government."[93] That Streit's book could provoke reactions from such luminaries outside the United States – and as far away as India – is another indication of its visibility.

Criticism from anti-imperialists is understandable, for *Union Now*, as already mentioned, was markedly Western and even white-centered. Streit tip-toed around issues of empire and race, partly because to include imperial possessions risked undermining the United States' demographic and thus representational advantage in the equivalent of the Union's house of representatives. Interestingly, Streit did not include the majority black population when calculating South Africa's possible proportional weight (if Atlantic federal union were to include the "white" dominions) but does appear to have included black Americans notwithstanding the apartheid (Jim Crow) system in the United States at the time.[94]

At the same time, it is noteworthy that the accusation of perpetuating empire came principally from outside the United States. To be sure, the accusation found some echo at home. The African-American scholar and political activist, W. E. B. Du Bois, who had famously described a color line running through US and global politics, reacted with considerable skepticism to Streit's claims that the United States and Britain were democracies. Remarking that Streit's proposal had "aroused much interest," Dubois identified it with a tendency to approach the war's stakes

---

[92] George Orwell, "Not Counting N-----s," *Adelphi*, July 1939; and H. G. Wells, *The New World Order* (London: Secker & Warburg, 1940).

[93] LOC, CKS, Box I: 65, file: India 1942–48, Nehru to Samuel Spalding (Federal Unionists), February 23, 1940; and CKS, Box I: 4, file: Chronological correspondence, 1938–1939, Curtis to Streit, May 4, 1939. And Streit, *Union Now*, 185–86.

[94] Streit, *Union Now*, 187–89. I am grateful to Dr. Andrew Johnstone for this point.

"solely from the point of view and interest of the white race."[95] Yet as central as race and empire were to the perspectives of African-Americans in the opening years of the war, they were far less so to the small group of foreign policy experts, almost all of whom were white, engaged in a burgeoning debate on the postwar international order. And it is this debate, as we shall see, which is central for understanding Streit's influence.

Among progressives in the United States, criticism of Streit was rooted more in pacifism than in anti-imperialism, though the latter was certainly not absent. A good example is Rosika Schwimmer, the Hungarian-born international pacifist and feminist, whom Du Bois favorably cited. Initially, Schwimmer hoped to win Streit over to her vision of an anti-militarist world federation, but when this failed she quickly became a fierce opponent, goaded by *Union Now*'s visibility. Over the next eighteen months, Schwimmer waged a determined campaign, which included a pamphlet printed and circulated at her own expense denouncing Streit's project as too pro-British, too exclusive (for leaving out South American states, the Soviet Union, and India, among others) and, above all, too militarist. Atlantic federal union, she charged, simply reproduced the failed power politics generating international tensions and conflict. In this regard, Schwimmer found Streit's distinction between democracies and totalitarian states particularly dangerous, insisting it would unfailingly lead to "the most savage clash between the group of Mr. Streit's so-called democracies and the rest of the nations."[96] Only a universal federation could serve the cause of peace. If Schwimmer's unyielding pacifism was not widely shared, her juxtaposition of Streit's exclusive federalism with a more inclusive version prefigured later wartime discussions.

Another group of Streit's opponents were the nationalists who rejected any form of federalism. A striking example is Clare Hoffman, a fiery anti-Roosevelt congressman from Michigan, who, in two speeches in January 1942, accused Streit of sacrificing US national sovereignty and

[95] W. E. B. Du Bois, "A Chronicle of Race Relations," *Phylon* 3 (1942), 322–23. Also see W. E. B. Du Bois, "As the Crow Flies," *Amsterdam News*, April 12, 1941. And more generally, Penny M. Von Eschen, *Race against Empire: Black Americans and Anticolonialism, 1937–1957* (Ithaca, NY: Cornell University Press, 1997), 1–95.

[96] NYPL, CFWG (CO), Box 88, file 13, Rosika Schwimmer, "Union Now for Peace or War? The Danger in the Plan of Clarence Streit" (New York: Campaign for World Government, August 1939), 2; and CFWG (NY), Box 19, file 7, Schwimmer to Liv, July 30, 1939. Also see Arnaldo Testi, "Alle origini di una utopia tranznationale: Rosika Schwimmer e la fondazione della Campaign for World Government (1937–1938)," *Genesis* 8 (2009), 65–83.

independence on the altar of world government. Streit's project, Hoffman thundered, amounted to a treasonous betrayal of the constitution, suggesting, if nothing else, that the cult of the latter was open to multiple meanings. Hoffman worked hard to disseminate his two speeches, prompting a flood of supporting letters to his office.[97] Some letters displayed an allergy to federalist frameworks, a condition shared by Hoffman's fellow Michigan congressman, Paul Shafer, who proposed to organize a "Wake Up Now" movement to combat Streit's proposal.[98] Other letters were infused with Anglophobia, a current of opinion evident elsewhere, for example, in the syndicated newspaper columns of Boake Carter, who accused Streit of being a front for Britain's "world-dominating empire."[99] But many of the letter-writers revealed another and probably more representative sentiment: one of malaise at the prospect of the United States assuming a more activist global role after the war. Before December 1941, this malaise expressed itself in opposition to direct US involvement in the war in Europe; afterward it manifested itself more often in calls to restrict the scope of a postwar international organization meant to be both a successor to and an improvement on the interwar League of Nations.

Streit's influence on the emerging debate in the United States on the postwar international order in the United States is most apparent with the third group of responses: the sympathizers. Dulles, Lamont, and Luce all belonged to this group. Collectively, they viewed Streit's proposal not as a roadmap but as a useful contribution in efforts to stimulate thinking about the international order and the United States' place in it. And, initially at least, this appeared to be the prevailing response among foreign policy commentators. Thus, at a meeting of the ASIL in April 1939, Allen Dulles, John Foster's brother and a future CIA director, recommended Streit's proposal as "a subject for more thorough consideration." "In this field of all others," he added, "we should not reject ideas merely because they appear novel, or out of the reach of practical politics at a given moment." Having received an advanced copy of *Union Now*, Raymond Clapper, one of the most popular syndicated columnists at the time, assured Streit "your thesis is challenging and provides a vehicle for

[97] BHLUM, Clare E. Hoffman Papers, Box 3, file 1942, "Don't Hall Down the Stars and Stripes," January 27 and 30, 1942. Box 3 contains several files of letters.
[98] For Paul Shafer, see "Union Now Idea Is Denounced on Floor of House," *Chicago Tribune*, January 28, 1942, 3.
[99] For example, see Boake Carter, "What about 'Union Now," *Boston Globe*, November 24, 1939, 21.

fresh thinking about the whole problem of international cooperation." Over the next two years, Clapper repeatedly urged readers to consider the book: Echoing Luce's "American Century" editorial, he judged Streit's plan "worthy of the study of everyone who wants this to be the last war."[100] In an article published in late 1941, William Maddox, a University of Pennsylvania political scientist, reported that, thanks largely to Streit, federalism had become a "catch-word" and "ready-made formula" in informed discussions of the postwar international order. While urging a more "critical examination" of federalism, Maddox admitted he found Streit's "union of democracies" particularly intriguing.[101]

In stimulating thinking on the United States and international politics, Streit's project influenced the developing nature of public discussion. When imagining the postwar international order, several prominent participants sketched two possibilities: a revived League of Nations or, drawing on Streit, some form of federalism. In a book published by Harper in 1940, James Warburg, a Wall Street banker and Council for Foreign Relations stalwart whom Streit had courted, presented the choice in precisely these terms. Rejecting the League as a proven failure, Warburg urged consideration of some type of federal union, an idea that had received "a new and vital impetus" from Streit's book. "Union," he assured readers, "means nothing more than the application to all nations, or to certain groups of nations, of the federal principal of government, with which we are all familiar." A book by Buell the same year framed federalist frameworks, of which Streit's was the best known, as an alternative to a League of Nations, which had few supporters. While voicing doubts about its practicality, Buell clearly considered the project worthy of serious discussion. Similarly, in 1940 Herbert Agar cosigned with several public figures a "Declaration on World Democracy," published by Viking. Along with affirming the postwar "City of Man must be much more than a League of Nations," the declaration offered the US federal system as an inspiring guide to thinking about international order. Soon afterward, Carl Becker, the historian and prominent commentator, contended the future belonged not to the League of Nations but to a

---

[100] Allen W. Dulles, "Collective Security," *Proceedings of the American Society of International Law* 33 (April 1939), 119. For Clapper, see LOC, CKS, Box III: 8, file 8, Clapper to Streit, February 7, 1939; "Clapper's Comment," *Honolulu Advertiser*, March 4, 1941, 10; and "Union Now Plan Is Worthy," *The Miami News*, December 20, 1941, 4.

[101] William P. Maddox, "The Political Basis of Federation," *American Political Science Review* 35 (1941), 1120–27.

federation of democracies whose precise form, he admitted, could not be determined in advance.[102]

It would be easy to multiply the examples, but the point would remain the same: In the two years following the publication of *Union Now*, Streit succeeded not simply in getting his proposal talked about but also in influencing the incipient debate on the postwar international order and the United States' role in it. Federalist frameworks, as a result, became a referent, one of two poles (the other being international organizations and the League of Nations in particular) structuring the discussion. This was no small achievement. If Streit benefited from the generalized cult of the constitution and of the US federal system, he also contributed mightily to this result through his tireless publicity activities.

Two additional points are worth underscoring. One concerns the relationship in the emerging debate on the postwar international order between federalist frameworks and the League of Nations. Streit clearly considered the two as distinct and even irreconcilable approaches, as they appeared to be for Warburg and Agar, among others. Nevertheless, the relationship between federalist frameworks and the League also allowed for the possibility of harnessing the former to the pursuit of the latter – to creating a more effective League. If, as mentioned, Felix Morley so admired Streit's publicity campaign it was because he hoped "it will make American entry into a reconstituted League of Nations easier."[103] It is worth recalling that James Brown Scott and, more recently still, Clyde Eagleton had framed federalism precisely in such terms. From Streit's perspective, the danger was that federalist frameworks would be used to rehabilitate – rather than replace – the interwar League for a US public.

The second point concerns the question of what now. In December 1938 Streit described his task with *Union Now* as to "get this snowball started rolling and gaining speed and size till it swaps [sic] everything before it." But an analogy is not a political strategy. After listening to a Streit lecture in March 1939, Schwimmer grumbled that he "had no other

---

[102] James P. Warburg, *Peace in Our Time?* (New York, 1940), 58–69; Raymond Leslie Buell, *Isolated America* (New York: Harper & Brothers, 1940), 419–45; Herbert Agar, Frank Aydelotte, Guiseppe Antonio Borgese et al., *The City of Man: A Declaration on World Democracy* (New York: Viking, 1941), 23–25; and Carl Becker, "Making Democracy Safe in the World," *Yale Review* 31 (March 1942), 442–53.

[103] LOC, Arthur Sweetser Papers, Box 33, Felix Morley to Arthur Sweetser, February 12, 1940. A July 1940 workshop at the University of Chicago discussed Streit's proposal in similar fashion. See Walter H. C. Laves and Francis O. Wilcox, *The Middle West Looks at the War* (Chicago: University of Chicago Press, 1940), 25–27.

advice but for everyone to go out and tell his neighbors and make everyone who can be reached believe in the plan."[104] While certainly not the most objective of observers, Schwimmer was right that it would take more than visibility to make Atlantic federal union a reality. If, much to Schwimmer's annoyance, Streit succeeded in attracting considerable attention to his proposal, he still needed to work out an effective means to influence policy.

---

[104] LOC, CKS, Box III: 4, file 9, Streit to wife, December 24, 1938; and NYPL, CWG, RNY, Box 19, file 7, Schwimmer to William B. Lloyd, March 11, 1939.

3

The Wartime Pursuit of Federal Union, 1940–1945

The previous chapter examined Streit's success in attracting attention to his book, *Union Now*, and its proposal for an Atlantic federal union. But for Streit, this achievement was nowhere near enough. Visibility constituted a means to the end of realizing the project. Streit, moreover, was impatient: He calculated in terms not of decades but of years. "We lose nothing that I can see by striving to get action quickly, and we have everything to gain," Streit announced to an audience of supporters in June 1941.[1] From this perspective, the outbreak of hostilities in Europe in September 1939 offered opportunities: War's attendant upheavals, uncertainties, and urgencies opened new vistas. What might in more peaceful times be dismissed as overly bold, if not quixotic, in wartime appeared intriguing and perhaps even feasible. William Fulton, a long-time *Chicago Tribune* journalist hostile to *Union Now*, remarked as much in a column in February 1941. "Before the war Streit's proposal slumbered within the pages of his book or popped up in academic discussion whenever Anglophiles got together ...," he uncharitably remarked. "The war came along and gave the idea a mighty fillip."[2]

This chapter examines Streit's efforts to realize an Atlantic federal union during the war. In addition to pursuing his publicity activities, Streit adopted two strategies. One was to build a nation-wide organization to publicize his proposal and to mobilize popular support for it.

---

[1] LOC, CKS, Box I: 46, file: Convention 1941, "Proceedings First Annual Convention, Federal Union, Inc. June 28–29, 1941," Streit, 149.
[2] William Fulton, "War Bloc Tries to Put U.S. in British Empire," *Chicago Tribune*, February 17, 1941, 1, 4.

A strategy common to political movements at the time, Streit's case is suggestive of the difficulties involved in mobilizing locally – difficulties oft-cited figures for membership and chapter numbers poorly capture. The second strategy consisted of direct political action comprising three elements: unsuccessful attempts to arouse the Roosevelt administration; a desultory campaign to interest Congress; and half-hearted and self-defeating collaboration with the Commission to Study the Organization of the Peace (CSOP), an unjustly neglected semi-official body that played a vital role in the emergence of the United Nations Organization (UNO), the principal postwar international organization.[3] As we shall see, the CSOP's wartime history witnessed a political struggle to articulate, to integrate, and ultimately to sideline federalist frameworks in discussions about the postwar international order.

The nexus between the CSOP and federalist frameworks is pertinent to the burgeoning scholarship on wartime US internationalism. Rejecting the traditional isolationist-internationalist binary, scholars such as Or Rosenboim and Samuel Zipp offer "globalism" as a more apt paradigm, characterizing the war years as an unprecedented moment of global awareness as Americans came to conceive of the world as an interconnected whole and their country as a globe-spanning force. Rosenboim identifies a number of "global schemes" articulated by various US and British intellectuals, among them Streit's Atlantic federal union, but provides little sense of their relative political weight. With Wendell Willkie, the defeated Republican candidate for president in 1940 who aimed to run again in 1944, Zipp focuses on a political heavyweight. Yet the claim that Willkie's globalism embodied a distinct internationalism, one whose principal elements were the equality and independence of all nations, anti-imperialism, and liberal economic exchanges, is questionable. After all, these elements had long been associated with liberal internationalism, a vision and even project of international order, other scholars contend, which World War II would make ascendant. Willkie's thinking, moreover, operated in the realm of grand principles, rendering his

---

[3] Scholarship on the CSOP is meager, but see Waqar H. Zaidi, *Technological Internationalism: Aviation, Atomic Energy, and the Search for International Peace, 1920–1950* (Cambridge: Cambridge University Press, 2021), 111–21; Glenn Tatsuya Mitoma, "Civil Society and International Human Rights: The Commission to Study the Organization of the Peace and the Origins of the UN Human Rights Regime," *Human Rights Quarterly* 30 (2008), 607–30; and Robert P. Hillman, "Quincy Wright and the Commission to Study the Organization of the Peace," *Global Governance* 4 (1998), 485–99.

internationalism more aspirational than programmatic.[4] Somewhat more concrete, in this sense, is Stephen Wertheim's study, which locates the beginnings of Washington's insatiable and destructive quest for "global supremacy" after 1945 in the earlier deliberations of elite advisors. Wertheim, though, leaves little room for the wartime politics of internationalism, a domain of activity encompassing not only a wider array of actors, including Streit and the CSOP, but also considerable contestation, not least on the issue of a postwar United Nations.[5]

ONGOING PROMOTIONAL ACTIVITIES

Streit continued to promote his project during the war, engaging in a punishing schedule of activities. In May 1940, he boasted to Clark Eichelberger of having traveled some 12,000 miles in the last thirty-five days and of giving talks to thirty-seven different audiences. In the spring of 1941, Streit gave commencement addresses to several colleges, and in a tour of western states in the autumn racked up another 8,000 miles of travel, visiting seventeen cities and towns. A similar tour of mid-western states the following year saw him lecture to a variety of groups, among them the Women's City Club in St. Paul, Minnesota, the North Dakota State Teachers' Convention, and the Sequoyah Dining Club in Oklahoma City. "Everywhere my talk was warmly received," Streit reported on the 1942 tour, "nearly always I got a curtain call, sometimes two."[6] Over the

---

[4] Or Rosenboim, *The Emergence of Globalism: Visions of World Order in Britain and the United States, 1939–1950* (Princeton, NJ: Princeton University Press, 2017); and Samuel Zipp, *The Idealist: Wendell Willkie's Wartime Quest to Build One World* (Cambridge, MA: Belknap Press, 2020). Also see Andrew Buchanan, "Domesticating Hegemony: Creating a Globalist Public, 1941–1943," *Diplomatic History* 45 (2021), 301–29. For wartime liberal internationalism, see G. John Ikenberry, *A World Safe for Democracy: Liberal Internationalism and the Crises of Global Order* (New Haven, CT: Yale University Press, 2020), 144–211; and Elizabeth Borgwardt, *A New Deal for the World: America's Vision of Human Rights* (Cambridge, MA: Belknap Press, 2005).

[5] Stephen Wertheim, *Tomorrow the World: The Birth of U.S. Global Supremacy* (Cambridge, MA: Belknap Press, 2020). For Wertheim, the United Nations is an afterthought, basically an instrument of US policy.

[6] LOC, CKS, Box I: 5, file: Chronological correspondence, 1940, Streit to Eichelberger, May 3, 1940; Box I: 76, file: Publications: Headquarters Bulletin, "Report on Streit's Western Speaking Tour September 20th–November 9th, 1941"; and Box I: 40, file: Board: Correspondence, 1942–43, Streit to FU Board, November 12, 1942.

next two years, he continued to crisscross the country, presenting his proposal and attracting local newspaper coverage.[7]

Streit's status as a prominent voice in the debate on postwar internationalism garnered him invitations to well-publicized events. At a two-day symposium in New York in May 1942 on the "future world order," Streit spoke alongside Senator Claude Pepper and Herbert Agar, editor of the *Louisville Courier*. At a similar event the following month, he shared the podium with Agar, Clyde Eagleton, and Eleanor Roosevelt.[8] In September 1943, Streit was back in New York as part of a *New York Times*' forum on "plans for winning the peace." The other participants included the former diplomat Hugh Gibson, James Shotwell, John Foster Dulles, Senator Joseph Hall, and Representative (and future Senator) J. W. Fulbright. At the forum, Streit underscored his prolonged experience as the *Times*' correspondent in Geneva, explaining it convinced him that "the reigning dogma of unlimited national sovereignty, must be eliminated first from the democracies" through the creation of "a full-fledged federal union." In the ensuing discussion, he pointed to the revolutionary period as an instructive precedent. "We have got to learn that there comes a time when you have got to make a break with the pattern, just as we did in 1787."[9]

Meanwhile, Streit persisted with his courting of influential people such as Henry Luce and Dulles, while working to lengthen the list of names. Having arranged a meeting with Wendell Willkie in April 1941 with Russell Davenport's help, Streit afterward sent him a copy of *Union Now* and requested an endorsement "for public use that would help get people to read the book." In subsequent correspondence, Streit sought to instruct Willkie on why federal arrangements modeled on the 1787 Constitution could be more effective than a renewed League of Nations, which he typically likened to the United States under the articles of confederation.[10] Although Willkie maintained a polite distance, Streit had more success with Owen Roberts, the Supreme Court justice whose

---

[7] For example, see UM, Clarence Streit Papers, Box 9, file 10, Union Now, HQ Bulletin, For one example, see "Report on Mr. Streit's Western Speaking Tour September 20th–November 9th, 1941," November 15, 1941.

[8] "U.S. Urged to Share in Building Future," *New York Times*, May 13, 1942, 9; and "Future World Order Topic of Symposium," *New York Times*, June 10, 1942, 7.

[9] LOC, CKS, Box I: 124, file: General 1943, "Plans for Winning the Peace," September 24, 1943; and "8 Leaders Offer Plans to Assure Permanent Peace," September 24, 1943, 1, 9.

[10] LOC, CKS, Box I: 91, file: Willkie, Wendell, 1941–44, Streit to Willkie, April 15 and August 11, 1941.

decisions regarding Roosevelt's New Deal legislation remain controversial. Armed with a glowing recommendation from Grenville Clark, a Wall Street lawyer, international activist, and government advisor, Streit first met Roberts in 1941, eventually winning him over the cause of Atlantic federal union. As discussed in Chapter 5, Roberts, following his retirement from the Supreme Court in 1945, would become a pivotal figure in the Atlantic Union Committee.[11]

Not surprisingly, *Union Now* occupied an important place in Streit's promotional activities. Throughout the war, he pressed his publisher, Harper, to increase publicity for the book. Canfield, Harper's editor, accepted the book "cannot be put just in the same category as ordinary commercial ventures," offering a more favorable agreement on royalties, for example. But Harper was a for-profit enterprise. Canfield thus turned down Streit's repeated requests for a new and updated version of *Union Now*, though he did publish an abridged version. Worse still from Streit's viewpoint, Harper in 1943 proceeded to destroy the book's type, citing the wartime shortage of metal as well as declining sales. In addition to bemoaning Harper's lack of a "very energetic promotional spirit," Streit responded by canvassing other publishers about a cheap paperback edition. With no offers forthcoming, he considered printing *Union Now* himself but the scarcity of finance and paper greatly limited the possibilities.[12]

As we shall see, Harper in early 1941 published *Union Now with Britain*, Streit's plea for an immediate union with Britain and the Commonwealth countries. The book was a response to the immediate crisis caused by Germany's military victories in Western Europe. When the crisis passed, Streit, faced with Harper's refusal to re-issue *Union Now*, decided to write a new book in the hope of reproducing the enthusiasm of 1939. In early 1942, he thus sought a contract for *Not Again in Vain*, a book that would "bring our proposal down to date." "I am eager to get on with it," Streit informed Canfield in May, "and feel I can do something better than before, nearer the needs of the occasion." Canfield proved receptive, anticipating the book "will have great vitality" and "should do much to advance your good cause."[13] The subsequent

---

[11] DUAM, Grenville Clark Papers, Box 172, file 19, Clark to Roberts, July 17, 1941.

[12] FLPU, Selected Papers of Harper & Brothers, Box 28, file 26, Canfield to Streit, January 22, 1941; and Streit to Eugene Saxton (Harper), August 18, 1942.

[13] LOC, CKS, Box I: 129, file: Harper & Brothers, Streit to Canfield, February 15 and May 16, 1942 and Canfield to Streit, May 19, 1942.

haggling over the terms of the contract frustrated Streit. "This is more than a book to me," he lectured a Harper employee in August. "It is perhaps the decisive effort, the best opportunity to get the Union set up in time. Consequently I am particularly concerned that it should get off to a good start."[14]

Although the contract's terms were eventually worked out, Streit never finished the book. In September 1943, he sounded Harper on the possibility of revising the contract to publish two short books, one immediately and one the following year. When, soon afterward, Streit submitted an incomplete manuscript of the first book to Canfield's replacement (Canfield was on war leave), the reception was chilly. Remarking the manuscript "is not the book that we discussed a year ago," Harper's interim editor judged it fragmentary in form and under-developed in argument.[15] Afterward, Streit appears to have dropped the project despite the hopes invested. As his correspondence makes clear, Streit found it difficult to find time to write, which is not surprising given his hectic schedule and, as will be shown, his responsibilities as head of a national organization. That said, it is not clear Streit had something fundamentally new to say, and by 1942 his basic proposal had been well ventilated in public, thanks in no small part to his success in promoting *Union Now*. But perhaps the more important point is that Streit had exhausted the potential of his initial promotional strategy. If Atlantic federal union were ever to be realized, something else was needed.

CREATING A NATION-WIDE ORGANIZATION/MOVEMENT

One possible strategy was to create a national organization and movement. In early 1939, Lord Lothian, soon to become British ambassador in Washington, recommended precisely this course to Streit. There "is nothing more volatile in the world" than the US public, he ventured, and "[i]t will rush at your fly with immense enthusiasm and then forget all about it unless a pretty vigorous organisation is formed to keep in front of public opinion and enlist support."[16] In Britain, at this moment a small group of activists, inspired by Streit's book, were in the process of founding an

---

[14] FLPU, Selected Papers of Harper & Brothers, Box 28, file 26, Streit to William Briggs (Harper), August 10, 1942.

[15] LOC, CKS, Box file: I: 129, file: Harper & Brothers, Streit to Briggs, September 13, 1943 and Briggs to Streit, September 21, 1943.

[16] LOC, CKS, Box I: 4, file: Chronological correspondence 1938–1939, Lord Lothian to Streit, March 7, 1939.

organization – Federal Union. It would quickly expand, attracting prominent individuals such as Lionel Curtis, Norman Angell, Lionel Robbins, Friedrich Hayek, and William Beveridge.[17] The British organization, though, would develop independently, with little contact with Streit, whose Atlantic federal union project soon became controversial. We are "a long way from supporting Streit's rather complicated plan" one member admitted in March 1940.[18] Indeed, by the end of the war, it favored a European federation over an Anglo-American or Atlantic one.

In any case, soon after receiving Lothian's letter, Streit met with a group of supporters in New York to form a local committee, a step his brother soon replicated in Washington, DC[19] The same month, the two brothers established a Union press to produce publicity material, including a bulletin with a print run of 17,000 by the end of the year. In May 1939, meanwhile, Streit circulated a prospectus for a new organization. Declaring an "urgent need for action, big action," it envisaged collecting the "local groups of Unionists" already sprouting in several places into a national structure equipped with an executive committee to "lay down general policies"; it would include a paid director and staff as well as a speakers' bureau. With such an organization, Streit enthused, "the Union idea would leap forward." With Russell Davenport's help, Streit participated in several luncheons in which he presented the prospectus to possible donors.[20]

Developments moved quickly thereafter. At a meeting in July 1939, the participants resolved to found a national organization with provisional headquarters in New York and another office in DC. Strangely, perhaps, agreeing on a name proved more contentious, and it would be several months before settling on Federal Union, Inc. (as in Britain). In August, the fledgling organization launched a mailing campaign for members in which Streit rousingly announced that "[t]here is still room for you on the foundation floor, room for you take as big and active a part as you can

[17] BLPES, Federal Trust Papers, Box 6, file 1, "Early Members of Federal Union," undated. Also see Richard Mayne and John Pinder, *Federal Union: The Pioneers: A History of Federal Union* (New York: St. Martin's Press, 1990); and Andrea Bosco, *June 1940, Great Britain and the First Attempt to Build a European Federal Union* (Newcastle upon Tyne: Cambridge Scholars Publishing, 2016).

[18] NYPL, CWFG (CO), Box 88, file 11, John Usborne (Federal Union) to Rosika Schwimmer, March 20, 1940.

[19] LLUI, UWF Papers, Box 13, file Federal Union, "Report of the Temporary Committee for Organization," March 27, 1939.

[20] BSHU, Thomas William Lamont Collection, Box 28, file 9, "Memorandum on the Enterprise for the Federal Union Now of the Democracies," Streit, May 4, 1939.

carry through."[21] In the autumn of 1939, Federal Union began to hire office staff as well as to solicit members for its Board and to draft articles of incorporation, which were approved in early 1940. A limited restructuring in May 1940 finalized the arrangements, equipping Federal Union with a national executive committee, whose monthly meetings ensured hands-on direction, and a national council whose members gathered less frequently to provide general oversight.[22]

From the beginning, local activism figured prominently in Federal Union's plans. As its secretary explained in July 1939, the organization aimed "to organize as many local committees as we can ... with special attention to the establishment of a committee in every Congressional district."[23] If this proviso hinted at a direct political purpose, for Streit initially the value of chapters lay principally in their potential for publicizing his proposal across the country. Chapters would function as a microcosm of the national organization, energized by militants who, much like Streit, would preach federal union to friends and acquaintances. A guide for local organizers drafted in November 1939 underscored the importance of individual commitment and enterprise. The organizer, presumed to be "the only known fully convinced Unionist in his community," should endeavor to build a local organization step by step, one convert at a time. For Streit, membership numbers mattered less than personal commitment. Urging new members to throw themselves into the task of organizing locally, Streit explained in December 1939 that Federal Union needed not "adherents" but "founders, their enthusiasm and their work for the greatest cause on earth today."[24]

The results appeared impressive. Chapters formed across the United States – for example, in Phoenix, Boston, Cincinnati and Bridgewater, New Jersey in 1940; in Chapel Hill, North Carolina, Lewisburg,

---

[21] LOC, CKS, Box I: 65, file: Inter-Democracy of Federal Unionists, 1939–42, "National Organizing Meeting," July 16, 1939; and NYPL, CFWG (CO), Box 88, file 13, Inter-Democracy Federal Unionists letter, Streit, August 9, 1939.

[22] LOC, Russell W. Davenport Papers, Box 34, file 7, R. Frazier Potts (Manager), circular, May 2, 1940.

[23] YUL, Chase Kimball Papers, Box 12, file 122, William Blake to Kimball, July 29, 1939. More generally, see Sacha Loignon, "De la popularité à l'obscurité: les rouages de la montée de Federal Union, Inc. aux États-Unis, 1939–1945," Masters' thesis, Université Laval, 2016.

[24] LOC, CKS, Box I: 65, file: Inter-Democracy of Federal Unionists, 1939–42, "Guide for Local Organizers," Streit, November 1939, emphasis in original; and YUL, Elizabeth Page Harris Papers, Box 83, file 1819, Streit to Fellow Unionist, undated but December 1939.

Pennsylvania, Chicago, and San Francisco in 1941; and Eugene, Oregon, Tucson, Arizona, and Alaska in 1942. There was even a Hollywood chapter whose members, predictably perhaps, discussed making a film about Atlantic federal union. The founding of a chapter was almost always the result of local initiative, though a Streit visit during one of his tours often provided a spur. By September 1941, Federal Union counted 108 chapters, and early the following year 118 with another 158 "organizing groups" with the potential to become chapters.[25]

Sympathetic observers nodded in admiration. A combination of Streit's energy and the "theoretical strength of the idea," Felix Morley, the *Washington Post*'s editor, remarked in early 1940, "is enabling his organization to make real headway." The "'Union Now' idea," Morley added, "is pulling ahead of the work of the League of Nations Association and this is due primarily to the very successful crusading efforts of Streit and his associates."[26] Even Streit's foes were impressed. The America First Committee, the leading anti-interventionist organization, kept a close watch on Federal Union, viewing Streit as a dangerous advocate of an Anglo-US alliance. Its chapter structure, a confidential report in August 1941 warned, endowed Federal Union with a national reach, facilitating the distribution of some 1.5 million "pieces of literature" to the far corners of the country.[27] Streit, in any case, repeatedly drew attention to Federal Union's rapid growth. Thus, in early 1943 Streit reminded a *New York Times*' editor that he was no longer a journalist "but the head spokesman for a rather extensive movement."[28]

THE REALITIES BEHIND THE NUMBERS

Federal Union's wartime history can be considered as part of a larger phenomenon of popular political mobilization. In a celebrated study, the political scientist Robert Putnam identified a tradition of local

---

[25] LOC, CKS, Box I: 5, file: Chronological correspondence, 1941, "Report on Chartered Chapters and Organizers, June 1 to September 1, 1941," September 1941; and Box I: 77, "Report of the Acting Director ...," January 8, 1942.

[26] LOC, Arthur Sweetser Papers, Box 33, file Morley, Felix, Morley to Sweetser, February 12, 1940.

[27] "Union Now?" August 16, 1941, in Justus D. Doenecke, *In Danger Undaunted: The Anti-Interventionist Movement of the 1940–1941 as Revealed in the Papers of the America First Committee* (Stanford, CA: Hoover Institute Press, 1990), 240–48.

[28] LOC, CKS, Box I: 4, file: New York Times, 1940–43, Streit to Lester Markel, February 3, 1943.

voluntarism in the United States dating back to the nineteenth century. Although suffering a decline during the Depression years, this tradition renewed itself during World War II – a renewal manifest in local political participation or what Putnam called "a massive outpouring of patriotism and collective solidarity."[29] Much of the scholarship on US wartime politics bolsters Putnam's argument. Referring to the early war years, Lynne Olson writes of untold numbers of people mobilizing for and against US intervention. The result, she maintains, was a "true exercise in democracy" in which "[g]rassoots activism flourished throughout the nation as volunteers on both sides circulated petitions, phoned their neighbors, ran ads, and lobbied their congressmen." Following Pearl Harbor, ordinary Americans continued to invest in politics and especially international politics, a commitment evident in the multiplying numbers of organizations, Streit's Federal Union among them.[30]

Although too much should not be inferred from one case study, a closer look at Federal Union suggests some of the limits of popular political mobilization during the war. Practical difficulties abounded, most notably when it came to raising money and recruiting members. Chapter numbers could conceal as much as they reveal: Studies of the America First movement, for instance, indicate that numerous chapters were barely active and even inactive.[31] In a 1942 analysis, a Stanford political scientist concluded that the vibrancy of foreign policy groups at

[29] Robert D. Putnam, *Bowling Alone: The Collapse and Renewal of American Community* (New York: Simon & Schuster, 2000), 17, 54–55. Also see Theda Skocpol, Ziad Munson, Andrew Karch and Bayliss Camp, "Patriotic Partnerships: Why Great Wars Nourished American Civic Voluntarism," in Ira Katznelson and Martin Shefter, eds., *Shaped by War and Trade: International Influences on American Political Development* (Princeton, NJ: Princeton University Press, 2002), 134–80.

[30] Lynne Olson, *Those Angry Days: Roosevelt, Lindbergh, and America's Fight Over World War II, 1931–1941* (New York: Random House, 2014), xxi. Also see Justus D. Doeneke, *Storm on the Horizon: The Challenge to American Intervention, 1939–1941* (Lantham, MD: Rowman & Littlefield, 2000); Robert Divine, *Second Chance: The Triumph of Internationalism in America during World War II* (New York: Atheneum, 1971); Andrew Johnstone, *Against Immediate Evil: American Internationalists and the Four Freedoms on the Eve of World War II* (Ithaca, NY: Cornell University Press, 2014); Andrew Johnstone, *Dilemmas of Internationalism: The American Association for the United Nations and U.S. Foreign Policy, 1941–1948* (Farnham: Ashgate, 2009); and Mark Lincoln Chadwin, *The Hawks of World War II* (Chapel Hill: University of North Carolina Press, 1968).

[31] Wayne Cole, *America First: The Battle against Intervention, 1940–1941* (Madison: University of Wisconsin Press, 1953); and James C. Schneider, *Should America Go to War: The Debate Over Foreign Policy in Chicago, 1939–1941* (Chapel Hill: University of North Carolina Press, 1989), 122–23, 198.

the grassroots level depended on a "small nucleus of individuals" – people he called "enthusiastic sparkplugs" – who possessed the time and local media and other contacts (and money) to attract and to maintain public attention. For Streit and others, such "enthusiastic sparkplugs" proved to be all too rare. But the problem was not simply one of recruiting engaged and energetic people. A fractious dynamic lurked in the very activism of participatory politics of this kind: The more committed a person was to a cause, the greater the stakes could seem, infusing policy debates within organizations with immense and even existential significance. As Streit would discover, commitment, ardor, and deference were not necessarily complementary traits.

For Federal Union, money was a perennial problem. As mentioned, Streit began fund-raising in 1939, targeting wealthy donors in particular. But despite occasional successes, the overall results were disappointing. The example of the Rockefeller Foundation highlights some of the difficulties. Streit officially approached the foundation in the autumn of 1939, using Russell Davenport as an intermediary. John Rockefeller initially appeared receptive, describing Streit's plan as "an interesting one even if somewhat visionary and idealistic." An advisor agreed, judging in October 1939 that the plan "possesses some arresting thoughts, which it seems to me well deserve some ventilation and consideration among people who are trying to think through the next phase of world affairs." The following month, however, the foundation chose to hold off on funding for the time being on the grounds that the "organization is still very much in the formative stage ..." Prompted by Davenport, Nelson Rockefeller did offer free office space in New York as a personal gesture. Nevertheless, the foundation reaffirmed its unfavorable decision in April 1940. While recognizing the value of bold thinking in "the cause of peace and a saner arrangement of national and international relationships," an internal assessment concluded the organization had yet to demonstrate its ability "to go on to bigger and better things." Left unexplained was how it might do so without adequate financing.[32]

Afterward, Streit continued to pursue well-heeled donors, presenting Federal Union as an opportunity to do something ambitious. And with

---

[32] See the file in RAC, Office of the Messrs. Rockefeller Records, World Affairs, Series Q, Box 24, file 205, and especially John D. Rockefeller to Arthur W. Packard, October 10, 1939 and "Union Now," Packard, November 3, 1939 and April 22, 1940. In 1943, the Guggenheim Foundation also rejected a request for funding. See LOC, CKS: I: 6, file: Chronological correspondence, 1943, John Simon Guggenheim Foundation to Streit, March 15, 1943.

the help of well-connected supporters such as Clare Boothe Luce, who chaired Federal Union's finance committee in the early years, Streit occasionally received a sizeable cheque. Boothe Luce's contacts also proved useful in convincing the Internal Revenue Service in the spring of 1942 to reverse its previous decision and to grant Federal Union tax-exempt status as a nonprofit organization. "A great day for F.U.," Streit jotted in his notebook regarding the news, which "makes it ... easier for us to raise funds."[33]

Even so, it soon became clear Federal Union would have to diversify its revenue sources. Making a virtue of necessity, Streit told Davenport in early 1940 that the organization should be "financed by the people and not by any small group of wealthy individuals."[34] In practice, this entailed a continual quest for money, which risked becoming the organization's primary activity and even an end in itself. As early as August 1939, one member of the executive resigned, denouncing Federal Union as a "fund-raising machine."[35] At the same time, the alternatives were limited. In the summer of 1940, Federal Union's executive opted to impose annual membership fees for the first time of $3.00. The decision brought in some money but not enough because Federal Union, the occasional dreams of grandeur notwithstanding, never developed into a mass membership organization, with at most 10,000 adherents at its peak.[36] The decision did, however, trigger considerable grumbling from militants. Membership fees being inadequate, Federal Union was forced to launch periodic fund-raising campaigns: in early 1940, in the autumn of 1941, in late 1942, and again in late 1943. The campaigns targeted both members and a larger public, employing a variety of means ranging from generic direct mailings to more specialized pleas to college students, housewives, businesses, and educators. As the organization's best-known member, Streit was a conspicuous and tireless fund-raiser through paid speaking engagements, letter writing, and personal encounters.

[33] LOC, CKS, Box I: 1, file: Notebook and Notes 1943–43, May 28, 1943. For the tax status, see ibid., Clare Luce Boothe Papers, Box 394, file 4, Streit to Boothe Luce, March 27, 1943; and UM, Clarence Streit Papers, Box 9, file 10, Treasury Department to Federal Union, August 12, 1943.

[34] LOC, Russell W. Davenport Papers, Box 34, file 1, Davenport to L. W. Makovski, March 7, 1940.

[35] LOC, CKS, Box I: 69 file: "M" Miscellany, 1939–46, Grace Gates Mitchell to Members of Executive Board, August 22, 1939.

[36] In early 1942, Federal Union undertook a membership drive with the declared aim of reaching 100,000 members. See McMaster University, George Catlin Fonds, Box 151, file Federal Union, Patrick Welch (FU) to Catlin, January 23, 1942.

These efforts notwithstanding, money remained tight. In November 1939 an internal memorandum warned of the "danger of debt," adding Federal Union might have to close its office in New York. The organization's revenue for the second half of 1939 was just over $17,000 (about $317,000 today), a respectable but not imposing sum and one falling short of expectations and, more important, of spending. Annual revenue peaked at $89,000 in 1941, before falling back to an average of $32,500 for the last three years of the war.[37] Pointing to a persistent deficit, the financial director in October 1942 described the situation as "deplorable" and recommended not only additional cuts in staff and salaries but also tailoring activities to existing resources. The latter idea found support among board members, several of whom were frustrated by the ad hoc nature of financial management. "We have never been on a sound financial basis" complained John Mason, an executive committee member and President of Swarthmore College. "There have been times when we have had money in the treasury, but it has not stayed there long, and its presence led to an overoptimistic series of expenditures. I fear that this is symptomatic of certain difficulties with which the organization has contended from the beginning." Mason demanded "hard-headed and practical measures" to ensure Federal Union operated on a "pay-as-you-go basis."[38]

Financial realities effectively imposed Mason's solution, resulting in further spending cuts in 1943 and 1944. Margaret Blumenstiel, who ran the New York office, explained the consequences to Streit in December 1942: "The less money we have to spend, the less personnel we have to handle our work, the more things must be done in half measures."[39] Financial shortages adversely affected local chapters in particular. Federal Union found it difficult and soon impossible to pay the salaries of field workers, despite recognizing their vital importance to a nationwide organization. Worse still, in February 1942 the organization informed chapters it could no longer contribute to their budget, citing

---

[37] LOC, CKS, Box I: 65, file: Inter-Democracy of Federal Unionists, 1939–42, Ray memo to Clarence, November 9, 1939; Box I: 96, file: Whitney, John Hay, Streit to Blum, July 31, 1946; and ibid., Russell W. Davenport Papers, Box 34, file 7, "Statement of Income and Expenses . . . from date of organization, July 16, 1939, to Dec. 31, 1939."

[38] LOC, CKS, Box I: 69, file: Miguel, J. A. 1941–1944, untitled report, October 2, 1942; and Mason to J. A. Miguel, August 20, 1942.

[39] LOC, CKS, Box I: 40, file: Blumenstiel, Margaret, 1943–43, Blumenstiel to Streit, December 14, 1942.

the heavy drain on resources.[40] By then, many chapters were barely solvent, if not in deficit, forcing further reductions in their activities. The following month Emery Baldurf, the director of the Chicago office, wrote Streit that he would soon have to quit his duties having received no salary for several weeks. Streit typically responded with a burst of fund-raising activity but could not prevent Baldurf from taking a government post. The Chicago office continued to function but at a much-reduced level. "We are financially able to operate the office, and have tried to keep up the interest among members as much as possible, as a good many of the chapters are fairly inactive . . .," the new director glumly reported in mid-1943.[41]

To be sure, Federal Union managed to remain visible throughout the war. Luncheons and dinners, round-table discussions, individual lectures, radio addresses, letters to the editor, newspaper advertisements, bulletins, pamphlets, flyers, buttons, auto stickers, Christmas cards: All this and more kept Streit's project in the public eye at the local and national levels.[42] Yet financial woes took a toll, fostering recurrent crises that strained the energies and nerves of all concerned. No less importantly, they created a yawning gap between ambitions and resources. In the spring of 1944, Federal Union's treasurer outlined an expansive campaign "to educate the masses in federal principles," priced at upwards of $100,000 ($1.5 million today). The lack of such a sum predictably bred frustration. "Our funds have never allowed us to plan and carry out a nation-wide campaign on even a mediocre scale for a year," Streit admitted in 1944.[43]

If financing posed problems, policy questions proved still more fraught. Two related issues dominated Federal Union: that of Streit's leadership and that of its precise policies. From the outset, Streit involved himself intimately in Federal Union's daily functioning, intervening in

---

[40] LOC, CKS, Box I: 76, file: Publications: Headquarters Bulletin 1942–1944, no. 28-1, February 12, 1942.

[41] LOC, CKS, Box I: 5, file: Chronological correspondence 1942, Baldurf to Streit, March 31, 1942; and Streit to Baldurf, April 2, 1942; and Box I: 44, file: chapters; Chicago, Illinois, 1942–48, Connie Hellyer to Streit, undated.

[42] For example, in 1943 Streit's plan figured among the proposals offered to New Jersey high school students for debate. See Heber Hinds Ryan, "Post-War Planning: Here Are 65 Questions on 7 Problems, for Use by High-School Classes and Discussion Groups," *The Clearing House* 17 (1943), 401–404, 404.

[43] LOC, CKS, Box I: 42, file: Board meetings, general, 1941–44, John Howard Ford memorandum to Streit, March 1944. Streit is cited in Loignon, "De la popularité à l'obscurité," 105.

frequent and sometimes peremptory fashion. As early as July 1939, Vernon Nash, an early and indefatigable activist within Federal Union, warned the organization must encourage a diversity of approaches and not devolve into a mere "shadow of C.K.S. [Streit]." The following month another member of the executive complained not only of Streit's "hasty judgments" but also of his "excessive veto power" over all decisions.[44]

Things first came to a head at the end of year over financial matters. Streit's unilateral decisions regarding spending on publicity material, together with his incessant meddling in the production of pamphlets, finally provoked the ire of Frazier Potts, the New York office manager at the time. The incident provided an opportunity for Nash and several others to call into question Streit's leadership. In a letter to Streit in November 1939, Nash pleaded for a more consensual approach: "we are not an executive committee at all if decisions of front-rank consequences can be and are made without full and adequate consideration and formal decision." Nash hoped to confine Streit to an advisory and even honorary role, confiding to another executive committee member that the majority of the executive had "lost all confidence in his organizational judgment." As a first step toward this goal, the executive committee voted in December 1939 to close the DC office (where Streit lived), a move Streit successfully resisted by rallying the "pro-Washington lobby" among his supporters.[45] Although defusing the crisis required deft personal diplomacy on the part of third parties, Streit remained unchastened. Federal Union, he scolded Potts, must avoid "being legalistic," by which "I mean seeking to gain one's ends by pressing fine legal points, or concentrating on fine legal points to the exclusion of the practical and political . . ."[46]

Even outside Federal Union, it is worth noting, Streit soon acquired a reputation for intransigence. "[N]obody could work with Streit," a League of Nations Association official reported in 1940, as "he considers himself a messiah."[47] While perhaps exaggerated, the charge did reflect Streit's imperious leadership style – a style on full display in the summer of 1940. In response to Nazi Germany's stunning military victories in

[44] LOC, CKS, Box I: 5, file: Chronological correspondence 1939, Nash memorandum, July 26, 1939; ibid, Box I: 69 file: "M" Miscellany, 1939–46, Grace Gates Mitchell to Potts, August 5, 1939 and Mitchell to members of executive board, August 22, 1939.
[45] LOC, CKS, Box I: 5, file: Chronological correspondence 1939, Nash to Streit, November 15, 1939, emphasis in original; and Nash to Gordon Mannerstedt, October 1939.
[46] LOC, CKS, Box I: 76, file: Publications: "Union Now" pamphlet 1939, Streit to Potts, December 31, 1939.
[47] NYPL, CFWG (CO), Box 7, William Lloyd to Edith Wynner, February 10, 1940.

Western Europe, Streit unilaterally revised his project: Rather than a federation of the North Atlantic democracies, he now called for an immediate union of the United States, Britain, and the Commonwealth countries. In early July, Streit informed Federal Union's executive he was issuing a press release in this sense "in my personal capacity as author of *Union Now*," claiming time pressures precluded prior consultation. Accompanying the release was a "Declaration of Interdependence," modeled on the 1776 Declaration of Independence, extolling "a Federal Union on the broad lines of the American Constitution." Streit personally raised the money to place a full-page advertisement in the *New York Times* calling on "the U.S.A. and the Six British Democracies [to] form a Federal Union before it is too late." In early 1941, Streit would publish a short book with Harper, *Union Now with Britain*, which elaborated on the proposal.[48]

Streit's call for union with Britain triggered another crisis, one which reflects the complex nature of contemporary disputes over US foreign policy. Hitherto, Federal Union had adeptly navigated the polarizing public debate over the war, pitching Atlantic federal union as a means to end the war quickly, thereby precluding US intervention. Whatever its inherent plausibility, this position satisfied disparate elements within Federal Union, both those who favored helping the Allies and thus inclined toward intervention and those who were more pacifist-inclined and thus opposed to intervention. Although Streit contended that his revised project of Anglo-US union might avoid war by convincing Nazi Germany and Fascist Italy to cease all aggression, the argument strained credibility. In any case, an immediate union with Britain and the Commonwealth was generally interpreted as being pro-interventionist in its anticipated effects, if not in its intentions. "I cannot see that it would amount to anything just now except getting the United States into the war," Thomas Lamont commented in this sense in September 1940. Even some of the more pro-interventionists among Federal Union's supporters expressed misgivings. Frank Aydelotte, the director of Princeton's Institute for Advanced Studies, warned Streit it risked undermining "the general idea of federal union" while distracting attention from the

---

[48] LOC, Clare Luce Boothe Papers, Box 94, file 5, Streit to National Executive, July 2, 1945; and "Defense Now Needs Union Now," *New York Times*, July 15, 1940, 11. Streit, *Union Now with Britain* (New York: Harper & Brothers, 1941).

campaign for immediate material aid to Britain, which he believed should take priority.[49]

Federal Union's executive committee was soon in turmoil. Roger Baldwin, a founder of the American Civil Liberties Union, openly challenged Streit's "questionable strategy," insisting "the purpose of federal union cannot be achieved by participation in war."[50] Predictably, strong opposition came from Nash. If continued frustration with Streit's leadership style constituted one factor, another and more important one was what Nash considered an overly short-term and war-oriented approach to federalism. Several committee members sympathized with Nash, prompting a search for a compromise formula for those "who cannot quite swallow whole the probably Anglo-American switch of FU." The effort proved fruitless, and at an executive meeting in late October 1940 Streit and his supporters pushed through a resolution endorsing an immediate union with Britain.[51] Stewing over the result, Nash privately groused that Federal Union's "Cult of Streit-ism" was inflicting "great harm to the common aim and objective of world federalism." Streit, meanwhile, consoled himself with the thought that "every great movement seems to have had early supporters who ended up betraying it for one reason or another."[52]

The divisive effects of Streit's policy change were also felt at the local level. In addition to the New York chapter, those in Chicago and Philadelphia reported "some dissent" in their ranks with the new policy as well as with the impression that "all Federal Unionists were supposed to have one opinion."[53] The response of Elizabeth Page Harris provides a personal perspective. Best-known as the author of the historical novel, *The Tree of Liberty*, Harris joined Federal Union's Pasadena chapter in late 1939, becoming the type of "founder" of which Streit dreamed:

[49] BSHU, Thomas William Lamont Collection, Box 28, file 10, Lamont to J. Whitfield Scott, September 11, 1940; and SCFHL, Frank Aydelotte Papers, Box 38, file Federal Union, 1940, Aydelotte to Streit, August 19, 1940.

[50] YUL, Elizabeth Page Harris Papers, Box 83, file 1838, Streit circular to chapters, July 15, 1940.

[51] LOC, CKS, Box I: 5, file: Chronological correspondence 1940, Nash to J. Howard Ford, October 17, 1940; and YUL, Elizabeth Page Harris Papers, Box 83, file 1827, Sam Spaulding memorandum to Nash, September 13, 1940.

[52] YUL, Elizabeth Page Harris Papers, Box 83, file 1828, Nash to Page, November 1, 1940; and LOC, CKS, Box I: 5, file: Chronological correspondence 1940, Streit to A. Powell Davies, November 24, 1940.

[53] LOC, CKS, Box I: 41, file: Board meetings, general 1940, "Minutes of the National Committee, Federal Union, Inc.," December 10, 1940.

A tireless activist, she gave talks and organized meetings across southern California. At the same time, Harris worked to harmonize her activism with her pacifist leanings, presenting federalism as a means toward a more cooperative and peaceful international order. Even before Streit's change of policy, she warned against tying federalism to the "Allied cause exclusively" or even to that of democracies, fearing the latter would divide the world between two ideological camps.[54] Following the policy change, Harris bounced back and forth between two impulses: working within Federal Union for a more expansive federalism and abandoning it as a lost cause. After much hesitation and consultation with local members, Harris resigned from Federal Union in January 1941. With your proposal, she wrote Streit, "[I]t is extremely hard to refute the constant taunt that no matter what we call our Union we are in fact just another military alliance to dominate the world in our selfish interests."[55]

The unease within Federal Union over policy was in full display at its annual convention in June 1941 in Cleveland. Streit arrived with the intention of receiving clear-cut approval of his policy, which he defined as beginning with "a kernel, a nucleus, the English-speaking people" that could subsequently be enlarged. However, as an ally admitted afterward, "[O]ur efforts to get through more specific resolutions endorsing the policies of the past year were defeated." Instead, Streit had two accept two major concessions: an open-ended policy resolution regarding the countries to be included in a federal union and the promise to appoint a director other than himself.[56] In reality, the concessions amounted to little. It was never likely Streit would find a suitable replacement – someone who combined zeal, energy, and purpose in sufficient measure. Nor did he feel the need to tone down his policy, as his spirited campaign to publicize *Union Now with Britain* during 1941–42 soon demonstrated.

In November 1941, several months after the convention, Federal Union's New York chapter, whose more active members included Nash, openly accused Streit of contradicting the convention's resolutions. A week later, the organization's executive committee moved to revoke the chapter's charter. Although Streit pretended the measure was for

---

[54] YUL, Elizabeth Page Harris Papers, Box 83, file 1824, Harris to Streit, May 20, 1940.
[55] YUL, Elizabeth Page Harris Papers, Box 83, file 1829, Harris to Streit, January 15, 1941.
[56] LOC, CKS, Box I: 46, file: Convention, 1941, James E. Downs to Streit, July 7, 1941; file: Convention 1941 proceedings, "Proceedings First Annual Convention, Federal Union, Inc. June 28–29, 1941."

financial reasons, the real motive was to eliminate an irritant and, more generally, to grasp more firmly the reins of control. The immediate result was to galvanize a group of militants to secede from Federal Union and to group themselves into a countermovement in favor of a more inclusive vision of international federalism – one not limited to Britain and the Commonwealth or even to the North Atlantic democracies. Announcing that "[w]e want to keep on working for world government under the Federal plan," Nash and others began to organize themselves under the banner of world federalists.[57]

International events soon overtook Streit's policy change. With the United States' entry into the war and with Britain's immediate survival seemingly assured, an Anglo-US union appeared less urgently relevant. Streit, accordingly, sought to return Federal Union to its initial position in favor of an Atlantic union of the democracies. "Under existing circumstances," he explained to a supporter in January 1943, "I would prefer the original Union Now proposal."[58] Such a return, though, was likely to be anything but straightforward. One reason was that Streit became publicly associated with union with Britain. For example, in his influential 1942 book on *America's Strategy in World Politics*, the Yale political scientist Nicholas Spykman lumped Streit with the advocates of "American-British Hegemony."[59] Another and related reason concerns the global nature of the war in which the United States found itself in alliance with non-Atlantic countries and non-democracies, most notably the Soviet Union and China.

That the war's global realities would pose additional difficulties soon became apparent. The question of membership in a federal union of states was raised at an executive meeting in early February 1942. Kicking off the discussion, one member reported that "[m]any other organizations favoring the general idea of Federal Union are springing up" – all with proposals more inclusive than that of an Atlantic union. "The fact that Russia is now our ally," he added, "complicates our original program." Echoing these remarks, several members questioned the tight association of federalism with democracy. Asked to comment, Streit defended the

[57] NYPL, CFWG (NY), Box 20, file 4, circular letter, November 19, 1941.
[58] LOC, CKS, Box I: 6, file: Chronological correspondence 1943, Streit to Hudson G. Rosebush, January 5, 1943.
[59] Nicholas J. Spykman, *America's Strategy in World Politics: The United States and the Balance of Power* (New York: Harcourt, Brace, 1942), 458–60.

emphasis on democracy. In addition to presenting a union of the "English-speaking democracies" as the first step toward a larger union of Atlantic democracies, he maintained "the war would not be won for democratic principles if the world went communist after defeating fascism."[60] Soon after the meeting, Streit circulated a statement of "basic principles" that rejected any "watering down" of his initial project:

Peace and freedom require strength. Shall we continue to seek strength in mere numbers in uniting the greatest possible number of nations at the start by watering down the principles whereby we unite them? Or shall we start by uniting fewer nations, but uniting them by much stronger principles, and letting this nucleus grow in numbers as our Thirteen States grew to Forty-Eight, without watering down their basic principles? I believe it wiser to base our hopes for peace and freedom on the second method. It is stronger than the first, as a regiment is stronger than a mob that far outnumbers it.[61]

Streit's position prompted Frank Aydelotte to draft an alternative statement whose understanding of federalism markedly differed. Rather than reproducing an existing political-constitutional structure (such as the United States), Aydelotte envisaged federalism as a form of international governance defined in terms of collective constraints on national sovereignty:

The whole purpose of Federal Union, Incorporated, is to work for the adoption of the federal principle in international organization with the limitations of international sovereignty which that principle implies as over the League [of Nations] principle, which preserves sovereignty intact. It is the fundamental belief of the members of our organization that the international anarchy which prevails in the world today is a direct result of the doctrine of unlimited national sovereignty and that we shall never be able to substitute the rule of law for the rule of force in relations between nations unless the members of whatever international association may be organized after this war can be brought to consent to such limitation of national sovereignty as will make practicable the control of national action by international law and, if necessary, by international force.

Although Aydelotte did not rule out "smaller federations of groups of states of a similar character and with similar aims and interests," his thinking pointed toward a postwar international organization that would be universal in membership. In this schema, federalism became a means to

---

[60] LOC, Percival F. Brundage Papers, Box 15, file: Federal Union, "Minutes of the National Board of Directors ... February 6, 1942."

[61] LOC, CKS, Box I: 41, file: Board General 1942–1947, "The Basic Principles of 'Union Now,'" Streit, February 22, 1942.

design a more inclusive international organization – an improved League of Nations.[62]

Although Streit agreed to re-work his initial statement, the new version reaffirmed his position. Federal Union, it read, advocated a "Union of the Free," whose nucleus would consist of the United States, the British Commonwealth, and "other American and European democracies." In an attempt to reconcile the two competing positions, another executive member, Armin Elmendorf, a writer, inventor, and businessman, offered a compromise. While recognizing the incongruity of excluding "Russia, China and India" from a postwar federal union, Elmendorf admitted that a "federal union of democratic people cannot be made to function successfully if it is to include Russia and the Oriental peoples." His solution was a dual-track policy: Streit's Atlantic union as well as a postwar international organization to "provide collective security" for all states. Wishing to downplay differences, executive committee members tacitly accepted Elmendorf's formulation.[63]

Whatever its merits, this fragile compromise did little to satisfy local activists who increasingly lobbied for a more inclusive approach to federalism, one that, at the very minimum, encompassed all the United States' wartime allies. The majority of members, Federal Union's director in Chicago reported, "lean toward a broadening of policy." Some of "our best supporters," he elaborated, "feel that we are making a great mistake by insisting upon our ideological basis for Union. They point out that we can hardly expect to get much sympathy at home or abroad if we say now ... that Russia and China, and possibly even Brazil, cannot come into the Union at the outset."[64] Early in 1943, Federal Union's Philadelphia chapter seceded, denouncing the organization's federalism as too narrowly conceived. Worse still from Streit's perspective, brewing unrest within various chapters fueled calls for cooperation and even a merger with other and rival federalist organizations emerging during the war, among them Nash's world federalists. In the spring of 1943,

---

[62] LOC, Percival F. Brundage Papers, Box 15, file: Federal Union, "Statement of Policy," Aydelotte, March 16, 1942. Aydelotte soon became a public advocate for a revamped League of Nations.

[63] LOC, CKS, Box I: 41, file: Board General 1942–1947, "Design for Freedom," Streit, April 3, 1942; and "Comments on Revising the Policy of Federal Union, Inc.," Elmendorf, March 31, 1942.

[64] LOC, CKS, Box I: 5, file: Chronological correspondence 1942, Emery Baldurf to Streit, February 28 and April 3, 1942; and CFWG (CO), Box 7, William Lloyd to Edith Wynner, November 14, 1942.

J. A. Migel, an executive committee member and businessman from Providence, Rhode Island, held talks with Nash about "the possibility of all Federalists getting into one organization." Justifying this step, Migel insisted it was the only way to keep several major local organizations (Boston, Philadelphia, Delaware) within the Federal Union fold.[65]

Streit predictably resisted calls for a merger, cautioning Migel that collaboration with Nash "would cost us much more support than we would gain, and lead to unending internal friction."[66] More generally, he continued to denounce any "watering down" of policy. Federal Union's difficulties, Streit explained to Powell Davies, another executive committee member, came from attempts "to gain strength by diluting and generalizing our policy." Striving to "put aside the merger ideas" and to "leave policy as it was," he pushed to have Federal Union's office relocated to DC "where I can keep a closer eye on the direction."[67] Yet once again he was compelled to gesture at concessions. At Federal Union's convention in Peoria Illinois in November 1943, the majority of delegates voted for an open-ended policy resolution. Making no mention of Atlantic democracies, it called for "a nuclear Federal Union of all those peoples willing and able to accept an international federal constitution ..."[68]

Ignoring the resolution, Streit seized on every opportunity to declare publicly that a "nuclear Federal Union" must be limited to the Atlantic democracies. The reaction arrived quickly. From Boston came complaints that Streit refused to "scrupulously adhere to the Statement of Policy as agreed upon at Peoria" – a complaint even Streit's closest supporters could not deny. Similarly, the head of the Delaware chapter concluded that "[e]ach of us is free to say what he thinks, but every one is wrong so far as FU is concerned if C.K.S. says the opposite." Soon afterwards, he sniped, Streit "ought to get in the hands of a good psychiatrist."[69]

By then Federal Union as an organization was disintegrating. Within the executive committee, prominent members such as Aydelotte had

---

[65] See LOC, CKS, Box I: 68, file: Migel, J. A. 1941–1944, and especially Migel to Streit, April 29, 1943 and Migel to Blumenstiel, May 18, 1943.

[66] LOC, CKS, Box I: 68, file: Migel, J. A. 1941–1944, Streit to Migel, March 5, 1943.

[67] LOC, CKS, Box I: 52, file Executive committee 1940–1944, Streit to Powell Davies, February 28, 1943; and Box I: 5, file: Chronological correspondence, Streit to Mrs. Lamont, March 28, 1943.

[68] LOC, CKS, Box I: 76, "Federal Union World," vol. v, no. 7, December 1943.

[69] LOC, CKS, Box I: 44, file: Chapters, Boston, MA, 1943, A. J. G. Priest to Streit, December 29, 1943; and Box I: 40, file: Barr, Stringfellow, 1944–47, Robert Wheelwright to Stringfellow Barr, January 25 and February 28, 1944.

already drifted away while others, such as Migel, quit in exasperation. Streit accused the malcontents of intriguing against him, an accusation not entirely unfounded, but the reality is that Federal Union continued to shed supporters. A telling case is that of the Student Federalists, a group active on several university campuses and energetically led by Harris Wofford, a future US Senator. By mid-1944, Wofford, who had been converted to federalism after hearing Streit on the radio, had become disillusioned. While undoubtedly a "great philosopher of this age," he reflected, Streit "is not the fiery organizer or mass leader who will build up a revolutionary movement, and succeed." The Student Federalists soon distanced themselves from Federal Union, having concluded Streit's version of federalism no longer corresponded to the realities of international politics.[70] Concurrently, local activists were voting with their feet. In some chapters, such as Boston, the majority voted to join groups advocating for a more inclusive federalism, while in others, such as Delaware, the chapter reconstituted itself under this banner.[71]

Ironically, Federal Union's disintegration coincided with the rising public popularity of federalist frameworks for international politics in the last years of the war. An array of actors offered a variety of plans for world government, many of them inspired by federalism. Probably the best-known one was the "World Federation Plan" by Ely Culbertson, a champion bridge player. The plan envisaged a three-layer governance structure comprising nation-states, multiple regional bodies, and a world federal government armed with international police powers. Significantly, Culbertson packaged his plan as both a development of, and alternative to, Streit's "Union Now," reproving the latter for its self-defeating insistence on democracy as a criterion of membership.[72] Also highly visible was Emery Reves's 1945 best-seller, *The Anatomy of Peace*, published by Harper (Streit's editor). Although vague on details, Reves, as Streit recognized, favored something more universal than Atlantic federal union, though he too presented federalism as the best means of overcoming the

---

[70] NYPL, Student Federalist Records, Box 2, file 8, Harris Wofford to Tam, July 13, 1944; and file 5, TLH to Neal, October 24, 1945. Also see Harris Wofford, Jr., *It's Up to Us: Federal World Government in Our Time* (New York: Harcourt, Brace, 1946), 3–7.

[71] See LOC, CKS, Box I: 44, files on the Boston and Delaware chapters.

[72] Ely Culbertson, *Summary of the World Federation Plan: An Outline of a Practical and Detailed Plan for World Government* (New York: The World Federation, 1943). One compilation in 1944 identified over thirty federalist-inspired plans since 1942. See Edith Wynner and Georgia Lloyd, eds., *Searchlight on Peace Plans: Choose Your Road to World Government* (New York: E. P. Dutton, 1944).

"nation-feudalism" (national sovereignty), deemed responsible for recurrent crises, tensions, and war. And like many others, including Streit, Reves admired the US federal system; unlike Streit, though, he viewed it more as an inspiration than a blueprint.[73]

Streit could take considerable credit for the surge in federalism's popularity. After all, he had done more than anyone since 1939 to promote federalism as a framework for international order. Nevertheless, as Federal Union's wartime history shows, federalist frameworks broke loose from Streit's hold after 1942 in response to changing international developments but also to Streit's refusal to adapt. As one former Federal Union member noted in November 1942, Streit "has not kept pace with the evolution of the [federalist] idea."[74] Streit feared that "watering down" his proposal would gut a federal union of its essential element: a truly federal political-constitutional structure. Given the tendency of advocates of a more inclusive federal union to elide federalism and a postwar international organization, his fear was not unfounded. Still, in resisting compromise, Streit helped to marginalize Federal Union not only within the public political domain but also among the clamoring pro-federalist voices during the war's closing years.

Overall, it is hard not to judge a failure Streit's wartime efforts to build a nation-wide organization. In addition to constant financial pressures, which led to the periodic downgrading of ambitions, fostering disappointment and frustration, Federal Union was rent by policy disputes. One informed observer in 1943 charged those he called "federationists" of being perfectionists, which in turn bred "fanaticism" and "intolerance." The description appears to fit Streit and his Federal Union, though tensions over means and ends are arguably a frequent (and perhaps even) inherent, element of political activism.[75] The results, in any event, were no more encouraging at the local level. To be sure, Federal Union chapters sprouted across the country as local enthusiasts agreed to devote time and effort to the cause. Yet the initial enthusiasm proved difficult to sustain. Most chapters owed their existence to the dedicated efforts of a handful of people; many soon became barely active or even inactive as one or more members drifted away for personal or other reasons. Scholars of grass-

---

[73] Emery Reves, *The Anatomy of Peace* (New York: Harper & Brothers, 1945), 26. And LOC, CKS, Box I: 84, file: R, Streit to Emery Reves, August 8, 1945.

[74] NYPL, CFWG (CO), Box 2, Edith Wynner to William Lloyd, November 12, 1942.

[75] P. E. Corbett, "World Order – An Agenda for Lawyers," *American Journal of International Law* 37 (1943), 207–8.

roots participation often cite chapter and sometimes membership numbers as indices of activity, but Federal Union's wartime history calls into question such numbers. There appears to have been far less to Federal Union's local activism than either Streit's sympathizers or opponents claimed.

Finally, Streit's efforts to create a nation-wide organization suffered from a basic conceptual problem, one arguably shared by others at the time, whether federalist-inspired or not: the lack of an effective political strategy. Streit and his followers, such as other political groups, believed it necessary to create a "strong and active political body" at the national and local levels. The purpose, though, remained unclear. Streit sometimes described Federal Union's mission as didactic: to educate people about his proposal (and federalist frameworks more generally) across the United States. But then what? Even if Federal Union's nation-wide organization had been considerably more substantial, even if it had built a mass movement (which was never likely) present in every state, it is questionable whether Streit would have been any closer to realizing an Atlantic federal union.[76] To have any chance of doing so, he needed to find ways to enter more directly into the policymaking process.

STREIT AND THE POLICYMAKING PROCESS: FDR AND CONGRESS

This section and the next one examine Streit's search for a means to influence policymaking. Two possibilities presented themselves. One was a direct approach targeting the executive and legislative branches. Early on, Streit endeavored to convince President Roosevelt to pursue Atlantic federal union, exploiting contacts with members of the president's entourage. The endeavor largely failed, leading Streit to pay more attention to Congress. Although Streit's wartime efforts to court Congress members remained haphazard, they did register some limited successes, laying the groundwork for the more sustained lobbying campaign undertaken after the war.

Beginning in 1939, Streit trained his persuasive skills on the administration, pursuing cabinet members such as Frances Perkins (Labor Secretary), Cordell Hull (Secretary of State, who he knew from his

---

[76] Interestingly in this regard, the America First movement had decided in late 1941 to intervene directly in the 1942 elections, a decision obviated by the US entry into the war. See Cole, *America First*.

Geneva days), and Henry Stimson (Secretary of War from 1940), all of whom responded with expressions of interest. With William Bullitt's help, Streit also entered into contact with Eleanor Roosevelt who called *Union Now* "grand" in her "My Day" column in August 1939.[77] The same month Streit sent a telegram to Roosevelt urging the president to consider his federal union plan. Despite the lack of response, Streit remained determined, mobilizing Bullitt, Perkins, and Eleanor Roosevelt to arrange an invitation to a White House dinner in January 1940. Not surprisingly, Streit took the President's extended dinnertime questioning as a sign of support. Although Roosevelt "at no time made any direct statement either in praise or criticism of the book . . .," Streit reported, "he left no doubt in my mind that he is, at heart, for The Union and will push it forward as rapidly as popular support of it allows him to do."[78]

His hopes buoyed, Streit extracted a promise from Eleanor Roosevelt in May 1940 to "put before" the president a memorandum on federal union.[79] Soon afterward, military developments in Western Europe convinced Streit the decisive moment had arrived. The result was a barrage of letters to Roosevelt in June, which included an advance copy of the "Declaration of Interdependence" appearing in the *New York Times* the following month. Pleading for an immediate offer of federal union to France and Britain, Streit implored Roosevelt to "recognize what others fail to see clearly enough – that we are in a very exceptional situation where the ordinary procedures are bound to fail and where the normally impossible is alone possible." Although Streit privately expressed confidence Roosevelt "will have the courage and wisdom to take the sole road to salvation," the president once again failed to respond. Afterward, Streit continued to court Roosevelt, succeeding in getting invited to another White House dinner in April 1941. The result proved disappointing, however, as Streit was unable to discuss federal union personally with Roosevelt. "I may be crazy," Streit conceded in his account of the dinner to the Luces, "but I believe I could persuade him if only I could have an hour with him privately."[80] Several months later, Eleanor Roosevelt

---

[77] For the text, see www2.gwu.edu/~erpapers/myday/displaydoc.cfm?_y=1939&_f= mdo55343.

[78] LOC, CKS, Box I; 33, file: Roosevelt, Franklin D., "My Dinner at the White House, January 5th," Streit, January 7, 1940.

[79] LOC, CKS, Box I: 4, file: Alphabetical correspondence, Streit to Mrs. Roosevelt, May 15, 1940.

[80] LOC, CKS, Box I; 33, file: Roosevelt, Franklin D., Streit note to Jeanne Streit, June 17, 1940; and ibid., Clare Boothe Luce papers, Box 99, file 14, Streit to Luces, April 8, 1941.

refused to sponsor a Federal Union group in DC, stating "I am not convinced on 'Union Now'."[81]

Unable to convince the executive branch, Streit looked to Congress. During 1940, he had worked with John Foster Dulles to draft a congressional resolution calling on Roosevelt to convoke a constitutional convention of the Atlantic democracies.[82] The resolution was never submitted, partly because Dulles soon lost interest in the project and also because Streit realized the ground needed to be better prepared. Accordingly, he began courting Congress members in 1941, sending copies of his books as well as publicity material. At meetings of Federal Union's directing board in the autumn of 1942, Streit admitted a lack of resources precluded an extensive "political campaign" in Congress in support of a resolution; he nevertheless promised to continue wooing congress members in the hope of convincing them to appoint a bipartisan commission to examine plans for the postwar international order – and federal union among them.[83]

Although Streit could devote only intermittent attention to Congress during the war, his efforts met with some success. In the summer of 1941, the *Congressional Digest* published a lengthy exchange on a "federal union of the world's democracies," with multiple texts arguing for and against.[84] An interesting example is Karl Mundt, a House (and later Senate) member from South Dakota, who in 1940 rejected outright a union with Britain. Mundt eventually softened under the sway of Streit's solicitation. "I have heard some nice reactions from my colleagues to the last letter gotten out by Federal Union," he intimated to Streit in June 1942. After the war, Mundt became a strong supporter of Atlantic union, but even before then he began to draw Congress' attention to Streit as the "author of one of the post-war plans now being discussed in this country."[85] To be sure, not all attention was favorable: In 1941, several

[81] LOC, CKS, Box III: 9, file 1, Eleanor Roosevelt to Mrs. Adams, December 26, 1941.

[82] For the draft, see LOC, CKS, Box II: 17, file: Atlantic Union Resolution, "Declaration and Joint Resolution of the Congress of the United States," October 21, 1940. Also see the file in SMLPU, John Foster Dulles Papers, Box 19, reel 4. Jean Monnet, who would become a father of European unity, collaborated with Streit and Dulles on the constitution.

[83] LOC, CKS, Box I: 42, file: Board meetings, General, 1941–44, "Minutes of Meeting of National Board of Directors ... October 2, 1942"; and "Report," Barr, November 20, 1942.

[84] "Should America Join a Move for a Federal Union of the Democracies," *Congressional Digest*, June–July 1941, 169–92.

[85] LOC, CKS, Box I: 69, file: Mundt, Karl E., Mundt to Streit, June 30, 1942; and *Congressional Record*, March 19, 1943, Mundt.

representatives asked the infamous Dies Committee on Un-American activities to investigate Streit's Federal Union as a subversive organization "that would destroy things that have made America great."[86] That said, their alarmism is a testimony to Streit's growing visibility within Congress.

Streit, in any case, stepped up his lobbying efforts during 1944–45, appearing before both the Republican and Democratic party resolution committees and, still more importantly, adopting a more systematic approach in his courting of Congress members. "It was a great pleasure to have had that stimulating talk with you at dinner the other night," he jotted to Millard Tydings, the Maryland senator, in March 1945. "I think you will find that we have more points of agreement than seemed true in our discussion." Quietly and tentatively, Streit was building a network within Congress.[87]

STREIT AND THE POLICYMAKING PROCESS: THE CSOP AS A MISSED OPPORTUNITY

For Streit, the principal policy makers occupied the executive and legislative branches of government. Nongovernmental actors such as universities, foundations, and think tanks interested him far less, other than as potential sources of financing. Significantly, this second group of actors has attracted considerable attention in recent years, as scholars work to trace the origins of the Cold War national security state back to developments in the interwar and especially wartime years.[88]

As mentioned in the Introduction, once actor deserving more consideration than it has received is the CSOP. The CSOP played a vital role in drafting what became the UNO's charter. Equally pertinent, it was the site of a prolonged struggle between three groups to shape the United Nations and, by extension, the postwar international order. One group, well

---

[86] "Union Now Idea Is Denounced on Floor of House," *Chicago Tribune*, January 28, 1942, 3.

[87] LOC, CKS, Box I: 89, file: U.S. Senate, Streit to Senator Tydings, March 15, 1945. The file contains numerous other examples.

[88] See Wertheim, *Tomorrow the World*; Dexter Fergie, "Geopolitics Turned Inwards: The Princeton Military Studies Group and the National Security Imagination," *Diplomatic History* 43 (2019), 644–70; and Inderjeet Parmar, *Think Tanks and Power in Foreign Policy: A Comparative Study of the Role and Influence of the Council on Foreign Relations and the Royal Institute of International Affairs, 1939–1945* (London: Palgrave, 2004).

represented by James Shotwell and other League of Nations Association (LNA) holdovers, advocated an international organization broadly modeled on the League of Nations. The other two groups both favored federalist frameworks but differed in their approach to federalism: one group, which included Streit supporters, argued for federal entities at the regional or global level, while the other, which became dominant and which included Clyde Eagleton among its members, sought to harness federalism to the project of forging a postwar international organization capable of imposing greater limits on national sovereignty than the League of Nations.

Streit was an initial member of the CSOP, and membership offered him an opportunity to preach federal union not only to an influential group of insiders but also to the larger public, given the Commission's immense publicity resources. But for this to happen Streit would have had to cooperate with members who did not embrace his position, something he refused to do. Instead, Streit chose to distance himself from the CSOP, ignoring Eagleton's pleas to compromise. The result was to weaken the federalist voices within the CSOP, making it easier for Shotwell and his allies to instrumentalize federalism for their project. Admittedly, the CSOP was never likely to become a simple mouthpiece for Atlantic federal union. Nevertheless, the Commission amounted to a missed opportunity for Streit to exert some influence, if only indirectly, on policymaking.

The CSOP was the brainchild of Clark Eichelberger, its director, and Shotwell, its chairman, whose close ties to the Carnegie Endowment ensured a level of financing of which Streit could only dream. Eichelberger and Shotwell had been closely involved with the LNA during the 1930s and both were partisans of an internationalism combining international organizations of nation-states with a well-developed structure of international law providing states with a clear code of conduct. Basically, they envisaged the creation of a revamped League of Nations. By the end of the 1930s, though, the League was unpopular in the United States, viewed generally as an abject failure. The League, Shotwell conceded in October 1939, "is not a term to conjure here with at present ..."[89] The challenge for Shotwell and his allies was to find some way to rehabilitate the League and international organizations more generally.

---

[89] LOC, Arthur Sweetser Papers, Box 33, file: Shotwell, James T., Shotwell to Sweetser, October 4, 1939.

With this challenge in mind, Eichelberger in the spring of 1939 proposed that the LNA establish an "Unofficial Enquiry," loosely modeled on Woodrow Wilson's earlier wartime "Inquiry," to plan "the organization of international society to follow the present state of war." Not surprisingly, Eichelberger took the League of Nations as the starting point:

The fundamental need of the world is a dynamic process of international community life capable of providing for advancement of peoples within the bounds of justice and peace. The effort of the League of Nations to provide for the peaceful settlement of disputes, collective security, international justice and peaceful change, are manifestations of a greater effort that must be made to provide the dynamic organization of a changing world.

A key element of the new enterprise, moreover, would be public education. "The Inquiry will be of value," Eichelberger wrote, "if its conclusions may be widely accepted by people on a non-partisan base and form the basis of American foreign policy."[90]

Scholarly assessments of the CSOP differ. Whereas Robert Hillam believes it embodied an "extreme internationalism," Wertheim detects more muddled thinking in its ideas on postwar international order. But Andrew Johnstone is probably closer to the mark in viewing the CSOP as an extension of the LNA.[91] That said, several points are worth underscoring. One is the CSOP's clear desire to appear "non-partisan," which explains Eichelberger's more public claim that the CSOP aimed not to promote a revamped League of Nations but simply to "help the American people think their way through the problems of the fundamental bases of world peace and the responsibility of the United States."[92] Another point concerns the sympathy of several prominent members for federalist frameworks. This was true of Eagleton who served as the CSOP's secretary, coordinating and animating its activities. Eagleton not only harbored big ambitions for the CSOP, envisaging its development into a nation-wide mass membership lobby group but also resisting arguments for a simple return to the League. "The Commission, as far as I can influence it," he confided to a potential recruit, "will not work for the

---

[90] NYPL, Clark M. Eichelberger Papers, Box 151, file: CSOP 1939, "Commission of Enquiry," April 8, 1939.

[91] Hillman, "Quincy Wright and the Commission," 496; Wertheim, *Tomorrow, the World*, 76; and Johnstone, *Dilemmas of Internationalism*, 2; and Johnstone, *Against Immediate Evil*, 62–64.

[92] NYPL, Clark M. Eichelberger Papers, Box, 151, file: CSOP 1939, "Commission of Enquiry," September 16, 1939.

restoration of the League of Nations, but for the most practicable form of international government."[93] In thinking about forms of international government, Eagleton was clearly intrigued by the possibilities of federalism, as was Dulles, another early participant. The CSOP also counted as members more ardent federalists such as Frederick Schuman, a well-known political scientist who sat on Federal Union's board and who lectured publicly on Streit's project, and Livingston Hartley, a former diplomat turned expert on foreign affairs who would work closely with Streit in the postwar Atlanticist movement.[94]

The vital point is that dominant thinking within the CSOP was far from fixed at the beginning. At an initial meeting in December 1939, the majority of participants spoke in favor of a postwar international organization "stronger" than the League and capable of imposing significant limits on "the exercise of [national] sovereignty, in respect to the use of force, armaments and economic regulations." While accepting that any proposal must be "practical," the CSOP, they added, "should not hesitate to recommend solutions deemed desirable, merely because public opinion may not be prepared for them." In terms of "radical changes," the participants not only agreed that "a transition from an international system to a federal system, either in the world generally or in any part of it" merited consideration; they also framed the stakes in Streitian terms as between "a federal and a league organization." Before ending, the meeting drew up a list of topics for further study, the first one of which was "Regional areas, union and federal system."[95]

All this provides the context for Streit's early involvement with the CSOP. Streit caught Eichelberger and Shotwell's attention in early 1939, having sent both of them advanced copies of *Union Now*. Shotwell responded with complimentary comments, which Streit typically circulated as proof of the book's appeal. Eichelberger also expressed interest but soon grew cooler, resenting the competition Streit's fledgling

[93] BLCU, CEIP (NY and Wash), Series VII, Box 283, Eagleton to Eichelberger, December 8, 1941; and LOC, Philip C. Jessup Papers, Box A112, Eagleton to Jessup, January 12, 1942.

[94] For Schuman's wartime activities for Federal Union, see WCASC, Frederick Lewis Schuman Papers, Box 1, file 6. For Hartley's interest in federalism, see his *Is America Afraid?: A New Foreign Policy for the United States* (New York: Prentice-Hall, 1937), 33–75.

[95] NYPL, Clark M. Eichelberger Papers, Box 151, "Meeting of the Sub-Committee on Political International Organization, December 27, 1939."

organization posed to the LNA at the local chapter level.[96] But whatever Eichelberger's misgivings, Streit was too visible a figure not to be included. Accordingly, he counted among the "thoughtful citizens" invited to participate in the CSOP. In accepting, Streit noted his reservations regarding what he detected as the CSOP's preference for a renewed League of Nations. Rather than starting with the League's Covenant, he lectured to Eichelberger, "[o]ur Federal Convention of 1787" provided a "sounder basis" for the postwar international order. In private, Streit expressed considerable doubts, criticizing Eichelberger's "effective world organization" as too narrowly conceived.[97]

Whatever the details of his recruitment, Streit and federalism figured prominently in the CSOP's early work. In 1940, for example, Streit was one of the rare members, aside from Shotwell and Eichelberger, chosen to give a CBS radio broadcast under the Commission's aegis. In the talk, subsequently issued as a CSOP pamphlet, Streit explained his proposal to "organize the [Atlantic] democracies as a nucleus of world government of, by and for the people." Earlier in the year, Shotwell had asked Streit to outline his federal union proposal to a plenary meeting of the CSOP. In his comments, Streit emphasized the need for a "federal rather than a league system" of democracies, while accepting that a League of Nations might be useful in dealing with "the rest of the world" (i.e., nonmembers).[98] In his own radio address in May 1940, Eichelberger identified two approaches within the CSOP: one centered on "a universal League of Nations using the present League as the foundation" and another on a federation of the democracies forming "the nucleus of the organization of the future." While suggesting that the majority of members favored a "universal society of nations," Eichelberger assured listeners the CSOP kept an open mind toward both approaches. "No hard and fast plans,"

---

[96] SMLPU, Hamilton Fish Armstrong Papers, Box 60, file: Streit, Clarence, Streit to Fish, with attachment, January 22, 1939. For Eichelberger, see Johnstone, *Against Immediate Evil*, 68–72.

[97] NYPL, Clark M. Eichelberger Papers, Box 151, file: Enquiry – Correspondence concerning members, Streit to Eichelberger, October 12, 1939; and LOC, Russell W. Davenport Papers, Box 34, file: Union Now correspondence, 1939, "Confidential Report of Clarence K. Streit ... Made to the National Executive Committee at meeting of October 13."

[98] NYPL, Clark M. Eichelberger Papers, Box 151, "Which Way to Lasting Peace," Streit, March 16, 1940; and "Meeting of the Commission to Study the Organization of Peace, January 28, 1940."

he insisted, "were laid down for the actual machinery to make the organization of peace effective."[99]

Tellingly, federalism permeated the CSOP's preliminary report released in November 1940. Echoing Streit in pointing to the League's interwar failure as proof that the "sovereignty of the nation-state is no longer adequate" as a basis of international order, the report identified the alternatives as "world empire, achieved by conquest, or some form of association, such as world federation, achieved by consent." Federalism, it continued, offered the only means to reconcile the nation-state as the "[basic] unit of world society" with the need to rein in the exercise of national sovereignty:

Federation organizes consent on the international scale while empire organizes coercion on that scale. Though coercion of the part of the whole is the essence of government, in the system of federalism that coercion can only be in accord with law, to which those bound had directly or indirectly consented. World federation, balancing the autonomy of the nation-state with the authority of the family of nations was the system implied by the founders of modern international law after the breakup of the medieval empire. Organization to make international law effective was, however, hampered by exaggerated developments in the idea of sovereignty.[100]

If anything, the emphasis on federalism was even more marked in the press release accompanying the report, which announced that "[t]he idea of Federation is advanced as a permanent basis for world peace by the Commission."[101] With good reason, Streit thanked Eagleton for a report that "has gone a long ways in the direction I believe is sound."[102]

Following what for Streit seemed a promising start, federalist frameworks grew increasingly marginalized within the CSOP over the next several years. The commission's second report, ready in February 1942 and dealing with the transitional period between war's end and the establishment of a stable international order, failed to mention federalism. The CSOP's subsequent reports, moreover, focused more and more

---

[99] BLCU, James T. Shotwell Papers, Box 195/196, "Is World Organization Possible?" Eichelberger, May 11, 1940.

[100] "Preliminary Report," November 1940, reproduced in *Building Peace: Reports of the Commission to Study the Organization of Peace, 1939–1972* (Metuchen, NJ: Scarecrow Press, 1973), 1–10.

[101] BLCU, James T. Shotwell Papers, Box 195, CSOP press release, November 11, 1939 [but 1940].

[102] SCFHL, Frank Aydelotte Papers, Box 38, file: Federal Union, 1940, Streit to Eagleton, November 4, 1940.

on the functioning of a postwar UNO, a focus reflected in the commission's internal activities, which included the drafting in 1943, by a former LNA executive director, of a first draft of the UNO's charter. Instructions circulated to the CSOP's various study committees the same year, meanwhile, oriented their work around the UNO's projected activities.[103] By 1944 the CSOP, under Eichelberger and Shotwell's guidance, had basically become a cheerleader for the UNO, campaigning for public approval of the Dumbarton Oaks proposals.[104]

Several factors worked to marginalize federalist frameworks within the CSOP. Most obviously, neither Eichelberger nor Shotwell were genuinely in favor. Their goal was a revived League. Any postwar international organization, Shotwell confided to a Columbia University audience in February 1942, will resemble the League "even if it bears another name ..." Admittedly, Eichelberger sometimes appeared more uncertain, reiterating into 1942 that the CSOP's ambit extended well beyond "a revision of the League of Nations Covenant."[105] But soon afterward, and probably even before, Eichelberger embraced Shotwell's preference for an institutional approach to postwar international order with a renewed League at its core. Within the CSOP, the two men worked closely in tandem.

Shotwell and Eichelberger found a key ally in Quincy Wright, a prominent political scientist at the University of Chicago. It was probably Eichelberger who recruited Wright as a CSOP member, having been his student in the 1930s. Wright, in any case, soon took over direction of the Commission's all-important studies committee, emerging in the process as its dominant thinker. That Wright would oppose federalist frameworks was not self-evident, given his prewar interest in some form of world federation. And during the war Wright often used federalist language, speaking publicly in 1943 of "federalistic organization" of the postwar world. Within the CSOP, meanwhile, he accepted that "effective world organization" required not simply "national and local governments" but also "certain universal principles and institutions" as well as "certain

[103] NYPL, Clark M. Eichelberger Papers, Box 152, Eichelberger to Studies Committee, April 15, 1943.

[104] For example, *Your Stake in the Peace: A Study Course on the Problems of the Future We Face* (New York: CSOP, n.d.).

[105] BLCU, CEIP (NY and Wash), series VII, Box 283, "Underwriting the Victory," Shotwell, February 14, 1942; and Eichelberger to Studies Committee, February 13, 1942.

regional organizations" of which one possibility was a "federal union of the democracies of the world."[106]

But the vital point is that Wright, like Shotwell and Eichelberger, exploited federalism for their own project of rehabilitating international organization. At the beginning, federalist talk offered a means to conceive of a renewed League of Nations, one which, it was hoped, might be more effective than the original. As it became apparent that the emerging UNO would resemble its predecessor, however, federalism became little more than a means to package the old as new.

Tellingly, within the CSOP Wright never took federalist frameworks seriously. In fixing the Commission's work schedule for 1940, he sought not only to sideline Hartley and his federalist inclinations but also avoided consulting Streit, informing Eagleton the latter's "views are so well known that I thought he wouldn't contribute much beyond that."[107] As chair of its studies committee, Wright was well placed to shape the CSOP's message. Working on a draft of its third report in late 1942, which would focus exclusively on the UNO, he framed federalism not as a tool for strengthening a postwar institution but for limiting its scope. Perhaps "we ought to come out for the need of a federal organization of the world as a whole," he proposed to Eagleton, "but with quite limited powers in the hands of the federal authority ..." As for Streit's federal union, Wright echoed Spykman in dismissing it as a project for "Anglo-American hegemony."[108] By mid-1943, Wright was questioning the very pertinence of federalism to the postwar international order. Examples of federal structures created in earlier periods, including that of the United States, he explained, "cannot be followed blindly" but must "be adapted, because the world is composed of people more diverse, culturally and economically, than those of any one nation or federation ..." From the perspective of complexity, a "universal political organization" was far

---

[106] Quincy Wright, "International Law and the Balance of Power," *American Journal of International Law* 37 (1943), 97–103, 98; and NYPL, Clark M. Eichelberger Papers, Box 152, Wright to Eagleton, December 12, 1939, with attachment: "Study of the Organization of Peace," December 5, 1939. For an emphasis on Wright's wartime federalism, see Samuel Moyn, *Humane: How the United States Abandoned Peace and Reinvented War* (New York: Farrar, Strauss & Giroux, 2021), 130–31, 143. Also see Daniel Gorman, "International Law and the International Thought of Quincy Wright, 1918–1945," *Diplomatic History* 41 (2017), 339–42.

[107] NYPL, Clark M. Eichelberger Papers, Box 151, Wright to Eagleton, December 8, 1939.

[108] UOC, Quincy Wright Papers, Box 118, file 1, Wright draft letter to Eagleton, December 23, 1942. For the report, see "Third Report: The United Nations and the Organization of Peace," February 1943, in *Building Peace*, 32–65.

more suitable because it would be "more flexible than the lesser organizations of states and federations."[109]

Together, Eichelberger, Shotwell, and Wright formed a formidable trio. The three, moreover, exerted considerable influence beyond the CSOP, most notably with the State Department and especially with under-secretary Sumner Welles, who directed its postwar planning activities and who quickly emerged as a staunch supporter of an interstate organization modeled on the League of Nations. Although no single factor probably determined Welles's position, it is noteworthy that Shotwell and Eichelberger served as State Department consultants during 1942–43, and if the latter's notes are to be believed, they helped to steer the under-secretary and his officials in their direction.[110] One sign of their influence, as already noted, is that the CSOP's draft constitution for the UNO provided the basis for its charter. Another sign is Welles's gratitude. "You have in fact been a tower of strength," he wrote to Eichelberger in August 1943, "at times when your vision, your faith and your ability were greatly needed."[111]

In praising the CSOP's first report, Streit had promised Eagleton his close cooperation. "The existing world situation and its probable trend should make it easier ...," he penned, "for us to reach much fuller agreement in the coming months."[112] In reality, Streit turned his back on the CSOP. After 1940, he stopped attending meetings, sometimes sending proxies, and did not sign the subsequent reports. By 1944, it was unclear whether he remained a member. Streit undoubtedly judged the cards to be stacked against him, and in this he was not wrong: Eichelberger, Shotwell, and Wright did work to marginalize federalist frameworks. Yet Streit arguably misjudged the situation within the CSOP, for Eagleton waged a determined struggle to keep the federalist fires alive. To recall, Eagleton was intrigued by the idea of reconciling federalism in general and Streit's project in particular with a renewed

---

[109] BLCU, CEIP (NY and Wash), Series VII, Box 284, "Security and World Organization," Wright, June 24, 1943.

[110] For the notes, see NYPL, Clark M. Eichelberger Papers, Box 152, file: Welles Committee 1942. Also see Christopher D. O'Sullivan, *Sumner Welles, Postwar Planning, and the Quest for a New World Order, 1937–1943* (New York: Columbia University Press, 2008); and Department of State, *Postwar Foreign Policy Preparation, 1939–1945* (Washington, DC: Department of State, 1950).

[111] NYPL, Clark M. Eichelberger Papers, Box 153, Welles to Eichelberger, August 31, 1943.

[112] SCFHL, Frank Aydelotte Papers, Box 38, file: Federal Union, 1940, Streit to Eagleton, November 4, 1940.

League of Nations, viewing the former as a means to strengthen the latter. To "convert the League into the Federal Union which Mr. Streit desires," he reasoned in 1939, "it is only necessary to give more powers to the League, taking them from the member States, as was done in 1789." So conceived, Streit's plan and a postwar international organization were separated by "differences of degree rather than of principle." Or as Philip Jessup, another international lawyer who Eagleton regularly consulted, opined to Eichelberger in 1940, "federalism is a very advanced form of international organization."[113]

It is tempting to lump Eagleton with Eichelberger, Shotwell, and Wright. After all, they sought to harness federalism to the project of a postwar international organization. The difference, though, is that Eagleton genuinely strove to cooperate with Streit. Within the CSOP, he used his influence as secretary to counter attempts to sideline federalist frameworks. In May 1942, for example, Eagleton sought to place "Federalism: Union Now" once again on the CSOP's research agenda, asking members to consider whether it "differ[s] in principle or in degree from the League of Nations." No less importantly, Streit's *Union Now* figured prominently in the attached bibliography.[114] A year later, Eagleton tried again, urging the CSOP to place a quasi-federal structure at the center of the CSOP's deliberations. "I am more and more impressed," he informed Shotwell in February 1943, "with the necessity of deciding upon the necessary minimum of powers for the international government and the distribution of powers between the international, regional and local systems ..." Or, as he summarized, the CSOP should consider what kind of "international system" it wanted – "Universal or regional; federal or what?"[115]

Equally significant, Eagleton pleaded with Streit to be more flexible in his approach to federalism. Intransigence, he privately warned in June 1941, "would not only be disastrous to your Movement, which has acquired a splendid momentum, and which should carry on; it would

[113] Clyde Eagleton, "The League of Nations and Federal Union," *The New Commonwealth Quarterly* 5 (1939), 121, 125; and LOC, Philip C. Jessup Papers, Box A113, Jessup to Eichelberger, September 7, 1940.

[114] BLCU, CEIP (NY and Wash), Series VII, Box 283, CSOP, "A Study Outline on Post-War Reconstruction," Eagleton, May 1942.

[115] BLCU, CEIP (NY and Wash), Series VII, Box 284, CSOP, Eagleton to Shotwell, February 8, 1943, with attachments.

also injure the whole movement toward international government."[116]
A year later he publicly appealed for cooperation, contending the "system
roughly sketched" in the CSOP's second report, which Streit did not sign,
"moves towards federalism, but regards the development in this direction
as evolutionary, rather than the definite break with the past which the
author of *Union Now* regards as necessary." In another venue the same
year, Eagleton, while rejecting "Streit's thesis that the principles of the
League are all wrong and that a new structure must be built," searched
for common ground. The shared project would be "to develop federation
gradually from the older institution [the League]" in which there "should,
in effect, be, for certain purposes, some kind of fusion of states which
would not destroy individual autonomy of each but would create something above them."[117] Schuman, another CSOP member and federal
union supporter, likewise beseeched Streit to be more flexible, cautioning
him against "clinging to myths and illusions and refusing to face
realities."[118]

Eagleton and Schuman's pleas fell on deaf ears, as Streit insisted on the
incompatibility of Federal Union and any postwar league of nation-states.
Rather than working with potential allies within the CSOP, Streit preferred to retreat into his own organization, whose purity of position he
carefully watched over. Admittedly, Eagleton's vision of a third way
skirted real differences in terms of membership and authority between
an international organization and Streit's Atlantic union of the democracies. Nevertheless, some openness on Streit's part would have
strengthened federalist voices within the CSOP, pressuring their opponents to be more forthcoming, even if, to reiterate, the Commission was
never going to become an instrument of an Atlantic federal union. Wright
inadvertently highlighted the possibilities for developing federalism when
challenged by Raymond Buell in 1943 on Streit's project. "Numerous
shades of difference between a thorough-going federation and an international system are possible" he accepted, assuring Buell that the "matter

---

[116] LOC, CKS, Box I: 5, file: Chronological correspondence 1941, Eagleton to Streit, June
20, 1941.
[117] Clyde Eagleton, "Organization of the Community of Nations," *American Journal of
International Law* 36 (1942), 235–36; and SCRCGW, Carnegie Peace Pamphlet and
Microfilm Collection, Box 6, "The World We Want" (League of Nations Union, 1942),
Eagleton, 7–8.
[118] LOC, CKS, Box I: 5, file: Chronological correspondence 1942, Schuman to Streit, April
25, 1942, with attachment.

would be gone into further" in a subsequent CSOP report.[119] No such report would be written.

With Streit in self-imposed exile, Eichelberger, Shotwell, and Wright could more easily silence or wear down resistance within the CSOP. Eagleton, tellingly, became less active within the Commission in the last two years of the war. Worse still for Streit, Eichelberger and Shotwell strove successfully to efface all traces of federal union from the CSOP, recasting in the process the terms of the debate. Whereas in the early war years the CSOP framed the postwar international order as a choice between empire and federalism, with a League of Nations-type international organization and Streit's federal union sitting uneasily together as versions of the latter, during 1944–45 Eichelberger and Shotwell presented the UNO as the counterpart to federalism, which they conflated with hopelessly utopian proposals for "world government." Thus, in a 1944 CSOP pamphlet, Eichelberger admitted that some people might be disappointed with the UNO, which resembled the interwar League, but urged them nevertheless to recognize that "new federations and new loyalties" were impractical in the foreseeable future. Realism, he added, demanded the recognition that "today we are living in a time in which the nation-state is the basic unity of international society." Similarly, Shotwell, in a book publicizing the CSOP's work, defended the approach embodied in the Dumbarton Oaks agreement as infinitely more realistic than both "the do-nothing policies and half-measures of the past and those theories of world peace which at a single leap would merge the sovereign nations of today under some form of world government."[120]

As the head of Federal Union, Streit sought to counteract the conflation of federalism with world government, insisting (much like Shotwell and Eichelberger) that the latter was unrealistic.[121] But for all his skills as a publicist, Streit was handicapped during the war by Federal Union's limited budget. The CSOP, by comparison, possessed considerable resources. Indeed, from 1942 onwards it embarked on an extensive publicity campaign, which switched into high gear during 1944–45 – a campaign suggesting, incidentally, just how unsure Eichelberger and Shotwell were about the popularity of their UNO-centered approach.

---

[119] LOC, Raymond Leslie Buell Papers, Box 17, file 5, Quincy Wright to Buell, September 18, 1943.
[120] Clark M. Eichelberger, *Time Has Come for Action* (New York: CSOP, August 1944), 9–10; and James T. Shotwell, *The Great Decision* (New York: Macmillan, 1945), xix–xx.
[121] LOC, CKS, Box I: 89, Streit to Howard McMurray, August 29, 1944.

Operating at the national and regional levels, the CSOP circulated its reports as well as other material in substantial quantities, organized study groups and speakers' tours, and arranged hundreds of radio broadcasts and newspaper articles. The CSOP could also count on the government, whose Office of War Information launched its own well-funded publicity campaign in favor of the UNO.[122] In turning his back on the CSOP, Streit not only impaired federalism's potential appeal within the commission but also found himself in a public relations battle he could not win.

In a letter to the editors of *Time* magazine in April 1942, Streit complained of the obstacles facing his movement: Its financial resources were "trifling compared to the funds spent ... promoting popular get-peace-quick-and-easy schemes" and its "worst opponents have spread venomous lies about Union Now by the hundred thousand ..."[123] Streit's frustration was understandable: Federal Union suffered from a significant comparative financial disadvantage and from attacks from various quarters. The *Chicago Tribune*, owned by the irascible Robert McCormick, regularly unleashed its columnists against Streit's Federal Union, accusing it of treason. That the *Tribune* exaggerated Federal Union's influence, conjecturing in 1943 that it dominated the CSOP, offered no comfort to Streit who considered pursuing the newspaper for libel.[124]

But however justified, Streit's frustration deflected attention from the failure to craft an effective political strategy. In promoting his project, Streit sought to build a nation-wide movement with local chapters. But vague talk of educating the public aside, it was never clear what precisely Federal Union was meant to accomplish. The CSOP arguably offered more promising possibilities for influencing policy but Streit spurned cooperation with potential allies. If his early involvement with the CSOP testifies to the wartime visibility of federalist frameworks, it also underscores their open-ended nature. Streit's rigid approach to federalism, with the US federal system serving as a formula to apply on a

[122] For the publicity campaign, see NYPL, Clark M. Eichelberger Papers, Box 154, "Memorandum on the Work of the Commission to Study the Organization of Peace During 1944," undated. For the government, see Susan Brewer, *Why America Fights: Patriotism and War Propaganda from the Philippines to Iraq* (Oxford: Oxford University Press, 2009), 111, 128–37.

[123] NYPL, Henry R. Luce Papers, Box 102, file: Streit, Clarence, Streit to Editors, *Time*, April 12, 1943.

[124] George Tagge, "Union Now Fold Lead in Shaping of Propaganda," *Chicago Tribune*, September 25, 1943, 6.

transatlantic scale, differed from Eagleton's more flexible understanding of federalism as a conceptual tool for thinking about a postwar international organization to succeed the interwar League of Nations. Whether the CSOP could have devised some compromise between the two, for example in the form of regional arrangement under the umbrella of a universal organization (as Walter Lippmann appeared to envisage), is impossible to say.[125] But Streit's inflexibility facilitated the opportunistic appropriation of federalism by Shotwell, Eichelberger, and others in support of a repackaged League of Nations. Ironically, Streit unintentionally contributed to the very outcome he had worked so hard to prevent.

[125] See Lippmann, *U.S. Foreign Policy: Shield of the Republic* (Boston: Little, Brown, 1943), 114–36; and *U.S. War Aims* (New York: Da Capo Press, 1976 reprint), 73–88.

4

Clarence Streit and Federal Union during the Cold War

In March 1950, *Time* magazine featured Clarence Streit on its cover. The accompanying article, entitled the "Elijah from Missoula," presented Streit as a dedicated but somewhat quixotic crusader, someone convinced he had discovered the key to US foreign relations: an Atlantic federal union of the democracies. Streit's self-assigned mission, the article explained, was to persuade the United States to forsake the principle of national sovereignty, the root cause of recurrent conflict between states, and to enter into a federal union, much as the thirteen colonies had done in 1787. A hint of condescension notwithstanding, the article could not disguise its sneaking admiration for Streit. Like the abolitionist Lloyd Garrison or the suffragette Susan B. Anthony, Streit belonged "to the small legion of Americans born to be touched by an idea and to give their lives to it" – the "reformers, the crusaders, sometimes the bores or screwballs, sometimes ineffectual, sometimes movers of the world."[1] Though pleased with the publicity, Streit chided the magazine's editor for not emphasizing more Atlantic union's "really impressive progress since 1939" in what he called the "opinion-mobilizing field." As evidence of progress, Streit pointed not only to the numerous "influential leaders [who] have been won over to this cause in 11 years of campaigning" but even more so to the visibility of the "ideas in Union Now."[2]

---

[1] "Elijah from Missoula," *Time Magazine*, vol. 15, no. 13, March 27, 1950, 22–25.
[2] NYHS, Henry R. Luce Papers, Box 102, file 2, Streit, Clarence, Streit to T. S. Matthews (*Time*), March 27, 1950; and Streit to Henry Luce, March 29, 1950.

Streit, as *Time*'s cover story suggests, was no flash-in-the-pan whose wartime moment in the spotlight quickly vanished.[3] Contrary to prevailing impressions, Streit remained strikingly active after 1945, promoting his project well into the 1970s. This activism possessed two prongs. One prong, examined in the next chapter, was directly political and involved lobbying presidential administrations and congress. The other prong, the subject of this chapter, focused on popularizing Atlantic federal union and federalism more generally. If the principal instrument of this publicity endeavor remained Federal Union, the organization Streit founded in 1939, the latter's nature changed after 1945. Rather than a national movement with local chapters, Federal Union evolved into an individual membership organization whose primary purpose was to sustain Streit's promotional activities, which included follow-up books to *Union Now* and a monthly magazine, *Freedom & Union*. As in the early wartime years, Streit's postwar promotional activities provide a window into the public dimension of politics, highlighting some of the opportunities it offered to, as well as the limits it imposed on, policy entrepreneurs. And perhaps the greatest limit remained that of translating visibility into policy influence.

In addition to the public dimension of politics, Streit's postwar promotional activities with Federal Union are relevant to two particular issues. One concerns the appeal of world government in the early postwar years. This appeal is often understood as a reaction to the atomic bomb and the fear of nuclear annihilation: After Hiroshima and Nagasaki, numerous people seemed ready to consider the proposition that only a world government of some sort could ensure states did not weaponize nuclear energy.[4] But world government's appeal was also an outgrowth of wartime debates on federalism as a means to overcome the dangers of national sovereignty for international politics. Toward the end of the war, as Chapter 3 showed, federalism became a framework for thinking

---

[3] For example, see Robert A. Divine, *Second Chance: The Triumph of Internationalism in America during World War II* (New York: Atheneum, 1971), 163; Quinn Slobodian, *Globalists: The End of Empire and the Birth of Neoliberalism* (Cambridge, MA: Harvard University Press, 2018), 91–92.

[4] Joseph Preston Baratta, *The Politics of World Federation: United Nations, UN Reform, Atomic Control* (Westport, CT: Praeger, 2004); Lawrence S. Wittner, *One World or None: A History of the World Disarmament Movement Through 1953* (Stanford, CA: Stanford University Press, 1993), 44–45, 66–71; and Paul Boyer, *By the Bomb's Early Light: American Thought and Culture at the Dawn of the Atomic Age* (Chapel Hill: University of North Carolina Press, 1985), 29–45.

about postwar international organizations – and, above all, what became the United Nations (UNO). Significantly, the vast majority of world government proponents after 1945 proposed to build on the UNO, viewing it as a potential embryo. Though often lumped with these proponents, Streit, in fact, defined Atlantic union in opposition to world government: Rather than a strengthened UNO, his federalism involved something more formal in terms of structure and more restricted in terms of geography and membership.[5] If Streit's ongoing promotional activities point to the diversity of federalist thinking after 1945, they are also a reminder that such thinking outlived the decline of the world government movement after 1950.

The second issue is that of Cold War political culture. In opposing calls for world government, Streit emphasized democracy, insisting that an effective federal union could not include non-democracies, however defined. This emphasis, whose roots lay in the 1930s and in anti-fascism, helped to make Streit an early Cold Warrior. Indeed, early on anti-communism infused his postwar activism on behalf of Atlantic federal union. Arguably more intriguing, though, is the form of Streit's anti-communism, which expressed itself in abstractions such as "freedom" and "liberty," offered as essential characteristics of democracy. Furthering distancing himself from his Progressive roots, Streit increasingly fetishized democracy, draining the term of any substantial content. But there was more. Studies of Cold War political culture draw attention to the binary force of abstractions as the United States defined itself against the Soviet Union, its virtues forming a mirror image of Soviet (communist) vices.[6] Streit's case calls attention to another and complementary dynamic at work: the privileging of trans-Atlantic commonalities. Invocations of democracy worked to elide the very real differences (political, social, economic) between the United States and Western Europe (and Canada) – differences Streit occasionally recognized. From this perspective, Streit's Federal Union figures as a determined

---

[5] For the lumping of Streit with world government proponents, see Fritz Bartel, "Surviving the Years of Grace: The Atomic Bomb and the Specter of World Government," *Diplomatic History* 39 (2015), 275–302; and Wittner, *One World or None*, 44–45.

[6] John Fousek, *To Lead the Free World: American Nationalism and the Cultural Roots of the Cold War* (Chapel Hill: University of North Carolina Press, 2000); Nathan Abrams, "Advertising Freedom: *Commentary* Magazine and the Cultural Cold War," *Studies in the Social Sciences* 36 (1999), 65–80; and Daniel T. Rodgers, *Contested Truths: Keywords in American Politics since Independence* (Cambridge, MA: Harvard University Press, 1987), 215–16.

participant in a larger political process of defining what constituted the "West" after 1945.[7]

Although Streit remained extremely active during 1944–45, Federal Union appeared anemic. As the previous chapter showed, the organization suffered from financial shortages, personality and policy disputes, and declining membership. Numerous local chapters were inactive, existing largely on paper. Well aware of this situation, Streit, in a bid to re-energize Federal Union, had approached the Rockefeller Foundation in 1944 to fund an ambitious national "grass-roots education" campaign "in the basic principles of federal union as exemplified in the Constitution of the United States with a view to attaining world order by a federal union of the democratic peoples." Although admitting the organization "has had its ups and down in the past five years," Streit insisted the immediate future looked bright for both Federal Union and federalism. "We feel we have built on firm foundations," he explained. "We feel that we are now in position to expand to the huge degree that this year, fateful because of the situation both at home and abroad requires … and permits."[8]

After some deliberation, the Foundation decided against funding Federal Union, citing Streit's lack of flexibility. "Streit," wrote Arthur Packard, its director, "tends to give the impression that he is the only person who has the right idea, and everyone else is wrong." Yet, just as significantly, the foundation was clearly intrigued by federalism whose wartime visibility Streit had contributed so much to promote. Federalism, Packard explained, "represent[s] the ideal expression of our thoughts about the brotherhood of man, the common nature of his responsibilities and privileges …" As an idea, he added, "I find it difficult to see why the federal principle is not capable of indefinite extension as it has been extended in this country." The problem was not federalism but Streit. While interested in exploring federalism as a framework for postwar international order, the foundation concluded "there is the lack of

---

[7] Michael Kimmage, *The Abandonment of the West: The History of an Idea in American Foreign Policy* (New York: Basic Books, 2020).

[8] RAC, Office of the Messrs. Rockefeller Records, World Affairs, Series Q, Box 24, file 205, "The Purpose, Character, Technique, History, Present Position & Prospects of Federal Union, Inc.," Streit, March 14, 1944; and Federal Union Treasurer to Streit, March 14, 1944.

readiness [on Streit's part] to let the idea [federalism] go and find its place in and with the adjustment of other ideas."[9]

Although disappointed, Streit remained optimistic about Federal Union's prospects. If anything, the dramatic end of the war in 1945, precipitated by the use of atomic bombs against two Japanese cities, further stoked his optimism. The atomic bomb, he believed, would profoundly alter international politics and, in so doing, offer an undreamt occasion to persuade people of the merits of Atlantic federal union. The "terrible threat of the atomic bomb," Streit declared to Federal Union's directors in August 1945, "was a new opportunity like that at the time of the fall of France." As with the League of Nations in the case of disarmament, the newly founded UNO would invariably fail to impose any form of international control over nuclear energy. In this situation, the public and government would both be ripe for alternatives. The "bomb," he predicted, "would serve as a means to get the Union started, like the navigation of the Potomac river was the issue which brought together the Philadelphia Convention of 1787." Continuing, Streit urged Federal Union to concentrate initially on a union of the United States, Britain, and Canada – or what he called a "nuclear union" – which could be progressively enlarged to include other Atlantic countries.[10]

Streit's presentation to Federal Union's directors provided the basis for a letter published the following month in some fifteen newspapers, including the *New York Times*, the *Washington Post*, the *Christian Science Monitor*, and the *Los Angeles Times*. Written by Streit and signed by several public figures (most of whom were not Federal Union members), among them the philosopher-educator John Dewey, the editor Felix Morley, and the African-American writer and journalist Chandler Owen, the letter declared the atomic bomb "has given the people of the United States, the United Kingdom and Canada an enduring common responsibility that requires their united common sense and courage," before calling on the US government "to convoke a convention to form a nuclear union on a free basis." Hardly surprisingly, the union would be modeled on the "United States Constitution," whose "Federal system"

---

[9] RAC, Office of the Messrs. Rockefeller Records, World Affairs, Series Q, Box 24, file 205, "Federal Union," Arthur W. Packard, April 6, 1944; and Packard to John D. Rockefeller, April 26, 1944.

[10] LOC, CKS, Box I: 42, file: Board: Meetings: General 1945, "Minutes of the Board of Directors ... August 20, 1945."

provided guarantees of "individual liberty" as well as of "fair representa-
tion, equal justice, defensive strength, effective central power, independent home rule, domestic tranquility."[11]

In public appearances and published writings, Streit took pains to
emphasize a "nuclear union" was not a policy departure on Federal
Union's part. As with the call for "Union Now with Britain" in
1940–41, Streit contended he was merely adapting the original Atlantic
federal union proposal to international events. A "nuclear union" of the
United States, Britain, and Canada, he repeatedly insisted, was an emergency measure in response to the urgent need to impose some form of
international control over the atomic bomb. For Streit, the vital point was
to seize an opportunity.[12]

Streit was far from alone in highlighting the significance of the atomic
bomb to international politics. Among the more fervent voices, moreover,
were advocates of world government who, to recall from the previous
chapter, looked to federalism to give form to their proposals. Mention has
already been made of Emery Reves's best-selling book, *The Anatomy of
Peace*, published in the last months of the war, which castigated the
principle of "absolute national sovereignty" as a formula for endless
war. As a solution, Reves sketched a vaguely defined federalist arrangement in which jurisdiction over policy areas would be divided between the
international and national levels. That the atomic bomb provided a
powerful fillip to such arguments is evident from another best-seller
several months later: *Modern Man Is Obsolete*. Written by Norman
Cousins, an up-and-coming journalist and political activist, the book
insisted "the greatest obsolescence of all in the Atomic Age is national
sovereignty" – a principle dismissed as "an anomalous hold-over from the
tribal instinct in nations." Much like Reves, Cousins's answer was "world
government" imagined in federalist terms. And much like Streit, Cousins
advised readers to look to US history in the 1780s for inspiration, even
citing John Fiske's paean to federalism, *The Critical Period of American
History*. "The United States were created largely through their differences," he affirmed in this sense, "differences so intense that only a

[11] "World Union Proposed," *New York Times*, September 16, 1945, 8E; and LOC, Clare
Luce Booth Papers, Box 516, file: Streit, Clarence, Streit to Luce Booth, September
15, 1945.
[12] "Atomic Bomb Is Seen as Making Unity Urgent," *New York Times*, November 21, 1945,
10; and "Union Head Cites Bomb Danger," *The Evening Sun* (Baltimore, MD), August
13, 1945, 14.

common sovereignty could prevent international anarchy within the American group."[13]

While Reves and Cousins might be dismissed as idealists, even someone as hard-headed as Walter Lippmann publicly expressed the fear that national sovereignty as a basis of international relations was suicidal in an atomic age. In his contribution to a widely diffused collection on the impact of nuclear weapons on international politics, *One World or None*, Lippmann accepted the pressing task was to remove nuclear weapons from the control of individual nations. No less pertinently, and quoting from the *Federalist Papers*, he contemplated federalism as a potential means of doing so. The UNO, he conjectured, could act as a global government operating above individual states and endowed with authority over a limited number of matters, most notably military security (and nuclear weapons).[14]

As the international jurist Clyde Eagleton recognized, much of the early postwar talk of world government, which the advent of the atomic bomb galvanized (but did not create), echoed points Streit had been making since 1939.[15] Arguably, therefore, an opportunity existed for Streit to ally with the burgeoning world government movement in the United States in order to promote federalist frameworks. But this demanded flexibility. Despite the important differences between them, Reves, Cousins, and Lippmann all envisaged the UNO as the basis of some form of federal world government. The emphasis was on transforming the UNO. "What advocates of world government wish," Eagleton wrote elsewhere, "can be obtained, where possible of attainment, more easily through the development and strengthening of UNO ..." "Whatever changes are made ...," he elaborated, "must depend on the agreement of sovereign states; and it would surely be easier to achieve this agreement by the procedures and pressures available under the UNO, and by changes to the UNO itself, than by thrusting a new system *in toto* upon public opinion throughout the world."[16]

---

[13] Emery Reves, *The Anatomy of Peace* (New York: Harper & Brothers, 1945); and Norman Cousins, *Modern Man Is Obsolete* (New York: Viking, 1945), 20, 27–29. Also see Boyer, *By the Bomb's Early Light*, 27–81; and George Hutchinson, *Facing the Abyss: American Literature and Culture in the 1940s* (New York: Columbia University Press, 2018), 355–82.

[14] Walter Lippmann, "International Control of Atomic Energy," in Dexter Masters and Katherine Way, eds., *One World or None* (New York: Whittlesey House, 1946), 66–75.

[15] Clyde Eagleton, "The Individual and International Law," *Proceedings of the American Society of International Law* 40 (1946), 27.

[16] Clyde Eagleton, "The Demand for World Government," *American Journal of International Law* 40 (1946), 390–94.

True to form, Streit viewed proponents of world government as rivals rather than potential allies. Whereas his focus remained fixed on the Atlantic democracies, they envisaged something more expansive in scope, encompassing nations from several regions and with varied political regimes. As Streit explained to Reves in August 1945, "I favor – now as always – reorganizing the world on a federal as opposed to league basis. I have never believed, however, that this can be done with all or most of the nations at once, and I have always favored beginning the process by forming a nuclear union of the democracies ..."[17]

The result is that Streit found himself increasingly isolated in 1945. Whatever its merits, his "nuclear union" of democracies neglected the realities of the recent war: The United States had been a member of global alliance that included the Soviet Union and China.[18] No less importantly, many Americans hoped the wartime alliance would continue into peacetime – a hope embodied in the UNO, whose birth and initial steps dominated public and political opinion. Against this background, Streit's disinterest in, if not disdain for, the UNO (dismissed as simply another League of Nations); his emphasis on democracy, which could only alienate the Soviets; and his seeming disregard for the non-Western world, all seemed out of step with the tide of international politics. While Federal Union's "slant on world government is challenging and stimulating," the Rockefeller Foundation admitted in a 1945 assessment, "efforts such as Streit's are breaking down rather than building confidence in UNO." An erstwhile supporter was even more damning. Streit's "backdrop in concrete world politics had left him ..." Together, his "nuclearism" and "Union of the West," meant Streit "is now quite generally regarded as a reactionary internationalist."[19]

Streit's isolation also manifested itself in the emergence of rival organizations. The most prominent one was Americans United for World Organization (AUWO). Founded in 1944, the AUWO soon attracted growing numbers of wartime Federal Union members and supporters who joined at the national and local levels. Significantly, its position fused world government, federalism, and the UNO. Having initially

---

[17] LOC, CKS, Box I: 84, file: "R" Miscellany, Streit to Emery Reves, August 8, 1945.

[18] A point Sumner Welles made in *Where Are We Heading?* (New York: Harper & Brothers, 1946), 46–48.

[19] RAC, Office of the Messrs. Rockefeller Records, World Affairs, Series Q, Box 24, file 206, Arthur Packard to Nelson Rockefeller, "Federal Union, Inc.," November 9, 1945; and NYPL, Student Federalists Records, Box 2, file 5, to Thomas Hughes to Neal, October 24, 1945.

championed US endorsement of the Dumbarton Oaks proposals, the AUWO afterward called for the establishment of "democratic world government in which sovereignty is pooled by all." The instrument of this incipient world government would be the UNO, following the revision of its Charter along vaguely federalist lines to strengthen the institution's authority over individual nations.[20] Reflecting this advocacy, the AUWO, in 1946, changed its name to Americans United for World Government (AUWG).

From Streit's perspective, the AUWO's stance amounted to sacrificing federalism on the altar of a failed experiment. Convinced since the 1930s that international organizations of sovereign nation-states were ineffective and even counter-productive, he did not believe the UNO could be meaningfully reformed. Here, it certainly did not help matters that Clark Eichelberger played a leading role in the AUWO from the beginning. As a driving force in the wartime Commission to Study the Organization of the Peace (CSOP), Eichelberger, to recall, had exploited federalist language to re-legitimize international organizations after the League of Nation's perceived failure.[21] For Streit, a vigorous response to the AUWO was required.

THE DUBLIN CONFERENCE, OCTOBER 1945

Streit, in fact, had been at work on such a response for some time. In December 1944, he began discussing the idea of a conference of prominent figures to "work out a plan for a Federal Union of the Democracies" to be published at the end of the war. The aim was to steer thinking about the postwar international order in the direction of an Atlantic federal union. As co-organizer, Streit could count on Owen Roberts, the Supreme Court justice, whose swing vote in the 1930s had helped to save elements of Roosevelt's New Deal. As a conservative voice on a liberal-dominated court, Roberts was looking to retire and would do so in 1945. No less

---

[20] PUFL, Hugh Moore Fund Collection, Box 5, file 9, "Report of Special Committee on Purpose, Aims, and Program of the 'Americans United for World Organization,'" May 22, 1944; and LOC, CKS, Box I: 47, "Statement of Principles Endorsed by the Executive Committee of Americans United," September 27, 1945.

[21] For the AUWO/AUWG, see Andrew Johnstone, "Americans Disunited: Americans United for World Organization and the Triumph of Internationalism," *Journal of American Studies* 44 (2010), 1–18; and Wesley T. Wooley, *Alternatives to Anarchy: American Supranationalism since World War II* (Bloomington: Indiana University Press, 1988), 3–59.

importantly, he had earlier been won over to Federal Union following several talks with Streit.[22] With Roberts's backing, Streit began organizing a conference of thirty or so invitees to be held in his home state of Montana. Its purpose, the invitation cagily explained, was not to replace the nascent UNO, whose inability to ensure postwar "peace, freedom and prosperity" was deemed self-evident, but to supplement it "with a nuclear Union of its more democratic members."[23]

Among the invitees was Grenville Clark, a wealthy Wall Street lawyer with an impeccable East Coast elite lineage. In 1940, Clark had circulated a draft constitution for a "Federation of Free Peoples" which, while expressing admiration for Streit's *Union Now*, proposed something looser than the latter's "international government with wide purposes and extensive powers."[24] Afterward, the two kept in touch, and it was Clark who introduced Streit to Roberts. By early 1945, however, Clark harbored serious doubts about Streit and his project. Streit's "ideas," he advised Roberts in response to the conference invitation, "would have to be much modified" to ensure success. "I like Streit and admire Streit very much ...," he added, but "I have repeatedly heard it said by very good people that he is unduly dogmatic and 'difficult'; so much so that they just can't work with him." But personality traits aside, basic policy differences separated the two – as Streit reported to Roberts. While sharply criticizing the Dumbarton Oaks proposals, Clark believed the UNO, however inadequate its initial form, constituted the only viable instrument for international government. The priority, therefore, must be revising the UNO's Charter.[25]

Not surprisingly, Clark sought to steer Streit's proposed conference toward his position. In a letter to Roberts in May 1945, Clark suggested a gathering of "a relatively small group of like-minded people" in the Northeast to discuss the UNO and especially proposals for "revamping it by amendment or framing an entirely new plan ..." Tellingly, Clark's

---

[22] LOC, CKS, Box I: 6, Streit to Grenville Clark, August 7, 1941.
[23] LOC, CKS, Box I: 42, "Confidential Memo," Streit, December 26, 1944; and "The Call for the Clearwater Conference," undated.
[24] NYPL, CFWG (NY), Box 20, file 5, Grenville Clark, "A Memorandum with Regard to a New Effort to Organize Peace and Containing a Proposal for a 'Federation of Free Peoples' ...," January 1940.
[25] DUAM, Grenville Clark Papers, Box 172, file 19, Grenville Clark to Owen Roberts, February 6 and May 8, 1945; and LOC, CKS. Box I: 45, Clearwater Conference correspondence, Streit to Roberts, February 9, 1945. Also see PUFL, Hugh Moore Fund Collection, Box 4, file 5, Grenville Clark to Hugh Moore, September 9, 1944.

list of suggested invitees omitted proponents of Atlantic union aside from Streit. Roberts reacted with sympathy to the idea of a conference to consider "a better and more workable form of [UNO] organization," placing Streit in a quandary as he counted on Roberts's prestige to entice invitees.[26] Streit, in fact, harbored hopes of convincing Roberts to become Federal Union's director once he retired from the Supreme Court. Accordingly, Streit agreed to cooperate with Clark while at the same time working to counter his influence by expanding both the list of invitees to include trusted supporters and the agenda to include Atlantic federal union. The project of revising the UNO, he apprised Roberts, must not exclude the possibility of "forming within it [the UNO] a nuclear Union of the free people guaranteeing its citizens at least the individual liberty that our Bill of Rights does."[27]

The immediate upshot was the "Dublin Conference" held over five days in October 1945 at Clark's estate in Dublin, New Hampshire. Norman Cousins, who participated, would remember the conference as an "unforgettable experience" that "commanded international attention."[28] If the assessment was perhaps overblown, the *New York Times*, which closely covered the conference, remarked positively on the "caliber" of the fifty or so participants ranging from university administrators and academics to lawyers, journalists, commentators, business leaders, and political activists. Although no minutes appear to exist, the conference produced two published reports. The majority report, signed by Clark among others, affirmed the UNO must either be developed into or be replaced by a "world federal government" endowed with "closely defined and limited power adequate to prevent war and designed to restore and strengthen the freedoms that are the inalienable right of man." The minority report, drafted by Streit and co-signed by Roberts, endorsed the goal of "world federal government" but went on to beseech the United States to "explore the possibilities of forming a nuclear union with nations where individual liberty exists, as a step toward the projected

---

[26] LOC, CKS, Box I: 45, file: Clearwater Conference correspondence, Owen Roberts to Streit, June 2, 1945 with attachment: Clark to Roberts, May 28, 1945.
[27] LOC, CKS, Box I: 51, file: Dublin, New Hampshire Conference, Streit to Owen Roberts, August 3, 1945; and file: Clearwater Conference correspondence, Streit to Roberts, May 29, 1945.
[28] Norman Cousins, "Grenville Clark: A Man of All Seasons" in Norman Cousins and J. Garry Clifford, eds., *Memoirs of a Man: Grenville Clarke* (New York: Norton, 1975), 4–5.

world government."[29] Streit had reasons to be pleased with the conference. Although in the minority, he had prevented the clamor for "world
federal government" through the UNO from quelling the idea of Atlantic
federal union.

But however pleased Streit might be, the conference results exacerbated
a crisis within Federal Union. Trouble within the latter had been brewing
for some time, one sign of which (as mentioned) was the AUWG's
growing appeal. By mid-1945, Federal Union members were openly
discussing the possibility of cooperating and even of merging with
the new organization. Significantly, the AUWG's appeal reflected dissatisfaction with Streit's unbending insistence on nuclear union. Writing
in October 1945, Harris Wofford, the leader of Student Federalists
(affiliated with Federal Union) and future civil rights activist and US
senator, pleaded with Streit to be more flexible. "We must all stick
together, act together, or none of us will achieve anything. What we must
each search for now is that area of agreement, that common ground
which can and must be found for all Federalists." Tellingly, Wofford
announced he now supported a "w.f.u." (world federal union), rather
than Streit's more circumscribed project.[30]

The Dublin conference brought the dissatisfaction within Federal
Union to a head. At least one Board member reproached Streit for not
consulting with them beforehand. But the real tensions concerned policy.
In preparation for a Board meeting in mid-November 1945, Streit circulated a paper framing "nuclear union" as a "happy medium" between
those who supported the UNO and those who wanted to transform it into
a world government.[31] At the Board meeting, though, Streit admitted this
position represented a compromise forced upon him at Dublin – and one
he deemed misguided. World government was "terribly dangerous,"
Streit contended, because "it would split the world into two camps" –
a criticism, ironically, several Board members returned against Streit's
own position. More importantly, Board members balked at endorsing
"nuclear union." "I am all for Federal Union," a member from St. Louis
asserted,

[29] "UNO Under Fire," *New York Times*, October 18, 1945, 17; and "Declaration of the
Dublin, N.H. Conference," *New York Times*, October 17, 1945, 4.
[30] LOC, CKS, Box I: 51, file: Dublin, New Hampshire Conference, Harris Wofford to Streit,
October 15, 1945.
[31] LOC, CKS, Box I: 47, file: Convention 1945, Streit to FU Board, November 8, 1945.

but I can't see how in the world you can have a Federal Union organization, how you can expect to bring it out and leave out Russia and China, who are our Allies; and if you enter an agreement with Great Britain, and the other so-called democracies, and omit, or don't even invite Russia and China, then you're just inviting a lot of trouble for the world.

As a weary Wofford recognized "there is no real compromise which can be reached at this Board meeting."[32]

The Board meeting announced a tumultuous annual convention in Pittsburgh later the same month. Two memoranda were circulated to the delegates in advance. The first one, written by Neal Potter, a government economist, advanced three arguments: that "nuclear union" was unpopular with the public and with most federalists, that the threat of nuclear war made it imperative to conceive of federation ("world government") in global and universal terms, and that the UNO offered promising possibilities on this score. The AUWG, Potter pointedly noted, has "done a very good job backing the UNO as well as the ultimate objective of world government, and there is no reason why we cannot follow the same line." The second written memorandum, written by John F. Schmidt, an army officer, favored Streit's "nuclear method." World government, it argued, was impossible with the Soviet Union because Moscow would not cooperate and, if it did, the resulting union could not function democratically. World government, Schmidt entreated, cannot come at the expense of democracy, adding that what Potter proposed "is not merely a change of tactics: it is the abandonment of our principles."[33]

With divisions running deep, the convention delegates passed two resolutions whose compatibility was questionable. One created a committee to "inquire into the possibility of effecting mutually acceptable reciprocal arrangements with Americans United for World Government or other organizations." The second resolution proposed to shift Federal Union from its "present membership emphasis to a magazine publishing emphasis" – a magazine directed by Streit. If nothing else, it was a tacit admission that the attempts to build a nation-wide structure with local chapters had failed. But it also amounted to a bid to maintain control of

---

[32] A copy of the lengthy Board minutes is in LOC, CKS, Box I: 41, file: Board: Meetings General 1945.

[33] LLUI, UWF Papers, Box B 13, Margretta Austin (FU executive director) to Convention delegates, November 6, 1945 with attachments: "Memorandum in Opposition to Federal Union 'Nuclear' Policy," Neal Potter, November 6, 1945; and "Memorandum in Support of the Nuclear Method of World Union," John F. Schmidt, November 6, 1945.

Federal Union. Frustrated with what he perceived as an effort to sideline him, Streit had for some time been contemplating a change of approach that would center the organization's activities more squarely on him. Federal Union, he ventured in August 1945, should focus less on precise policy and more on disseminating "our principles of liberty and union. We should stress how peace depends on individual liberty and the importance of moving the unity of sovereignty from the state to the individual."[34]

OUTLASTING THE WORLD GOVERNMENT MOVEMENT, 1945–1950

Streit had no intention of pursuing discussions with the AUGW in good faith. In an internal paper circulated in November 1945, he maintained a merger was desirable solely on Federal Union's terms, which meant accepting "our basic principles."[35] The committee created to examine the subject, though, arrived at a different conclusion, recommending in January 1946 that Federal Union "join" the AUWG. The latter's "size, resources, and policy" when taken together, it affirmed, "represents the greatest opportunity we have ever had to get things done." Soon afterward, Federal Union members were encouraged to join the AUGW as individuals. An unhappy Streit denounced the report as "inaccurate, misleading, and gave the impression that the FU had practically folded up." In seeking to mobilize opposition, Streit maintained a merger would jeopardize Federal Union's tax-exempt status as a nonpolitical organization and would undermine plans for a magazine by discouraging Federal Union members to take out subscriptions. Both arguments were dubious: Federal Union's activities were no less political than those of the AUWG, and a merger with the latter would just as likely expand as curtail the pool of potential subscribers.[36]

If Streit resisted a merger, it was principally because he believed the AUWG's position to be incompatible with his own. And as the better-financed and more active organization, the AUWG would be well-

---

[34] LOC, CKS, Box II: 25, "The Board of Directors of Federal Union ... July 14th and 15th, 1945." For the resolutions, see Box I: 42, Federal Union press release, undated but November 1945.

[35] LOC, CKS, Box I: 47, Streit to FU Board, November 8, 1945.

[36] UM, Clarence Streit Papers, Box 9, file 10, FU (Chair) to members, May 23, 1946; and LOC, CKS, Box I: 40, file: Board correspondence, 1944–1947, Streit to A. J. Priest, January 26, 1946, emphasis in original.

positioned to impose its terms on Federal Union. Significantly, in doubling down on the differences between approaches Streit emphasized two related elements. One was the centrality of personal liberty and freedom to Atlantic federal union. While the AUWG "avoided taking any stand on liberty that might cause controversy," he lectured a Board member, Federal Union affirms "individual liberty is the surest basis for peace." The other element was the comparative advantages of democracy. The "structure of dictatorship makes for war," he maintained in a *New York Times* letter, "whereas the structure of a Government that holds civil liberty supreme serves to guarantee the citizens and the world alike against aggression by that Government." Accordingly, a "Union of the free" offered "the best way to defend the blessings of individual liberty, and therefore peace."[37] An emphasis on these two elements, in turn, allowed Streit to concentrate attention on the Soviet Union, whose inclusion in universal proposals for world government he recognized as a potential weakness at a time of growing public concern about Moscow's ambitions. There is "no possibility of our forming a federal union with Russia" he lectured a friend in 1946, adding that with a union of "the advanced western democracies … we would get enough power behind freedom to remove any danger of Russian aggression …"[38]

Streit succeeded in preventing a merger. Instead, in early 1946 Federal Union and AUWG agreed to what amounted to a nonaggression pact: Each organization would promote its respective position while refraining from attacking the other – a constraint Streit would have difficulty respecting.[39] Although doing little to staunch the exodus of Federal Union members, the pact did ensure the organization's continued independent existence.

At the time, Streit and Federal Union appeared to have missed an opportunity to join a burgeoning movement. In February 1947, the AUWG merged with several other organizations to form the United World Federalists (UWF). Soon afterward, the UWF claimed to have 17,000 dues-paying members and over 200 chapters, figures that rose to 46,755 members and an astonishing 720 chapters by 1949. If such numbers are almost certainly inflated, the UWF did appear to have the

---

[37] LOC, CKS, Box I: 47, file: Convention 1944 General, Streit to A. L. Priest, November 9, 1945; and Streit, "Individual Freedom: This, with Unity, Regarded as Surest Way to Peace," *New York Times*, March 31, 1946, 80.

[38] LOC, CKS, Box I: 85, file: Sick, Emil, Streit to Emil Sick, November 15, 1946.

[39] LOC, CKS, Box I: 40, Streit to Ulric Bell (AUWG), May 21, 1946.

wind in its sails. In addition to a diverse group of influential backers, among them Grenville Clark, Norman Cousins, Cass Canfield, and the journalist-broadcaster Raymond Swing, the UWF attracted considerable media and political attention across the United States. Gabriel Almond, a leading political scientist at Yale, wrote admiringly of its range of activities, which included "mass petition campaigns, meetings and revivals, special work with church and student groups, as well as aggressive lobbying at both the state and national level." By 1949, Almond reported, the UWF could boast that resolutions in favor of world government had been introduced in all forty-eight state legislatures and passed in seventeen of them.[40]

Initially, the UWF's position closely resembled that of the AUWG: "to strengthen the United Nations into a world government of limited powers adequate to prevent war ..."[41] Soon, however, the UWF began striking distinctly Streitian notes. In addition to championing federalism in general, its publicity invoked the US federal system as a model of governance and the 1780s as a pertinent historical precedent, while also calling for a constitutional convention to forge the equivalent of the US Constitution on a global scale. In a book published by Harpers in 1949, Vernon Nash, a UWF vice-president and former Federal Union activist, explained that the "first great demonstration of the practicality of federalism began in the United States in 1787." The Founding Fathers, he continued, "*thought and felt* about their basic problem very much as we do now about ours. They phrased identical concepts in amazingly similar language ..." Nash even downplayed differences with Streit's Federal Union, noting that the UWF's universalism operated more as an ideal than a practical guide as several states would likely decline an invitation to a global constitutional convention.[42]

The UWF, in any case, was only one of several voices promoting world government. Surveying proposals for the latter, Percy Corbett, another Yale political scientist, marveled in 1950 at the scope of the phenomenon. "The drive that we are now witnessing is unique in its vigor and volume." "What was once the dream of poets and philosophers," he added, "has

[40] Gabriel A. Almond, *The American People and Foreign Policy* (New York: Harcourt, Brace, 1950), 219–20. Also see Wittner, *One World or None*, 67–71; and Baratta, *The Politics of World Federation*, I, 235–46.

[41] "6 Groups Project Federalist World," *New York Times*, February 27, 1947, 25.

[42] Vernon Nash, *The World Must Be Governed* (New York: Harper & Brothers, 1949), 27, 51, 174–76. Also see Cord Meyer, Jr., *Peace or Anarchy* (Boston: Little, Brown and Co., 1948).

become a serious factor in politics – something to be reckoned with by those who formulate and execute foreign policy."[43] A draft "world constitution" in 1948 by a committee of prominent academics and intellectuals directed by Robert Hutchins, the University of Chicago's president, figured among the more prominent proposals; others included Grenville Clark's *A Plan for World Peace*, which Canfield eagerly published, and Clark Eichelberger's more UNO-centered and functionalist-inspired approach.[44] As Corbett recognized, moreover, whatever their differences, the proposals all envisaged some form of federalist structure. And if federalism imposed itself as the means to realize world government, it was because it provided a framework for simultaneously preserving and attenuating national sovereignty. Equally telling, Corbett also pointed out that the proposals "rely heavily on the formation of the United States as a precedent," presenting its federal system as an inspiration and sometimes a model.[45]

None of the proposals endorsed Streit's Atlantic federal union and some criticized it.[46] Nevertheless, proponents of world government helped to popularize not only federalist frameworks in general but also, albeit indirectly and even inadvertently, at least some elements of Streit's project. In this sense, even critics of world government could make a contribution. A revealing example is Reinhold Niebuhr, the apostle of a Christian-infused realism, who considered world government to be naïve. "Virtually all arguments for world government," Niebuhr protested in a

---

[43] Percy E. Corbett, "Proposals for World Government before Congress," Yale Institute of International Studies, Memorandum no. 34, March 25, 1950; and Percy E. Corbett, "Congress and Proposals for International Government," *International Organization* 4 (1950), 383–99. Also see Gerard J. Mangone, *The Idea and Practice of World Government* (New York: Columbia University Press, 1951).

[44] Robert M. Hutchins, Guiseppe Antonio Borgese, Mortimer J. Adler et al., *Preliminary Draft of a World Constitution* (Chicago: University of Chicago Press, 1948). Also see Robert L. Tsai, *America's Forgotten Constitutions: Defiant Visions of Power and Community* (Cambridge, MA: Harvard University Press, 2014), 185–217; and Or Rosenboim, *The Emergence of Globalism: Visions of World Order in Britain and the United States, 1939–1950* (Princeton, NJ: Princeton University Press, 2017), 168–208. Grenville Clark, *A Plan for World Peace* (New York: Harper & Brothers, 1950); and DUAM, Grenville Clark Papers, Box 156, file 93, Canfield to Clark, June 13, 1950. Clark M. Eichelberger, "World Government via the United Nations," *Annals of the American Academy of Political and Social Science* 264 (1949), 20–25.

[45] Corbett, "Congress and Proposals for International Government," 390–91.

[46] For example, see Edgar Ansel Mowrer, *Challenge and Decision: A Program for the Times of Crisis Ahead – For World Peace under American Leadership* (New York: McGraw-Hill, 1950), 141–42.

1949 *Foreign Affairs* article, "rest upon the simple presupposition that the desirability of world order proves the attainability of world government." In addition to claiming world government required a pre-existing world community, which could only be built gradually if at all, Niebuhr accused its advocates of being out of sync with current developments in international politics – the UNO's paralysis as well as the developing Cold War.[47] Yet, significantly, Niebuhr's charge of naïveté, echoed by Corbett among others, was directed less at federalist frameworks for international politics (for which he expressed some sympathy) than it was at their association with world/universal government. If such frameworks could be detached from the latter, if they could be adapted to Cold War "realities," then even self-designated realists might give them another look.

As world government monopolized attention, Streit remained confident despite some frustration. Convinced of the soundness of Atlantic federal union, he waited for the interest in world government to subside as its unworkability became evident. Time is on our side, Streit adjudged in 1947, and "[c]oming events, I am confident, will prove this quite fully."[48] His confidence was well placed: The gathering Cold War had sapped the world government movement of much of its vitality by the beginning of the 1950s. In a sign of the times, Cord Meyer, the UWF's youthful and high-minded president, left the organization in 1951 to join the CIA.[49] More to the point, the world government movement's decline, together with Cold War political dynamics, created space for Streit's far less universal, more regional (and Western-centric) project of Atlantic federal Union. As an editorial in *Fortune* magazine suggested in April 1949, "History is Catching Up with 'Union Now.'"[50]

FEDERAL UNION AFTER 1945

The majority of delegates at the October 1945 convention approved the transformation of Federal Union from a chapter-centered into a

---

[47] Reinhold Niebuhr, "The Illusion of World Government," *Foreign Affairs* 27 (1949), 379–88. Also see his *The Children of Light and Children of Darkness: A Vindication of Democracy and a Critique of Its Traditional Defenders* (London: Nisbet & Co., 1945), 105–28.

[48] LOC, CKS, Box I: 40, file: Barr, Stringfellow, 1944–47, Streit to Edgar E. Rand, June 19, 1947.

[49] Wooley, *Alternatives to Anarchy*, 58.

[50] "History Is Catching Up with 'Union Now,'" *Fortune*, April 1949, 77–78.

membership-centered organization. Consistent with its tax-exempt status, achieved after considerable lobbying in 1943, Federal Union's primary mission would remain educational: to promote Atlantic federation and federalism more generally. Still, this re-centering had important implications for the organization. As mentioned, the decision amounted to a tacit abandonment of ambitions to build a nation-wide presence in the form of local chapters. To be sure, existing chapters were not closed down, and over the next several years several new ones would be created, for example, in New York, Syracuse, and Louisville, Kentucky.[51] Now, though, chapters were left entirely on their own. As Streit explained to the head of the Baltimore chapter, Federal Union would no longer devote resources to "local branches" as "[w]e found the latter generally took more effort than the return justified." Given that many chapters were barely active, independence often spelled demise. Significantly, the Baltimore chapter held its final meeting in December 1945.[52] As we shall see in the next chapter, the (few) remaining Federal Union chapters would be absorbed by the Atlantic Union Committee created in 1949.

The postwar version of Federal Union rested on several elements. A board of directors was made up of people possessing some influence or means (or both) such as William Clayton, a businessman and former Under-Secretary of State (sometimes identified as a father of the Marshall Plan); the pollster Elmo Roper; Howard Ditz, a Hollywood publicist; Beardsley Ruml, an economist and chairman of Macy's; Don Dennis, chairman of the Foreign Policy Association; Ted Achilles, a former State Department official; and the wife of Henry Luce's son. In the mid-1970s, the Board counted thirty members, including Percival Brundage, former US budget director; Gale McGee, senator from Wyoming; Edward Teller, the controversial scientist; and Jane Elliget, a prominent education specialist.[53] Another element consisted of Streit devotees, most vitally his wife, Jeanne, who toiled for decades at his side and mostly in his shadow, but also their son Pierre, a journalist. More generally, Streit relied heavily on the volunteer work (and pocketbooks) of middle- and upper-class women, a group he sedulously wooed. A final element comprised staff workers, whose number varied but whose salaries were consistently

---

[51] For example, see "Chapter of Federal Union Formed in Louisville," *The Courier-Journal*, November 13, 1947, 2; and LLUI, UWF Papers, Box 13, file Federal Union, *Federal Union File*, no. 6, February 1948.

[52] LOC, CKS, Box I: 45, file: Chapters General, 1940–45, 1951, Streit to George Schaun, December 23, 1945.

[53] LOC, Percival F. Brundage Papers, Box 15, "Board of Directors, 1974."

below market. This practice reflected Federal Union's limited resources, which spurred Streit to hire women who could be paid less than men. But it was also rooted in Streit's personal relationship to Atlantic federal union, which he viewed not as work but as a calling demanding fervent dedication and financial sacrifices – sacrifices he imposed on himself and his family. One consequence was repeated disappointment, as no board member or staff worker could match Streit's intensity of commitment.

More than anything, Federal Union after 1945 belonged to Streit. He dominated the organization not only as founder and guiding spirit but also in its day-to-day functioning. Streit repeatedly claimed to desire nothing more than to find someone who could relieve him of the burden of directing Federal Union; hardly surprisingly, he never found a "first-rate" person. If financial constraints were certainly a factor, Streit's imperious bent posed greater obstacles. Intolerant of dissent, he sought disciples more than collaborators, quietly pushing out people who, like Wofford Harris, offered to cooperate with Federal Union on equal terms.[54] At the same time, Streit had difficulty delegating, suspecting others of lacking the commitment required to remain true to the course he had set out. As late as 1975, Percival Brundage lamented to another Board member that any decisions

we may make will be unimportant unless Clarence ... is willing, and even anxious, not to interfere with any steps that may be agreed upon. He must realize by now that it's hard to keep his hands off any policies related to his life's work, but this will be essential for any reorganization that will be effective and in order to get the right men for the job.[55]

If Streit hoped a recentered Federal Union would make his life easier, the reality proved more complicated. In fusing Federal Union's purpose so closely with his own, Streit became more responsible than ever for the organization's continued existence. And after 1945, as before, this meant fund-raising. "Do you know what would be your hardest organization problem if you occupied my place," Streit lectured members in 1958. "To keep our cause financed."[56] The organization was perennially short of funds, compelling Streit to embark on recurrent financing campaigns. In early 1952, Federal Union had an $11,000 deficit, covered by a bank loan using donated stocks as collateral. Faced with another deficit in late 1958,

[54] LOC, CKS, Box I: 91, file: Wofford, Harris, Jr, Streit to Harris, May 18, 1947.
[55] LOC, Percival F. Brundage Papers, Box 15, Brundage to Don Dennis, September 8, 1975.
[56] UM, Clarence Streit Papers, Box 9, file 12, Streit circular, March 1958.

Federal Union's treasurer emphasized the "seriousness of the situation, and said that if we continued on this downward path we would soon be insolvent." In response, Streit, as he reported early the next year, chose "to abandon all work" in order "to redouble my efforts to buckle our budget." Not much had changed several years later, in November 1964, when Board members discussed yet another deficit, with Streit promising to launch a "financial drive" to raise $40,000 before the end of the year.[57]

With financial difficulties in mind, it is tempting to frame Federal Union's postwar history in terms of crisis, of inadequate means and wasted idealism. Frederick Schuman, a leading political scientist and wartime supporter, did just this in a 1952 book. Federal Union's spirit, he wrote, was imbued "with the fervor of conversion to a creative idea, the frustration of functioning with funds and personnel never adequate to the tasks in hand, the discouragement of public apathy, and the inspiration of trying to save the world from its own folly."[58] Yet however tempting, such a framing risks overlooking Streit's perseverance as well as Federal Union's staying power – both manifest in fund-raising. To be sure, Streit never succeeded in persuading a wealthy donor or major foundation to finance Federal Union, although he did, as we shall see, receive a one-time award from the Rockefeller Foundation in 1965. Nevertheless, Streit did manage to raise enough money to endow Federal Union with a respectable budget: Hovering around $80,000–$85,000/year for much of the 1950s, it rose to $134,000 in 1965 before falling back to just over $100,000 in the mid-1970s. All told, between 1939 and 1976, Federal Union raised $3,245,187 for an average of $85,000/year.[59]

Writing in 1956 to his former boss and *New York Times*' owner, Arthur Hays Sulzberger, Streit boasted his movement had raised over $1 million since 1939, and had done so in "the hardest way."[60] Some

---

[57] PUFL, Hugh Moore Fund Collection, Box 6, file 1, Streit to Hugh Moore, January 21, 1952; HTPL, William Clayton Papers, Box 123, file 5, "Minutes ... Board of Directors Meeting June 20, 1958"; and Streit to William Clayton, January 3, 1959; and LOC, CKS, I: 43, file: Board Meetings General, 1959–1965, "Minutes ... Board of Directors Meeting, November 21, 1964."

[58] Frederick L. Schuman, *The Commonwealth of Man: An Inquiry into Power Politics and World Government* (New York: Alfred A. Knopf, 1952), 432.

[59] Figures compiled from various files in LOC, CKS, Boxes I: 41 and 42. Also see Box I: 40, file: Biographical Material, "1939–76 Financial Data Compiled for Nobel Peace Prize Nominators Clarence and Jeanne Defrance Streit," undated.

[60] NYPL, NYTCR, Arthur Hays Sulzberger Papers, Box 171, file 9, Streit to Sulzberger, October 1956.

money came from membership dues, but given Federal Union's limited membership (never above 8,000, not all of whom paid dues), Streit needed to find other sources. One source consisted of a coterie of perennial donors, many of whom expressed bemused admiration at Streit's persistence: people such as Clayton; Roper; Harry Scherman, the president of the Book-of-the-Month Club; and Hugh Moore, the president of the Dixie Cup Company and activist on population issues. Another source consisted of a panoply of people, some Federal Union members, others not, who contributed amounts ranging from $100 to $1,000, often in response to a direct plea from Streit.[61] Together, these sources provided Federal Union with the means to promote Streit's project.

PROMOTING FEDERAL UNION: *FREEDOM & UNION*

To recall, Federal Union's November 1945 convention had decided to concentrate its educational efforts on a magazine. For Streit, a magazine offered several advantages: a partial return to journalism, his first profession; an alternative to the frustrations of running a national organization; and a distinct voice for his project. He would also be in firm control. Bodies such as Federal Union, he confided in 1946, "either split apart on such questions [as policy], or spend too much time arguing them out within the organization." A magazine, by contrast, promised a more managed debate, one undertaken "not by half-informed people but by leading thinkers whose names will attract readers." That Streit intended to impose a "strong editorial line" is clear from his insistence on possessing sole authority to select the editorial board.[62] "[V]ery few facts are able to tell their own story," he explained to Henry Luce, citing John Stuart Mill, "without comments to bring out their meaning." And Streit's magazine would supply these much-needed comments.[63]

From the outset, Streit targeted a fairly exclusive audience. The magazine, he wrote William Bullitt in December 1946, aimed at "reaching policy makers and those in a position to influence the masses." This choice was partly dictated by scarce resources: With a magazine, he

---

[61] For example, see BLCU, Declaration of Atlantic Unity, Box 16, file: Federal Union – 1953, "Federal Union, Inc. Chief Donors," undated but 1953.

[62] LOC, CKS, Box III: 9 file 1, Streit to Arthur Moore, May 26, 1946; and Box I: 40, file: Board Correspondence, 1944–1947, Streit to Board, November 27, 1945.

[63] NYHS, Henry R. Luce Papers, Box 102, file 4, Streit to Luce, August 16, 1946.

briefed Bullitt, "we can get the greatest influence with the little money we have."[64] But it also reflected his understanding of how US politics worked. There was considerable talk at the time of elite domination: The Yale sociologist C. Wright Mills, for example, famously identified a cohesive "power elite" of political, economic, and military "chieftains" who discreetly determined policy.[65] But while fully convinced of the importance of elites, Streit, because of his outsider status and his journalist experience, appreciated the value of visibility. Political ideas (and projects) like his own had to gain public traction. Scholars have highlighted the postwar preoccupation with public opinion manifest in the rise of polling, which promised to uncover what the public really wanted. But instead of a vast and elusive public, Streit targeted what Elmo Roper identified as the "great disseminators" – the 500–1,000 people who "are respected and listened to" at the national level. For Streit, these people collectively formed the public dimension of politics, functioning as a forum but also as a tribunal, capable of conferring legitimacy on policy proposals.[66]

Moving quickly, in the opening months of 1946 Streit circulated a prospectus for a monthly magazine. Tentatively titled "Headlight," the magazine would be "a Journal of Opinion and Discussion of the great life-and-death issues of our time," prominent among them the question of "[h]ow to advance the basic American principle of individual liberty through federal union beyond its present limits."[67] A principal purpose of the prospectus was to raise funds, which proved challenging. Streit initially hoped to interest a major foundation, but the Carnegie, Ford, Rockefeller, and Whitney foundations all turned him down. Consequently, Streit embarked on a rapid fund-raising campaign, tapping into his network of friends and contacts. Over the next few months, a number of well-known people (John Foster Dulles, Harold Ickes, Alf

---

[64] YUL, William C. Bullitt Papers, Box 79, file 2038, Streit to Bullitt, December 16, 1946.
[65] C. Wright Mills, *The Power Elite* (New York: Oxford University Press, 1956).
[66] Elmo Roper, "Forward," in Elihu Katz and Paul Félix Lazarsfeld, *Personal Influence: The Part Played By People in the Flow of Mass Communication* (New York: Free Press, 1955), xix. For public opinion and polling, see Sarah Igo, *The Averaged American: Surveys, Citizens, and the Making of a Mass Public* (Cambridge, MA: Harvard University Press, 2014). Also see James N. Rosenau, *Public Opinion and Foreign Policy* (New York: Random House, 1961).
[67] RAC, Office of the Messrs. Rockefeller Records, World Affairs, Series Q, Box 24, file 206, Streit to Nelson Rockefeller, March 15, 1946, with attachment: "A New Illustrated Monthly Magazine Tentative Called Headlight …," Streit, undated. Also HLSL, Manley O. Hudson Papers, Box 22, file 4, Streit to Hudson, March 11, 1946.

Landon, Walter Lippmann, Harry Scherman, William Shirer, Arthur Sulzberger) donated funds, signed up as "charter subscribers," and/or offered public endorsements. Others, such as the journalists Stringfellow Barr and Herbert Agar and the business magazine executive Russell Davenport, agreed to act as contributing editors.[68]

By the end of 1946, Streit had raised enough money to launch a monthly magazine now entitled *Freedom & Union* with 8,000 paid subscribers (many of them Federal Union members) and an initial run print-run of 20,000. The magazine, Streit declared in the first issue, "will champion the principle of individual liberty, equality & fraternity through an ever-peacefully-expanding federal union of the free, beginning with the new Atlantis." A variety of pieces filled out the issue, including a forum on world government with contributions from Grenville Clark and senators Carl Hatch and Elbert Thomas, among others; an article by Davenport on federalism and economic freedom; a survey by Roper of promising polling results on US attitudes toward world government; an essay by Owen Roberts on the UNO's limits; and the first in a series of "New Federalist" papers, modeled on the 1787 Federalist Papers, making the case for Federal Union as a better alternative to "a bloc, alliance, league or confederation."[69] Marking the event, Luce's *Time* magazine reported that "Streit has gathered an impressive array of aides, for most of whom the monthly is a labor of love."[70]

Although Streit succeeded in raising sufficient funds to launch the magazine, the financial situation remained precarious. Publishing a magazine, he remarked in 1967, "has been to me an annual miracle," given the lack of resources.[71] Streit predictably found himself devoting considerable time and energy to fund-raising – time and energy he would have preferred to invest elsewhere. Limited finances, moreover, forced Streit to trim his ambitions for *Freedom & Union*. For example, the magazine could not hire the managing editor initially identified because the salary offered was too low. Instead, Streit typically turned to "a woman I might get at a salary we could afford to pay," hiring Helen Hamer, who possessed considerable professional experience in the magazine industry.[72] In times

[68] LOC, CKS, Box I: 101, file: History General, 1946. "Freedom and Union. Illustrated Monthly Magazine," undated.
[69] *Freedom & Union*, vol. 1, no. 1, October 1946.
[70] "The Press: Streit and Straight," *Time*, September 23, 1946.
[71] LOC, CKS, Box I: 4, file: Alphabetical correspondence, 1967–1969, Streit to Robert Aron, June 8, 1967.
[72] LOC, CKS, Box I: 44, file: Cessna, Ralph, 1946, Streit to Ralph Cessna, July 20, 1946.

of financial crunch, Streit's reflex was to cut staff and salaries (including his own), rather than reduce either *Freedom & Union*'s length or frequency of publication. While staving off financial disaster, these cuts compelled Streit to assume much of the burden of running the magazine. As for Hamer, she finally quit in 1955 after "nine years of devoted service."[73]

Notwithstanding the difficulties, *Freedom & Union* would appear regularly for over three decades. This itself was no mean achievement: The overwhelming majority of magazines quickly failed. Indeed, the magazine industry in the United States became increasingly competitive after 1945 as the dominance of a handful of general interest publications, such as *Life* and *Time*, gave way to a proliferation of specialist ones. True, overall readership rose but less so proportionately than the growth in magazine numbers, resulting in fierce competition for readers and subscriptions.[74] *Freedom & Union*'s longevity in this environment owed much to Streit's tireless efforts. Along with fund-raising, Streit mustered much of the magazine's content, writing editorials and articles as well as soliciting contributions from people on both sides of the Atlantic, including Gardner Cowles, Michel Debré, Livingston Hartley, Christian Herter, Estes Kefauver, Cord Meyer, Nelson Rockefeller, and Adlai Stevenson. Finding sufficient content was handicapped by the inability to offer contributors anything but gift subscriptions to the magazine.[75] Streit, meanwhile, worked hard to get the magazine in the hands of influential people, providing free copies to Congress members as well as to "key leaders in various national business, farm, labor, veterans, women's and other organizations." "All this free controlled circulation of ours," he reported in 1956, "is carefully selected, high quality, and gets, we believe, good readership."[76]

As expected, Streit kept a firm editorial hand on the magazine. If open in principle to opposing views, he reacted allergically to criticisms of his Atlantic federal union project. In 1947, Streit forced out several

---

[73] LOC, CKS, Box 1: 41, file: Board meetings general, 1955, Janice Holland (FU) to Helen Hamer, November 9, 1955.

[74] David Abrahamson, *Magazine-Made America: The Cultural Transformation of the Postwar Periodical* (Cresskill, NJ: Hampton Press, 1996), 2–30; and Theodore Peterson, *Magazines in the Twentieth Century* (Urbana: University of Illinois Press, 1964), 44–79.

[75] For example, Streit offered Quincy Wright six gift subscriptions for Freedom & Union in return for permission to print a revised version of an article published elsewhere. See UOC, Quincy Wright Papers, Box 49, file 10, Streit to Wright, September 3, 1954.

[76] LOC, CKS, Box I: 93, Streit to Betty Ruth White, February 11, 1956.

contributing editors, including Stringfellow Barr, a popular writer, edu-
cator, and world government activist, over policy issues.[77] As editor,
Streit ensured *Freedom & Union* promoted federalism as the solution to
most of the ills of international politics and Atlantic union as the solution
to the particular challenges facing the United States. Although hardly an
objective observer, the *Chicago Tribune* was not far from the mark in
underscoring the magazine's single-minded purpose – or zealotry. "In
reading the latest issue of 'Freedom and Union,'" a 1956 editorial sardonically remarked, "we are struck by the same missionary zeal and same
addiction to a single test of political fitness prevailing among Clarence
Streit and his friends, whose one object in life is to promote the United
States into membership in an Atlantic political union."[78]

Under Streit's determined editorship, *Freedom & Union* fused democracy with liberty and freedom. Its publicity heralded the "basic principles
of individual liberty," not only as the best guarantee of peace and prosperity but also as the shared possession of the "western democracies."[79]
Clearly, the emphasis on liberty and freedom served to distinguish democracy from Soviet communism, which Streit, like so many others, conflated with interwar fascism in a larger totalitarian whole. Streit, though,
went beyond this standard Cold War fare, invoking the principles of
individual liberty and freedom as bulwarks against "national socialism"
defined not as Nazism but as socialism or social democracy, which
appeared as one and the same. From this perspective, Western Europe
seemed especially threatened with social democratic parties either hold-
ing, sharing, or close to governmental power. Singling out France and
Britain, Streit warned James Conant, Harvard University's president, that
"the basic principles of national socialism are winning the war politically,
economically and socially." Similarly, his magazine prospectus spoke of
the dangers of "statism" – of "philosophies that seek to solve economic,
political or social problems by giving the national government more
power over the citizen ..."[80] *Freedom & Union* would oppose the

[77] LOC, CKS, Box I: 40, file: Barr, Stringfellow, 1944–47, Streit to Stringfellow Barr,
August 31, 1947.
[78] "Zealots, Then and Now," *Chicago Tribune*, October 16, 1956, 14.
[79] LOC, CKS, Box I: 101, file: History general, 1946, publicity pamphlet, undated.
[80] LOC, CKS, Box I: 45, file: Clearwater conference 1945, Streit to James B. Conant, April
5, 1945; and RAC, Office of the Messrs. Rockefeller Records, World Affairs, Series Q,
Box 24, file 206, Streit to Nelson Rockefeller, March 15, 1946, with attachment: "A New
Illustrated Monthly Magazine Tentatively Called Headlight ..."

"Marxist character" of politics, whose dangerous advance in Western Europe offered ill omens. Less clear was why Atlantic federal union would blunt rather than sharpen the Marxist/socialist menace to the United States.[81]

Freedom & Union's advertising strategy further prodded Streit into becoming an outspoken advocate of free enterprise, reinforcing the magazine's anti-socialist orientation. Advertising developed into the principal source of revenue for magazines in general after 1945, and, from the beginning, Streit looked to business and especially corporate advertising as a means to finance the magazine.[82] *Freedom & Union*, he assured potential advertisers, "shall uphold the basic principles of free enterprise because we are convinced that they are more conducive to peace and liberty – the things that are important to us – than is state socialism."[83] More concretely, the magazine published an array of articles championing the merits of free enterprise, including a series eventually published in pamphlet form under the title "Free Enterprise Makes for Peace." The pamphlet equated Marxism with socialism, socialism with the nationalization of industry, and nationalization with war. Only free enterprise, which Streit conjoined with democracy, could guarantee peace, and only a federal union of the democracies could guarantee democracy and free enterprise in both Europe and the United States. In sending a copy to Henry Luce, Streit offered the pamphlet as "a good answer to socialism."[84]

Initially, Streit managed to persuade several major companies (Standard Oil, Purina, Heinz, Monsanto) to purchase advertising space. But such successes proved rare. Stanley Resor, the president of J. Walter Thompson Company, a major advertising firm, warned Streit that finding advertisers would be difficult. Powerful business organizations, most notably the National Association of Manufacturers and the Advertising Council, were already actively promoting free enterprise. *Freedom &*

[81] LOC, CKS, Box I: 6, file: Chronological correspondence, 1947–1949, Streit to Clayton Fritchey, June 24, 1947.

[82] David E. Sumner, *The Magazine Century: American Magazines Since 1900* (New York: Peter Lang, 2010), 9.

[83] LOC, CKS, Box I: 101, file: History general 1946, "Why Advertise from the Start in Our Magazine," undated.

[84] BLCU, Declaration of Atlantic Unity, Box 16, file: Federal Union – National, "Free Enterprise Makes for Peace"; and NYPL, Henry R. Luce Papers, Box 102, file 2, Streit to Henry Luce, April 10, 1949.

Union could add little of value to their well-financed efforts.[85] Meanwhile, individual companies, in the best spirit of free enterprise, were motivated by profit and benefit calculations rather than by larger political considerations. "[M]any of us think very highly of the work you are doing," General Electric's vice-president explained to Streit, but company policy precluded "using advertising money to 'support' a cause." Similarly, the president of a machine tool company informed Streit he advertised in order to "keep our company's name favorably before those people who may directly or indirectly be buyers of machine tools" and not "to spread the right principles of simple economics ..."[86]

All told, *Freedom & Union*'s championing of free enterprise paid few financial dividends. Advertising revenue fell well short of hopes, compelling Streit to scale down his ambition to make the magazine a hefty player in the postwar mediascape of international politics in the United States, akin perhaps to *Foreign Affairs*, edited by his friend Hamilton Fish. This raises the question of *Freedom & Union*'s influence – a question difficult to answer. Its subscription numbers remained modest, never exceeding 10,000 per month; that said, Streit targeted not a mass readership but a selected audience. And among this audience, as the *Chicago Tribune* grudgingly acknowledged, *Freedom & Union* distinguished itself as an emphatic advocate of Atlantic union and of federalism more generally. As such, it helped to keep federalist frameworks visible to participants in policy debates, whatever their views on Streit's particular project. "The reason I do subscribe [to *Freedom & Union*]," Walter Lippmann wrote Streit in 1958, "is that while I don't agree [with 'your thesis'] I think you are on the side of the angels nevertheless." Or as Dulles remarked a few years earlier, "I always find it stimulating to read F & U."[87]

---

[85] LOC, CKS, Box I: 93, file: Advertising general 1946–47, Stanley Resor to Streit, November 5, 1947. Also see Laura A. Belmonte, *Selling the American Way: U.S. Propaganda and the Cold War* (Philadelphia: University of Pennsylvania Press, 2008), 116–35; Andrew L. Yarrow, "Selling a New Vision of America to the World: Changing Messages in Early U.S. Cold War Print Propaganda," *Journal of Cold War Studies* 11 (2009), 3–45; and Robert Griffith, "The Selling of America: The Advertising Council and American Politics, 1942–1960," *Business History Review* 57 (1993), 388–412.

[86] LOC, CKS, Box I: 93, file: Advertising general 1949–50, Robert Peace (General Electric) to Streit, September 19, 1950; and Charles Stilwell (Warner & Swasey Co.) to Streit, August 29, 1949.

[87] YUL, Walter Lippmann Papers, Box 104, file 2021, Lippmann to Streit, April 1, 1958; and LOC, CKS, Box I: 21, file: Ford Foundation, 1952, "Some Evidence of Freedom & Union's Influence," undated but 1952.

The question of influence aside, *Freedom & Union*'s understanding of democracy, its anti-socialist and pro-free enterprise emphasis, was ironic for a magazine promoting Atlantic union. Such a definition, after all, could find little resonance in Western Europe, whose democratic politics during the initial postwar decades were infused with various forms of state interventionism in the social and economic realms, lending them a more collectivist bent than in the United States.[88] This irony, in turn, underscores the insular nature of Streit's project, which if anything became more US-centric over time.

PROMOTING FEDERAL UNION: BOOKS

If *Freedom & Union* became Federal Union's primary promotional platform, Streit did not limit his activities to the magazine. Indeed, he remained interested in the potential of the book market, influenced by *Union Now*'s earlier success. To recall, from the beginning Streit had resourcefully promoted the book, carving out a space for his Atlantic federal union project (and federalist frameworks for more generally) in the nascent wartime debate on the postwar international order. *Union Now* soon became something of a bible for Federal Union, a foundational text that Streit embellished with an origins story – a saga of its difficult genesis replete with repeated rejections, uncomprehending editors, and the author's unshakeable and ultimately triumphant resolve. Tellingly, Streit safeguarded the original manuscript, convinced its value as a historical document would rise exponentially with the realization of Atlantic federal union.[89] Arguably more pertinently for this chapter, Streit after 1945 hoped to reproduce *Union Now*'s effects.

Although busy editing *Freedom & Union*, Streit pitched various proposals to Cass Canfield, his editor at Harper. In the early postwar years, Canfield agreed to publish both new and abridged editions of *Union Now*, though only after Federal Union promised to purchase several hundred copies and Streit to forgo royalties. In 1950 Harper also

---

[88] See Martin Conway, *Western Europe's Democratic Age, 1945–1968* (Princeton, NJ: Princeton University Press, 2020); and Charles S. Maier, *Among Empires: American Ascendancy and Its Predecessors* (Cambridge, MA: Harvard University Press, 2006), 191–228.

[89] LOC, CKS, Box I: 6, file: Chronological correspondence, Streit to Mrs. St. John Garwood, May 16, 1950.

published *The New Federalist*, a series of short articles initially published in *Freedom & Union* on various aspects of the Atlantic federal union project and modeled on the *Federalist Papers*. Streit persuaded John Foster Dulles to contribute an introduction welcoming the exploration of "this principle of federalism ... as providing a possible way for free peoples to gain the added strength needed to meet the severe tests that fate may hold in store for them."[90] Canfield, though, did not take up all proposals, declining to publish a collection of Streit's speeches on the grounds that it was commercially unviable; he also poured cold water on Streit's idea of a history of Federal Union's first decade. Instead, Canfield urged Streit to drop such projects and "to take time and do a real book."[91]

Streit eventually accepted Canfield's advice, submitting in August 1953 a proposal for a book to be entitled "Freedom vs Freedom: Your Sovereignty – or Your Nation's." Hardly surprisingly, its argument was that Atlantic federal union alone could ensure the collective future of the free nations and peoples. Streit, in fact, had signed a contract for such a book in 1942 but the burden of running Federal Union sidelined the project. "Now I can finish the job," he assured Canfield, "and greatly improve on it, – and events in the 10 years that have elapsed have served to strengthen its theme, and make it more timely."[92] In a fund-raising letter, Streit insisted "I can write today a better book than *Union Now*," one exposing the "confusion in thought" among Americans regarding national sovereignty:

This confusion leads men to conclude that because the independence of their nation has contributed to their freedom as individuals, any transfer of its rights to a broader inter-state government, however, freely formed, must necessarily involve a sacrifice of their rights as individual men. They thus unwittingly sacrifice to the sovereignty of the state not only their lives and liberties but all the freedom and peace they could reasonably gain by instituting new democratic government in the international community where anarchy now rules, and dictatorship prowls.[93]

---

[90] Owen Roberts, John F. Schmidt, and Clarence Streit, *The New Federalist* (New York: Harper & Brothers, 1950), xvii; and SMLPU, John Foster Dulles Papers, Box 50, reel 17, Dulles to Streit, January 18, 1950. Dulles agreed to forgo royalties. See, SMLPU, John Foster Dulles Papers, Box 50, reel 17, Dulles to Streit, March 29, 1950.

[91] PUFL, Selected Papers of Harper & Brothers, Box 28, file 30, Canfield notes, "Streit," July 28, 1948.

[92] PUFL, Selected Papers of Harper & Brothers, Box 29, file 3, Streit to Canfield, August 5, 1953; and file 4, "Atlantic or Freedom Against Itself?" Streit, November 9, 1953.

[93] HTPL, William Clayton Papers, Box 96, file 2, "The Problem I Face in Writing a New Book," Streit, August 23, 1953.

More prosaically, Streit presented the book to Federal Union's board of directors as a potential answer to the organization's financial difficulties.[94]

Canfield proved receptive, quickly offering Streit a contract. If Federal Union's agreement to buy at least 500 copies certainly helped, the Harper editor appeared genuinely enthusiastic. An internal assessment in 1954 of the first draft judged it "a much broader book than Union Now," adding that "it is much less of a direct exhortation for Atlantic Union than the last book was."[95] For Canfield, the appeal of Streit's book reflected his ongoing interest in world government and federalism, as well as the hope of finding common ground among its diverse advocates. Complaining to Gardner Cowles, a well-connected magazine editor, that the programs of organizations such as Federal Union and UWF "have become too set," Canfield framed Streit's new book as an opportunity for "a new look at the subject of international federalism and analysis of the many problems this topic raises ..." As a first step, Canfield proposed to form a small study group, similar to those associated with the Council on Foreign Relations (of which Canfield was a longtime member), at whose meetings "all the outs to any plan for federation would be frankly discussed and re-examined."[96]

Although Canfield's study group never materialized, Streit's book did appear in the spring of 1954 under the title *Freedom Against Itself*. Streit constructed the book around a paradox. On the one hand, freedom, never concretely defined but instead assumed to correspond to democracy and US democracy, in particular, spawned inventiveness, a claim Streit sought to demonstrate by attaching a lengthy list of inventions by free peoples (Americans, British, and French) since the late eighteenth century. The result was spectacular technological progress shared by all. On the other hand, this progress was not matched by advances in the political realm. Indeed, freedom, in the form of a counter-productive commitment to national sovereignty, actively worked against political progress, predictably defined as an Atlantic federal union. "For generations now our freedom has been working simultaneously to pull men together and to pull them apart," the book affirmed. "While it unites them through the

[94] LOC, CKS, Box II: 25, file 3, "Federal Union, Inc ... Board of Directors ... June 25, 1953."
[95] PUFL, Selected Papers of Harper & Brothers, Box 29, file 5, Memo to CC, January 13, 1954.
[96] BLCU, Harper & Row Collection, Series II, Box 187, Canfield to Gardner Cowles, June 22 and 19, 1954.

machines its inventiveness produces, it divides them by the political policies it favors. With its right hand it creates an Atlantic community; with its left it keeps this community ungoverned, a prey to anarchy." The solution was both obvious and urgent: "Freedom must break through the shell of unlimited national sovereignty, or be destroyed by it. There is no other choice."[97]

Predictably, Streit threw himself into the task of promoting his new book. I am "working to get this book off to the best possible start," he wrote Bullitt in early 1954. "The Lord knows it will take a really big jolt to move public opinion. But I believe it can be done."[98] Along with pressuring Canfield and Harper to do more, Streit repeated much of the formula devised earlier for *Union Now*: He sent copies to an expanding circle of influential people while entreating wealthy friends to do the same; he solicited endorsements which he then circulated; he badgered newspapers to review the book; and he circulated a chapter in pamphlet form under Federal Union auspices.[99]

This time, however, the results proved disappointing. *Freedom Against Itself* failed to make much of an impression, receiving sparse reviews and generating little commentary. In 1939, the *New York Times*, Streit's former employer, had printed a front-page and adulatory review; this time, a short review appeared in the back pages. As the reviewer dryly commented, the book's "central theme is, or ought to be, well known by now for he [Streit] has expounded it before in 'Union Now' ..." Sales also lagged, prompting Canfield to veto further spending on promotion (already over-budget) and to hold-off on new editions.[100] Writing to his longtime friend, Henry Scherman, whose Book-of-the-Month Club had decided against (unlike with *Union Now*) offering the book as a gift to members, Streit puzzled over the limited results of his promotional efforts. Lamenting the "failure of all my hopes to get 'Freedom Against Itself' into any mass media," he admitted the "disappointment is a rather bitter one for me, and the sense of failure sharp." "I tried hard ...," he explained,

---

[97] Clarence K. Streit, *Freedom Against Itself* (New York: Harper & Brothers, 1954), 2, 222.

[98] YUL, William C. Bullitt Papers, Box 79, file 2039, Streit to Bullitt, March 8, 1954.

[99] For examples, see LLUI, UWF Papers, Box 130, "Freedom Against Itself Wins Nationwide Acclaim ..."; and YUL, Chester Bowles Papers, Part IV, Series I, Box 158, file 639.

[100] Saul K. Padover, "'A Union of the Free,'" *New York Times*, July 18, 1954, 78; and FLPU, Selected Papers of Harper & Brothers, Box 29, file 7, Canfield to Streit, June 23, 1954.

"to make this book easier to read, and wider in its appeal, because it must get into some mass media to do its work."[101]

Initially, Streit wanted to divide the manuscript of *Freedom Against Itself* into two books but Harper refused. Two years later Streit returned to the charge, proposing to Canfield a book on the "sovereignty issue ... primarily and fundamentally, and with Atlantic Union only secondarily." The two discussed the proposal over the next couple of years, with Streit conceiving of the book as a history of his "20-Year Campaign for Union Now." This history, he explained to a supporter, "is worth telling, and could draw to Atlantic Union the fresh support needed at this juncture, [and] I must tell it, for no one, alas, knows it as I do."[102] Canfield clearly had his doubts, reminding Streit his last two books (*The New Federalist* and *Freedom Against Itself*) "did not enjoy substantial sales." Nevertheless, Canfield offered Streit a contract for "your new project, partly because of my admiration for you and your work." Once again, Federal Union's promise to purchase copies (5,000 this time) undoubtedly helped to overcome Canfield's doubts.[103]

The book, entitled *Freedom's Frontier: Atlantic Union Now*, appeared in 1961. The long delay stemmed principally from Streit's active schedule, which included rounds of fund-raising for Federal Union. The book was divided into two parts. Part I largely re-hashed the "fundamentals" of *Union Now*: the value of the US federal system as a model for international relations, the pertinence of eighteenth-century US history, the superiority of Federal Union over confederation (League of Nations/United Nations), the need to rethink conceptions of national sovereignty, the equation of freedom and liberty with democracy and of democracy with peace, and the urgency of action. As if to underscore this continuity, Part II consisted of a reprint of *Union Now*. If *Freedom's Frontier* distinguished itself from earlier books, it was in its unrestrained celebration of Western civilization (or "Atlantica"), whose principles, rooted in liberty and freedom, had made it "the leading creator of the modern world." Atlantica's basic principles, Streit insisted, were "widely acclaimed by

---

[101] BLCU, Harry Scherman Papers, Series IV, Box 10, Streit to Scherman, June 18, 1954.

[102] PUFL, Selected Papers of Harper & Brothers, Box 29, file 7, Streit to Canfield, September 10, 1956; and LOC, CKS, Box I: 27, file 3, Streit to William Clayton, May 8, 1958.

[103] PUFL, Selected Papers of Harper & Brothers, Box 29, file 10, Canfield to Streit, June 27, 1958.

mankind now as the key to the future, the way to a better life for every man, woman and child, living and to be born." [104]

As always, Streit worked hard to promote the book. The challenge, he wrote to Hamilton Fish Armstrong, was to get "over-burdened men" to read it and to "understand fully the much greater opportunity there is, now, to turn interest into action." [105] Streit hoped to benefit from the upcoming convention of NATO countries, the result of a decade-long lobbying campaign in which he was intimately involved (discussed in Chapter 5). Yet, once again, the results were disappointing. Fish Armstrong's *Foreign Affairs* gave it the briefest of mentions; the *New York Times*'s review was admittedly longer but little more encouraging, describing the book as "an expansion and an updating of his [Streit's] earlier argument." [106] Beyond this limited circle, *Freedom's Frontier* appears to have had little public impact, particularly among the influential commentators, those "over-burdened men" whom Streit so ardently pursued.

Freedom's Frontier was Streit's last book. During the 1960s, he tried to find a publisher for a cheap paperback edition of *Union Now* but found no takers; Federal Union would be compelled to re-issue the book at its expense. It is possible and perhaps even tempting to poke fun at Streit's pretensions regarding a sequel to *Union Now*. Still, several points should be kept in mind. First, it was *Union Now*, which allowed Streit to become a public figure, thanks in good part to his promotional energies. Streit's belief in books as a powerful promotional vehicle rested on experience. Second, in trying to recreate the success of 1939–40, Streit failed to understand the unique nature of that moment. *Union Now* appeared at a time when war clouds loomed anew, when the League of Nations was widely judged to be a failure, and when Americans interested in foreign policy were looking for new approaches to international politics and the United States' role in them. In this situation, Atlantic federal union arrived as a fresh proposal, even if one well rooted in US history. And this leads to another point: If after 1945 the proposal no longer appeared fresh, it was because, as the reviews of his post-1945 books suggest, Streit had succeeded to an extent that is easily overlooked in popularizing Atlantic federal union – and federalist frameworks more generally.

[104] Clarence K. Streit, *Freedom's Frontier: Atlantic Union Now* (New York: Harper & Brothers, 1961), 30, 175.
[105] SMLPU, Hamilton Fish Armstrong Papers, Box 60, file: Streit, Clarence, Streit to Fish, April 6, 1961.
[106] *Foreign Affairs* 40 (1961), 143; and R. L. Duffus, "That Free Men May Be Kept Free," *New York Times*, July 2, 1961, 50.

ASSESSING INFLUENCE: THE CASE OF NELSON ROCKEFELLER

Through Federal Union, Streit after 1945 worked to promote Atlantic union and federalist frameworks more generally. In addition to a magazine and several books, the means included newsletters, pamphlets, flyers, newspaper advertisements, and letters to the editor. Assessing the results of this promotional activity is not easy. Looking to Google Ngrams, mentions of "Federal Union" and "Clarence Streit" show a decline from 1945 to the mid-1950s after which the numbers remained steady into the 1970s. Data from newspapers.com point to a similar trend: Although the éclat of the early wartime years waned, Streit and Federal Union retained a public presence. That said, Google Ngrams and newspapers.com measure visibility and not influence.

One way to think about the extent (and limits) of Streit and Federal Union's influence is through a brief case study – that of Nelson Rockefeller. To recall, Rockefeller had been intrigued by Streit in 1939, offering his fledgling organization free rent. Afterward, Rockefeller appears to have lost interest and the family's foundation rejected Federal Union's requests for funding in 1944 and 1945. It "wouldn't appear that Streit's plan ... has a ghost of a chance of getting anywhere in this human world at the present time," a 1945 assessment curtly concluded.[107]

Circumstances changed at the beginning of the 1960s as Nelson Rockefeller, then governor of New York, shifted his presidential ambitions into high gear. Following his early defeat in the 1960 Republican primaries, Rockefeller, eyeing the 1964 nomination, searched for signature policy positions to distinguish his candidacy. During the late 1950s, the Rockefeller brothers had gathered a group of experts to sketch out possibilities, which included alternatives to the "conventional national security [policy] of containment of hostile aggression ..." Sensing an opportunity, Streit began courting Rockefeller anew, offering political advice as well as material on federalism.[108] Two years later, Rockefeller delivered the Godkin lectures at Harvard, which an aide later admitted had been cribbed from Streit. Entitled "The Future of Federalism," the

---

[107] RAC, Office of the Messrs. Rockefeller Records, World Affairs, Series Q, Box 24, file 206, "Extract from Memorandum for Open File ... October 25, 1945."

[108] Rockefeller Brothers Fund, *Prospect for America: The Rockefeller Panel Reports* (Garden City, NY: Doubleday, 1961), xxi; and HTPL, William Clayton Papers, Box 123, file 6, Streit to Nelson Rockefeller, May 3, 1960.

lectures were replete with Streitian language: Federalism "fosters diversity within unity," it "invites the free play of innovation and initiative," and it is based on the "idea of shared sovereignty." Boiling down his message to "one basic proposition," Rockefeller intoned:

the federal idea, which our Founding Father applied in their historic act of political creation in the eighteenth century, can be applied in this twentieth century in the larger context of the world of free nations – if we will but match our forefathers in course and vision. The first historic instance secured freedom and order to this new nation. The second can decisively serve to guard freedom and to promote order in a free world. Sweeping as this assertion may be, I believe it to be anything but an academic proposition. Quite the contrary: it is a matter of cold political realism.[109]

Bursting with enthusiasm, Streit worked to publicize the lectures, serializing them in *Freedom & Union* with Rockefeller's approval and circulating them in pamphlet form.[110] More generally, Streit believed he had finally identified the great man (and great resources) his project needed: He accordingly bombarded Rockefeller with material and advice, presenting Atlantic federal union as a winning electoral issue. Importantly, Streit found an important ally in Hugh Morrow, Rockefeller's principal speechwriter. Streit, Morrow confided, might be "a fanatic – a Johnny One-note," but his project could nevertheless be useful. "I think we might have something here that we can develop on our own ... but translated into less high-flown language and made meaningful for the average Joe who is damn sick of 18 years of cold war." We must, Morrow elaborated, "get our thinking lifted out of this closed and neurotic world of expertise into something better – using Streit as we can, using others as we can, but not limiting our thinking to an essentially European view of American history and American foreign policy." Together with Morrow, Streit would write policy outlines and speeches for Rockefeller during 1963 and 1964.[111]

Despite entering the 1964 Republican primaries as the front-runner, Rockefeller lost out to Barry Goldwater. True to form, Streit urged Rockefeller not to despair but to "turn your own setbacks to great

[109] Nelson A. Rockefeller, *The Future of Federalism* (Cambridge, MA: Harvard University Press, 1962), 6–7, 10, 59. For the aide, see RAC, Rockefeller Brothers Fund Records, Box 332, file 2056, James N. Hyde to Dana S. Creel. August 24, 1965.
[110] UM, Clarence Streit Papers, Box 9, file 12, Streit (FU) circular, June 1962.
[111] RAC, Nelson A. Rockefeller Gubernatorial Records, Hugh Morrow, Series 21, Box 39, file 402A, Morrow to Dr. Ronan, undated. Also see LOC, CKS, Box I: 32, file: Rockefeller, Nelson A, general, 1963–64.

account" by seizing the Atlantic union banner more firmly than ever. Indeed, Streit in 1965 urged Rockefeller to renounce another term as New York's governor and to "devote yourself fulltime to speeding its [Atlantic union] creation."[112] Streit's fervor, however, had little effect as Rockefeller quickly moved on from Atlantic union and federalism more generally. True, in 1965 the Rockefeller Foundation awarded Federal Union a $25,000 grant, a result of Rockefeller's personal intervention following yet another rejection. Yet what Streit considered evidence of Rockefeller's genuine interest in Atlantic union was, in fact, a one-off grant best understood as a payment for services rendered. The foundation refused to renew the grant. As for Morrow, though retaining some sympathy for Atlantic union as a long-term aspiration, he no longer had any immediate use for the project. In 1972, Morrow instructed an aide to place Streit's most recent request for money in the "file of 'lost' stuff."[113]

Rockefeller was notoriously opportunist in terms of ideas. As Eisenhower cattily noted, Rockefeller "is too used to borrowing brains instead of using his own."[114] Still, it is telling that Rockefeller and his aides chose to exploit Streit's project for their political ends. This choice points not only to the political visibility of both Atlantic union and federalist thinking after 1945 but also to their respectability. That Rockefeller could, however briefly, consider federalist frameworks a promising electoral issue is a testimony to Streit's success in promoting his project since 1939. At the same time, Rockefeller's opportunistic use suggests a notable and even fatal limit to Streit's project: its narrowness. Like others, Rockefeller (and Morrow) found federalism as a framework for thinking about international politics more intriguing than they did the precise project of an Atlantic federal union. The more Streit insisted on the latter, the more their interest waned.

In 1964, Streit's editor, Harper, published a textbook on US politics written by Peter Odegard, a Berkeley political scientist. In an extended discussion of the federal system, Odegard acknowledged the latter's international dimension, commenting that "the federal solution ... might have

---

[112] LOC, CKS, Box I: 78, file: Republican Party: National Convention, 1964, general, Streit to Rockefeller, July 5, 1964; and CKS, Box I: 83, file: Rockefeller, Nelson A, general, 1965–78, Streit to Rockefeller, August 6, 1965.

[113] RAC, Nelson A. Rockefeller Gubernatorial Records, Hugh Morrow, Series 21, Box 16, file 160, Morrow to Ann Whitman, February 8, 1972; and Internal note from mn, undated.

[114] Cited in Cary Reich, *The Life of Nelson A. Rockefeller: Worlds to Conquer, 1908–1958* (New York: Doubleday, 1996), 620.

some [wider] applicability." Later in the same chapter, he referred to proposals to "enlarge the degree of union among the nations that make up the North Atlantic Community" as well as "to establish a federal union among the world's democracies." For reference, he cited Streit's 1939 book, *Union Now*.[115]

For Odegard, a prominent political scientist, a discussion of the US federal system naturally included a mention of federalism's larger international relevance – a relevance which, in turn, led back to Streit. Federalist frameworks, in short, had become familiar to informed observers, one element among others in ongoing debates about the international order and the United States' place within it. At the same time, skepticism about the viability of precise proposals such as Streit's Atlantic federal union was palpable. "Whether these proposals have practicality," Odegard coyly noted, "are questions for the future."[116] And as this future receded, so would the relevance – and visibility – of Streit and his project.

Streit kept going well into the 1970s, raising money for Federal Union and promoting Atlantic federal union to anyone who would listen. In 1971, *Freedom & Union* published a twenty-fifth-anniversary issue containing congratulatory messages from various well-known figures.[117] Ten years later Canfield praised Streit and his wife as "practical innovators" and assured them that "[y]our concept lives on."[118] Institutionally, Canfield's prediction proved accurate: In 1985, one year before Streit's death, Federal Union became the Association to Unite the Democracies before assuming its current name, the Streit Council for a Union of the Democracies. In terms of practical politics, though, little remains of Atlantic federal union or even of federalist frameworks for international politics. Neither has it any real presence in today's policy debates in the United States.

What remains is the emphasis on democracy. Looking back, Federal Union's most enduring legacy arguably concerns its understanding of democracy. To be sure, Streit was not a lone voice: A cult of democracy flourished in the United States during the Cold War, rivaling if not surpassing the earlier cult of the constitution and the federal system.

---

[115] Peter H. Odegard, *The American Republic: Its Government and Politics* (New York: Harper & Brothers, 1964), 567–68.

[116] Ibid., 572.

[117] McMaster University Library, George Catlin Fonds, Box 151, file: Federal Union, Streit to George Catlin, September 30, 1971.

[118] LOC, CKS, Box I: 129, file: Harper & Brother general, 1980–82, Cass Canfield to Clarence Streit and Jeanne Defrance, August 5, 1981.

That said, both before and after 1945 Streit featured as a determined and resourceful cheerleader for democracy. In contrast to his earlier Progressive-inspired politics, by the 1930s Streit fetishized democracy, invoking incantatory abstractions such as freedom and liberty. Two aspects of this process are worth highlighting. One is the fixation on the Atlantic world: While democracy might in theory be suitable for countries in other regions, in practice Streit's conception of democracy was forged in – and for – the United States and its Western allies and partners. The second aspect is the impoverished discussion of democracy, whose meaning was drained of any social, economic, or even political content.

5

Clarence Streit, the Atlantic Union Committee, and Postwar Atlanticism

On September 7, 1960, President Eisenhower signed Public Law 86-719. The product of a joint congressional resolution, the law enjoined Congress to form a citizens commission of individuals from "private life," who would meet with members of similar commissions from other NATO countries "in order to explore means by which greater cooperation and unity of purpose may be developed to the end that democratic freedom may be promoted by economic and political means."[1] Fourteen months later, the various delegates gathered in Paris for a twelve-day convention, the immediate upshot of which was a declaration calling on NATO members to forge a "true Atlantic Community" encompassing the "political, military, economic, moral and cultural fields."[2] The law and the subsequent convention crowned a decade-long political campaign spearheaded by the Atlantic Union Committee (AUC), a political lobby group founded in 1949 to promote greater unity among North Atlantic countries. From the outset, Clarence Streit was intimately involved with the AUC, acting as a guiding spirit, tireless activist, and increasingly controversial figure.

This chapter examines the AUC and its political campaign, using Streit's involvement to explore the extent and nature of the organization's activities – activities that offer insights into the public dimension of politics in the foreign relations realm after 1945. Existing studies of the AUC concentrate on its relationship with the State Department and the Eisenhower administration. Whereas Kenneth Weisbrode identifies

[1] www.govinfo.gov. [2] A copy of the declaration is in LOC, CKS, Box II: 15, file 2.

several Atlanticists within the State Department who sympathized with the AUC's goals and Lawrence Kaplan suggests the "fame" of its leadership rendered the AUC impossible for the Administration to ignore, others depict an organization and movement fatally handicapped by internal divisions and by the absence of mass membership.[3] None of these studies, however, accord much attention to the AUC's sustained political lobbying in favor of a constitutional convention of the North Atlantic countries modeled on the 1787 convention in Philadelphia. The AUC's campaign, moreover, increasingly focused on Congress in a deliberate effort to side-step the State Department and the Administration.

This chapter builds on the growing scholarly interest in Congress and its policymaking role during the Cold War. Much of this scholarship centers on domestic policy, but, as Robert David Johnson shows, Congress quickly emerged as a vital foreign policy actor after 1945. The breakdown of bipartisanship at the end of the 1940s raised the political stakes of foreign policy as congressional Democrats and Republicans maneuvered for partisan (and personal) advantage.[4] Equally important as a factor was a collective desire within Congress to claw back some of the authority the executive branch had arrogated to itself during the New Deal and World War II. In a co-written book published in 1947, Estes Kefauver, a representative and soon-to-be senator from Tennessee, urged Congress to assume a more prominent role because its members alone could identify the "foreign policy of the nation" and endow it with popular sanction.[5] Kefauver, the Democrats' vice-presidential candidate in 1956, would spearhead the AUC's lobbying campaign in the Senate.

---

[3] Kenneth Weisbrode, *The Atlantic Century: Four Generations of Extraordinary Diplomats Who Forged America's Vital Alliance with Europe* (Cambridge, MA: Da Capo Press, 2009); and Lawrence S. Kaplan, *The United States and NATO: The Formative Years* (Lexington: University Press of Kentucky, 1984). For internal divisions, see Istvan Szent-Miklosy, *The Atlantic Union Movement: Its Significance in World Politics* (New York: Fountainhead Publications, 1965) Also see Emmett E. Panzelle, "The Atlantic Union Committee: A Study of a Pressure Group in Foreign Policy," PhD, Kent State University, 1969.

[4] Robert David Johnson, *Congress and the Cold War* (New York: Cambridge University Press, 2006). Also see Julian E. Zelizer, *On Capitol Hill: The Struggle to Reform Congress and Its Consequences, 1948–2000* (New York: Cambridge University Press, 2004); Robert A. Caro, *The Years of Lyndon Johnson: Master of the Senate* (New York: Alfred A. Knopf, 2002); and Gary W. Reichard, "Divisions and Dissent: Democrats and Foreign Policy, 1952–1956," *Political Science Quarterly* 93 (1978), 51–72.

[5] Estes Kefauver and Dr. Jack Levin, *A Twentieth-Century Congress* (New York: Duell, Sloan & Pearce, 1947), 91–95.

Streit and the AUC thus offer a case study of political lobbying in the early postwar period. There is now a sizeable body of social science scholarship on lobbying. Rooted in pluralist perspectives on US politics, early studies argued that lobbying strengthened democracy by providing various groups with a voice in policymaking. Not surprisingly perhaps, more critical perspectives developed, suggesting lobbying could undermine democracy by affording some groups an unfair influence on legislation.[6] But whether laudatory or critical, much of the social science scholarship, influenced by work on interest groups and social movements, assumes lobby groups "represent" or "speak for" some definable interest group (workers, farmers, women, Jewish Americans, businesses, abolitionists, temperance crusaders, etc.). Reflecting this assumption, the predominant framework is informational: Lobbyists provide valuable information to legislators on the preferences of their constituents – or on the "salience" of issues. "Lobbies gain access when, in the judgment of congressional elites, they represent constituents," a leading scholar asserts. "They are influential because they determine the kinds of information about constituents that are available to legislators and the kinds of information that are not."[7]

The AUC, however, had no obvious constituency: There was no group out there waiting to be mobilized and represented. Instead, the challenge for the AUC was to persuade Congress members to support a proposal when they had little if any material or electoral reasons for doing so. Accordingly, an interest group approach is less helpful than one which conceives of lobbying as performance (or play) in which participants behave according to mutually accepted expectations.[8] The AUC worked

---

[6] The classic study is with Lester Milbrath, *The Washington Lobbyists* (Chicago: Rand McNally, 1963). Also see Conor McGrath, "Lester Milbrath's *The Washington Lobbyists*, 50 Years On: An Enduring Legacy," *Political Studies Review* 16 (2017), 217–29; and Anthony J. Nownes, *Pressure and Power: Organized Interests in American Politics* (Boston: Houghton Mifflin, 2001).

[7] John Mark Hansen, *Gaining Access: Congress and the Farm Lobby, 1919–1981* (Chicago: University of Chicago Press, 1991), 3. Also see Elisabeth S. Clemens, *The People's Lobby: Organizational Innovation and the Rise of Interest Group Politics in the United States, 1890–1925* (Chicago: University of Chicago Press, 1997); and Jeffrey M. Berry, *Lobbing for the People: The Political Behavior of Public Interest Groups* (Princeton, NJ: Princeton University Press, 1977).

[8] For play/performance, see Elizabeth Bell, *Theories of Performance* (Thousand Oaks, CA: Sage, 2008), 147–72; and Richard Schechner, *Performance Theory* (London: Routledge, 2003), 1–25. The Harvard political scientist V. O. Key spoke of lobbying in terms of "maneuvers" and "rituals." See his *Public Opinion and American Democracy* (New York: Alfred A. Knopf, 1965), 500–31. A more recent study that borrows from Key is Ken

to convince Congress that an Atlantic union both advanced US interests and possessed popular support. And it did so because Congress members casted themselves as guardians of the nation's well-being and as servants of their constituents. In terms of national interests, the AUC focused increasingly on NATO, arguing that a military alliance alone was inadequate and that it required a supplemental political structure. In a Cold War pitting two superpower blocs against one another, this argument resonated.

Perhaps more intriguing were efforts to demonstrate Atlantic union's popularity. An elitist organization, the AUC belonged to the Washington foreign-policy eco-system made up of experts, journalists, academics, think tanks, etc. Notwithstanding this reality, the Committee sought to adduce evidence of local support through letter-writing campaigns, petitions, articles and editorials in newspapers, and chapters in various states. In truth, much of this bordered on make-belief: The chapters, for example, were often little more than Potemkin villages, something easily apparent to anyone who bothered to look. Yet, significantly, few in Congress did so because chapters, much like letters or editorials, provided plausible fictions – that Atlantic union was popular and that Congress members, therefore, were responding to constituents. Plausible fictions, as we shall see, could also be useful in exhibiting Atlantic union's appeal across the Atlantic. The literary scholar Michael Warner claims "publics exist only by virtue of their imagining. They are a kind of fiction that has taken on life, and very potent life at that."[9] Studying the AUC's lobbying campaign illustrates the role of such fictions in the making of US foreign policy in the early Cold War years.

The AUC's political activities are also relevant to the postwar history of Atlanticism. Two basic ideas imbued Atlanticism: that the North Atlantic comprised a distinct region whose countries shared political, cultural, and historical roots and that the region should occupy a prominent and even preeminent place in US foreign relations.[10] Although Atlanticism had multiple advocates, the AUC would distinguish itself by its promotion of a political program revolving around NATO. Indeed, the

Kollman, *Outside Lobbying: Public Opinion and Interest Group Strategies* (Princeton, NJ: Princeton University Press, 1998).

[9] Michael Warner, *Publics and Counterpublics* (New York: Zone Books, 2002), 8.

[10] Work on the origins of Atlantic history often highlight the first idea. See Bernard Bailyn, *Atlantic History: Concepts and Contours* (Cambridge, MA: Harvard University Press, 2005); and William O'Reilly, "Genealogies of Atlantic History," *Atlantic Studies* 1 (2004), 66–84.

AUC succeeded in placing the question of NATO's nature prominently on the Washington policy agenda during the 1950s – well before De Gaulle's challenge to US leadership of the alliance. Streit's federalist project, moreover, powerfully influenced debate on the question, operating as a foil against which alternative conceptions of Atlanticism were forged. It is in this context that what Christian Herter, a former secretary of state and AUC ally, called a "true Atlantic community" emerged by the early 1960s as the dominant understanding of Atlanticism.[11] Its leading voice would be the Atlantic Council, the AUC's direct successor, which Herter initially headed. From the outset, it envisaged (and embodied) transatlantic relations in terms not of formal political structures but of overlapping networks of influential insiders centered in and on Washington. Today, the Atlantic Council is a well-connected and well-endowed Washington organization.

THE AUC: ORIGINS AND INITIAL ACTIVITIES

The previous chapter examined Streit's postwar work with Federal Union, Inc., especially his magazine, *Freedom & Union*, which began publishing in 1946. The magazine's purpose was primarily educational: to stimulate discussion of federalism and Atlantic union among a fairly elite group. Although editing the magazine demanded considerable effort, someone as driven and impatient as Streit was unlikely to be satisfied with such an indirect approach to politics.

Predictably, then, Streit during the early postwar years searched for ways to intervene more directly in politics. As always, he cultivated relations with influential individuals, some of whom he already knew such as John Foster Dulles and Henry Luce, and others he did not such as George Marshall and George Kennan. Increasingly, Congress became a focal point of his efforts: Streit cultivated relations with an impressively large number of senators and representatives, eager to explain to them why Atlantic federal union was both necessary and urgent. Writing in January 1948 to Arthur Vandenberg, Streit urged the chair of the Senate's Foreign Relations Committee to take the lead with Atlantic union just as Alexander Hamilton had done in the 1780s. "[N]ow is the time when you yourself must act as boldly as Hamilton did, if his great federal and financial principles are to give mankind the new birth of freedom for

---

[11] Christian A. Herter, *Toward an Atlantic Community* (New York: Harper & Row, 1963), 30.

which it hungers."[12] Similarly, Streit testified before several congressional committees, insisting economic and military aid to Western Europe were merely stopgap measures and certainly no substitute for a policy of "federating the free, forming the Great Union of the Atlantic."[13]

Streit soon latched on to the idea of a congressional resolution. Working closely with Owen Roberts, the former Supreme Court justice, he drew up a draft that he circulated to a wide audience in April 1948. The resolution called on the US president to convene delegates from the "world's top producing democracies" (the United States, Britain and the Commonwealth, Northern and Western European countries) to "meet in Convention ... to explore how best to advance world recovery, peace and individual freedom by the framing of a Constitution uniting their people in a Federal Union ..."[14] Estes Kefauver, who would be elected Senator in November, figured among the more enthusiastic respondents. Streit typically seized on the opportunity to recruit Kefauver, who would become a steadfast ally. Soon afterward, Streit began canvassing the possibility of forming a "supporting committee" to "[m]ake careful and detailed preparations for the political strategy to facilitate passage of the Resolution."[15]

By early 1949, the decision had been taken to create a committee, and organizing meetings were held in New York in January and February. In addition to Streit and Roberts, the initial participants included Elmo Roper; Robert Patterson, FDR's secretary of war; Hugh Moore, a businessman and cofounder in 1939 of the Committee to Defend America by Aiding the Allies; the newspaper editor Gardner Cowles; Henry Flower, an advertising executive; and William Clayton, who as under-secretary of state in 1946–47 had played a vital role in the Marshall plan's genesis. The participants quickly agreed on a name (Atlantic Union Committee), and in March 1949 the AUC opened offices in New York and Washington. At a press conference that month, Roberts announced the formation of a "nonpartisan movement by private citizens for a federal union of the North Atlantic democracies." In its report on the

---

[12] LOC, CKS, Box I: 89, file: Vandenberg, Arthur H, 1947–48, Streit to Vandenberg, January 2, 1948.

[13] UOT, Estes Kefauver Papers, Box 17, file 5, "Peace and Recovery through Federal Union of the Free," Statement to House Committee on Foreign Affairs, Streit, May 12, 1948.

[14] LOC, CKS, Box II: 17, file 9, "Draft Resolution for a Transatlantic Federal Union Convention," Streit, April 1948.

[15] LOC, CKS, Box I: 27, file: Moore, Walden, 1948–53, Walden Moore to John Howard Ford, December 13, 1948.

announcement, the *New York Times* spotlighted Roberts, Clayton, and Patterson as the AUC's big three, though also mentioning Streit as a Board member "who had been active in advocating such a federation for several years."[16]

From the outset, the AUC confronted several pressing challenges. One was financial. Board members had contributed $30,000 as seed money, but it was understood that larger funds were needed to organize an effective political campaign. The AUC soon embarked on an effort to raise $400,000, approaching foundations (including the Rockefeller brothers) and dispatching some 23,000 letters to individuals across the country. The results were disappointing: We received "numerous nice letters," Clayton remarked, "but not much money."[17] Although the AUC did manage to raise $100,000 over the course of 1949, the figure fell short of requirements. Finances quickly became a preoccupation, one that cut into other tasks. Equally unhappily, the committee was forced to reduce its operating budget – and its political activities accordingly. Given "our present stringent financial condition," its director judged at the end of 1949, the AUC could do little more than "keep the flag flying." "We are assuming," he noted, "that additional funds will be available and expansion [of activities] will be possible after the first of the year."[18]

Another early challenge concerned the AUC's program. The involvement of prominent individuals such as Moore, Clayton, and Roper, all of whom possessed considerable political experience, made it unlikely that Streit would dominate the AUC as he did Federal Union. More pertinently, it was unlikely that his Atlantic union project, to which Streit remained fervently attached, would go uncontested. Signs of tension could be detected early over the question of cooperation with the United World Federalists (UWF) who, to recall, looked to the United Nations as the starting point for developing forms of world government. The UWF appeared eager to cooperate, suggesting the possibility of drafting a joint resolution; it tasked Cass Canfield, Streit's editor at Harper, to pursue talks with the AUC. Several AUC board members welcomed the

[16] "Roberts Proposed an Atlantic Union," *New York Times*, March 16, 1949, 14. Also see LOC, AUC, Box 2, file 1949, "Formation of an Action Committee for an Atlantic Federal Convention," undated.
[17] PUFL, Hugh Moore Fund Collection, Box 9, file 19, J. E. Cecil (AUC) to Hugh Moore, May 23, 1949; and HTPL, William L. Clayton Papers, Box 68, file 1, Clayton to Owen Roberts, May 16, 1949.
[18] PUFL, Hugh Moore Fund Collection, Box 10, file 1, AUC, "Program Activity November–December [1949]," Bishop, undated.

possibility of cooperation, pointing to the UWF's visibility, national chapter structure, and congressional support as valuable assets. However, Streit, who disliked the UWF's more universal as opposed to North Atlantic approach, resisted any meaningful concessions, viewing talks merely as a means to sow divisions among world federalists. Although Streit could not prevent the onset of formal negotiations in 1950, major differences between the two organizations' positions, together with the UWF's rapid loss of steam after 1949 as sharpening Cold War's animosities paralyzed the UNO, effectively prevented any real cooperation.[19]

More portentous were early tensions over the issue of the North Atlantic Pact (creating NATO), which was the subject of extensive congressional and especially Senate debate during the first half of 1949. When AUC leaders first sounded Dean Acheson on the project of a resolution, the secretary of state, fearful of complicating the Senate proceedings, asked the committee to hold off until the Pact had been approved. Streit preferred to ignore the State Department's request, insisting the AUC should frame the choice for Congress and the wider public as one between "a Pact or Union." Several other Board members, however, proposed deferring to Acheson, maintaining the AUC could not oppose the Pact, if only for tactical reasons. Confronted with conflicting positions, Roberts, the public face of the AUC, commented that "if Mr. Streit could not go along with the group, he would not go along either. He said there would be no Committee without Mr. Streit."[20]

This initial mini-crisis was resolved through compromise. The AUC Board members agreed to support the North Atlantic Pact as "an important emergency first step toward Atlantic Union" but one that, in itself, was insufficient. In accepting this compromise, Streit emphasized the latter point: "unless we established ... that we felt the Pact was inadequate, we would be in a poor position to reopen the question later."[21] The more important compromise, though, involved side-stepping two related and potentially contentious questions: what form of Atlantic union the AUC should seek and what form it would settle for. Streit fully understood the nature of the compromise. While personally committed to

[19] PUFL, Hugh Moore Fund Collection, Box 9, file 20, Streit to Hugh Moore, July 3, 1949. Also see the file in LLUI, UWF Papers, Box: B 199, file: Atlantic Union Committee.

[20] LOC, AUC, Box 96, "Fourth Meeting of the Board of Directors ... February 27, 1949." For Acheson, see HTPL, Dean G. Acheson Papers, Memoranda of Conversations, 1949, 1953, Box 65, Acheson memorandum on talk with Justice Roberts, February 21, 1949.

[21] LOC, AUC, Box 96, "Meeting of the Board of Directors ... Wednesday, April 6, 1949."

the creation of a federal union of Atlantic democracies, he accepted the need for flexibility. Many more people, he explained to a supporter in November 1949, favored "an organization that sought merely to get a federal convention called" rather than one that insisted on federal union from the outset. "The big job now is to get members and financial support quickly – let's not make it any harder than necessary."[22]

With the North Atlantic Pact safely through Congress, Estes Kefauver in July 1949 introduced the AUC's resolution in the Senate. The sponsors (eighteen Senators and four Representatives), Kefauver declared, "are united in believing that it is high time we Americans began to explore in a federal convention how we can extend the federal principles of the United States between the free peoples of the North Atlantic."[23] The AUC launched a lobbying campaign, instructing members to promote the resolution – to write Congress members, to solicit petition signers, to give talks, and to recruit supporters. Predictably, Streit was an eager participant. In addition to a cross-country speaking tour, he badgered friends and contacts while also working closely with Kefauver during 1949–50 to solicit individual congress members. "I appreciate all the good letters you have been writing," Kefauver assured Streit in the spring of 1950. "I think we are making good progress."[24] Several months earlier, Senator Elbert Thomas personally informed Streit that his sub-committee would hold hearings on several proposed resolutions on international policy, including the AUC's.[25]

Streit's exertions went into over-drive as he helped AUC leaders prepare their testimonies while appearing himself before the Thomas sub-committee in February 1950. Difficulties, however, quickly emerged. As mentioned, the sub-committee considered several resolutions on "international government," including one from the UWF. The AUC feared that its Atlantic union project would either get lost in the shuffle or be associated with world federation proposals, which, by 1950, were widely coming to be viewed as hopelessly utopian. In the end, the sub-committee's report in July 1950 concentrated on reform of the UN Charter while refusing to pronounce on any single resolution or to

---

[22] LOC, CKS, Box I: 27, file: Moore, Walden, 1948–53, Streit to Walden Moore, November 20, 1949.

[23] *Congressional Record*, Senate, July 26, 1949, Kefauver, 10144.

[24] UOP, Sadie Alexander Papers, Box 56, file 18, Don Dennis (AUC) circular, March 9, 1950; and UOT, Estes Kefauver Papers, Box 16, file 2, Kefauver to Streit, June 12, 1950. Also see the file 3 in the same box.

[25] LOC, CKS, Box II: 18, file 2, Elbert Thomas to Streit, January 16, 1950.

propose its own resolution.[26] Worse still, the State Department poured cold water on the AUC's resolution, cautioning the sub-committee that Atlantic union implied, at the very least, major revisions to the country's constitutional functioning, revisions the American people alone should decide. As for a convention, it risked raising false hopes while also undermining more practical measures to strengthen relations between NATO members.[27] One result is that President Truman, who initially had expressed sympathy with the AUC resolution, revised his position, proclaiming at a news conference in February 1950, "I don't think now is the proper time to press a thing of that sort. We have other things much more important now."[28]

The combined skepticism of the administration and the State Department ensured the AUC's resolution made little progress in 1950. Undeterred, the AUC re-introduced a resolution in January 1951, with Kefauver once again taking the lead in the Senate. Invoking the Cold War, he framed Atlantic union as the most effective response to the Soviet menace, contending that merely convoking a convention "would electrify the free world." This time the resolution could count on the votes of twenty-seven senators (up from twenty in 1949), including Senators Fulbright and Vandenberg, both influential voices in foreign policy.[29] Streit, once again, threw himself into lobbying Congress, working closely with Kefauver and Guy Gillette, a senator from Iowa, as well as Richard Harless, a former representative from Arizona and the AUC's legislative director. With characteristic optimism, Streit informed the AUC's executive in June 1951, "[W]e had a chance to get our resolution through at least one House [of Congress] this year – the best chance we have had so far." The "power of events ...," he added, "were moving continuously in our direction."[30]

---

[26] For the various proposals, see Percy E. Corbett, "Congress and Proposals for International Government," *International Organization* 4 (1950), 383–99. For the report, see "Revision of the United Nations Charter. Report of the Committee on Foreign Affairs ..., Washington, 1950."

[27] CLA, RG 46, U.S. Senate, Box 18, "Statement by Assistant Secretary of State John D. Hickerson on S.Con.Res.57," February 15, 1950.

[28] "Atlantic Union Plan 'Good' Says Truman," *New York Times*, January 21, 1950, 3; and HTPL, Public Papers Harry S. Truman, News conference, February 16, 1950.

[29] *Congressional Record*, Senate, January 15, 1951, Kefauver, 262–64; and "Vandenberg Backer of Atlantic Union," *New York Times*, April 26, 1951, 8.

[30] HTPL, William L. Clayton Papers, Box 86, "Estimate by Sen. Kefauver in conference with CKS and Richard Harless & PDS on Feb. 4, 1951," undated; and LOC, AUC, Box 97, "Fifty-Third Meeting of the Executive Committee ... June 28, 1951 ..." Streit

In reality, the AUC's resolution had stalled. One cause was opposition from groups such as the Daughters (and Sons) of the American Revolution, the Society of Mayflower Descendants, the American Sovereignty Campaign, Veterans of Foreign Wars, and the American Flag Committee, all of which denounced Atlantic union as a sell-out of US sovereignty – a charge the *Chicago Tribune*, a longtime foe of Streit's Federal Union, repeated with obsessive insistence. "All that the Atlantic Unionists want to do," one editorial fumed, "is take the ultimate step – junk the Constitution, submerge the United States in a supra-national government, deprive America of decision over its course in world affairs, and strip the country of the right and means of protecting itself."[31] Worryingly, several Congress members echoed these attacks, including George Malone (Rep-Nevada), John Bricker (Rep-Ohio), and Joseph McCarthy, the anti-communist zealot. In 1955, several senators would seek to block John Marshall Harlan's Supreme Court nomination on the grounds he advocated "world government," citing his membership on the AUC's Council. Harlan passed easily, though, having assured the Senate judiciary committee he was "not an internationalist, a one worlder nor a union-nower."[32]

The biggest obstacle remained the State Department. Although the AUC succeeded in winning the public endorsement of nine former Department officials, Acheson remained opposed, even if he treaded carefully in deference to the resolution's congressional supporters. Thus, while privately dismissing the AUC's proposal as "stupid," Acheson in April 1951 informed the Senate Foreign Relations Committee that his department deemed the resolution "inadvisable" for the time being.[33] Without firmer State Department, the Senate committee, with its Democratic majority, declined to move ahead with the resolution.

worked hard to win over Mike Mansfield, representative and, from 1953, senator from his home state of Montana. See UM, Mike Mansfield Papers, Series 4, Box 15, file 5.

[31] "Junking the Constitution," *Chicago Tribune*, November 11, 1950, 8. Also see several of interventions in "What Form of International Organization Should the U.S. Support?" *Congressional Digest* (31), August–September 1952.

[32] "UN Affiliation May Defeat Harlan," *The Knoxville Journal*, March 4, 1955, 8.

[33] "Atlantic Union Regime Urged," *Baltimore Sun*, August 7, 1950, 10; and "Secretary of State to the Chairman of the Senate Committee on Foreign Relations (Connally), April 6, 1951," *FRUS*, 1951, vol. IV, part 1, 17–18. For "stupid," see Lawrence S. Kaplan, "Dean Acheson and the Atlantic Community," in Douglas Brinkley, ed., *Dean Acheson and the Making of U.S. Foreign Policy* (New York: St. Martin's Press, 1993), 44.

THE AUC IN CRISIS, 1951–1952

By the middle of 1951, the AUC was in crisis. With its resolution stalled in Congress and confronted with mounting political opposition, empty coffers, and stagnant membership numbers, the AUC appeared to be on a course for failure. "I think most of us who have been close to this Atlantic Union undertaking," an internal report noted in August 1951, "must feel as I do that there must be something basically wrong with the methods we have been using to enlist public support."[34] The report's initial recipient, Hugh Moore, had repeatedly expressed dissatisfaction with the AUC's political activities, suggesting "what was needed was a slogan with an emotional content."[35] Together with several Board members, including Henry Flower, a fellow corporate executive (with J. Walter Thompson advertising agency), Moore launched a sustained critique of the AUC's program, insisting it was too focused on a congressional resolution, on a constitutional convention, and on federal union. The time had come, Moore intoned in September 1951, "to make changes in methods, in strategy, and in organization." Concretely, Moore and his allies proposed revising the resolution to drop any mention of federal union, to pursue other routes to Atlantic union, including an "Atlantic Citizens' Conference" of private individuals, and to cooperate with other groups. Moore and Flower, in particular, championed NATO as a potential vehicle for Atlantic union, arguing the AUC should advocate for the "closer integration" of foreign and defense policies among alliance members. This "limited approach," Moore pleaded, would be easier to sell to Congress and to the larger public. It would "take us out of the class of starry-eyed idealists" and "enable us to hold and possibly largely increase our following among practical people ..."[36]

As might be expected, Streit worked hard to counter the fronde within the AUC. The latter, he asserted, must retain its focus on a congressional resolution, claiming, with characteristic optimism, that success was on the horizon. "[H]istory relates that when Columbus crossed the ocean his crew started to mutiny just two days before they sighted land." Watering

---

[34] LOC, AUC, Box 71, file: General 1951, Ralph Stoddard to Hugh Moore, July 6, 1951.

[35] HTPL, William L. Clayton Papers, Box 84, file 3, "Memorandum on conference at home of Mr. Justice Roberts, March 18, 1950," March 22, 1950.

[36] LOC, AUC, Box 97, "Fifteenth Meeting of the Board of Governors ... September 20, 1951," emphasis in original; and LOC, CKS, Box II: 16, "Thirteenth Meeting of the Board of Directors March 13, 1951 ..." Also see CKS, Box II: 18, file 3, Henry Flower to Walden Moore, February 16, 1951.

down the resolution, Streit declared at another meeting, "could not stop backsliders ... any more than the churches could stop backsliders by changing the Ten Commandments."[37] If Atlantic union were to be achieved it would not be by small steps, as Moore and Flower contended, but by a single leap. Accordingly, Streit especially disliked the idea of centering Atlantic union on NATO at the expense of federal union. Rather than revising the program, Streit urged the AUC to intensify its political lobbying, especially of Congress. In this internal battle, Streit could count on influential supporters, including Elmo Roper and Wally Moore, the AUC's administrative director. At the same time, he wished to avoid a rupture. "I'm sure you agree," Streit confided to an ally, "that we can't be too careful to preserve morale and make for better feeling all around."[38]

Complicating the internal battle over the program was a simultaneous debate over the AUC's nature. Two visions structured the debate: the AUC as an elite political group and as a nation-wide organization. Early on, the first vision predominated as the AUC looked to recruit people with the financial means and political clout to influence the Administration and Congress. But as the resolution stalled, some members questioned this vision, claiming significant grass-roots support and a nation-wide presence were necessary if Atlantic union were to be realized. Only with such a presence, Harless, the AUC's legislative director, advised in 1951, could a majority of Congress be persuaded to pass a resolution. "Many members of Congress have told me recently," he explained, "that although they are favorable to the Resolution, it would be unfortunate for them and the Resolution to have it considered before it is understood by the grass roots."[39] This argument prompted talk of a national educational campaign, an idea Hugh Moore vigorously promoted and whose cost Harless estimated at $3–$5 million. Rapidly, however, much of the discussion centered on the idea of recruiting large numbers of new members who would be organized on a local and regional basis.

---

[37] LOC, AUC, Box 97, "Fifteenth Meeting of the Board of Governors ... September 20, 1951; and LOC, CKS, Box II: 16, file 4, "Fourteenth Meeting of the Board of Governors ... May 18 ..."

[38] LOC, CKS, Box I: 38, Streit to Mrs. Frank C. Baker, September 27, 1952; and UOP, Sadie Alexander Papers, Box 56, file 18, "Minutes. Committee on Congressional Elections for 1950," December 15, 1950.

[39] LOC, AUC, Box 97, "Fifty-Sixth Meeting of the Executive Committee ... August 9, 1951 ..." Also see BLCU, Declaration of Atlantic Unity, Box 7, Jerry Henry to George Shea, Jr., July 28, 1952.

The "AUC's greatest need is to get a real chapter organization," staff members were informed in July 1951.[40]

Streit reacted cautiously to the calls to reconsider the AUC's structure, contending "Congressional support was more important than citizen support ..." The unhappy wartime experience with Federal Union's chapter-based national structure undoubtedly fed his doubts, as did the concern that the AUC would spread itself too thin. Any educational work, Streit reassured board members, could be best undertaken by his own organization – Federal Union. At the same time, Streit could not simply dismiss arguments in favor of enlarging the AUC's membership, if only because both Harless and friendly State Department officials maintained Congress members would be impressed by evidence of nation-wide backing for the resolution.[41]

In working to keep the AUC focused on a congressional resolution, Streit's principal ally was the AUC's cramped possibilities. As always, money was scarce and in late 1951 the committee had a $20,000 deficit. Reflecting its Washington focus, the AUC's total membership at the time hovered around 8,000, though the number of Council members did continue to creep upward. From such a small base, a massive effort would be needed to significantly increase membership, and the AUC simply lacked the resources for this.[42]

Nowhere was the chasm between ambitions and resources more starkly apparent than on the issue of chapters. Early on, the AUC found itself with chapters in various states, several of them simply re-named Federal Union chapters. But if the AUC boasted in November 1951 of having 139 chapters in 26 states, the individual chapters, with rare exceptions, led ephemeral lives. A typical case was the University of Oregon's chapter, first formed in 1949, but with little subsequent sign of life; recast in 1951 with eleven members, it organized one or two events before falling dormant the following year. As the AUC's public relations director acknowledged in October 1951, "most of the chapters are not really functioning in an organized fashion," adding that it "is a sheer waste of postage" to ask them to do anything.[43]

---

[40] LOC, AUC, Box 71, "Staff Meeting – Atlantic Union Committee," July 17, 1951.
[41] LOC, AUC, Box 97, "Forty-First Meeting of the Executive Committee, December 21, 1950"; and BLCU, Declaration of Atlantic Unity, Box 7, Herbert Hill (State Department) to Wally Moore, August 5, 1952.
[42] LOC, AUC, Box 2, "Report of Membership Committee," November 29, 1951.
[43] UOO, Atlantic Union Committee Records, files 4 and 5; LOC, AUC, Box 30, file: Oregon; and LOC, CKS, Box I: 77, file: radio project 1951, Sabra Holbrook (AUC) to John Rolfson, October 4, 1951.

In response to these discouraging results, the public relations director underlined the importance of transforming chapters into "active groups with functioning officers and a clearly defined program." And during 1951–52, the AUC elaborated plans to do just this: to undertake an extensive "field program" with salaried organizers working on regional and then local levels.[44] Yet at a time when the AUC was forced into budget cuts and when Harless resigned as legislative director for a higher-paying job elsewhere, such plans were illusory. Surveying proposals in the summer of 1952, the AUC's financial director reported "the main lines of policy of the organization have been under debate from its very start with some in favor of a grass roots movement and others inclined to a smaller, more concentrated effort." Financial imperatives, he continued, imposed a choice, which could only be "to strip the organization down to its essentials."[45] If nothing else, this effectively ruled out almost all field-work, any large-scale educational program, or a nation-wide membership drive. At the end of 1953, the AUC decided to create a small committee to look into "stimulating and coordinating chapter activities," but it appears never to have met.[46]

Tensions over the AUC's program and nature came to a head in 1952, prompting several decisions. One was to reaffirm the committee's initial purpose "primarily as an organization for political action" headquartered in Washington. To be sure, the AUC did not disavow a national structure, for the mirage of the latter (as we shall see) possessed political value. Nevertheless, the priority would be on getting an "Atlantic Union Resolution" through Congress. Another decision, formulated at a strategy conference in May 1952, was to align the AUC's political campaign more closely with NATO, framing Atlantic union as a means to develop and reinforce the military alliance. As Streit understood, these two decisions, endorsed at the AUC's annual congress in Buffalo in November, were potentially in conflict, given that one could support the strengthening of NATO while opposing Atlantic union.[47] But for now a

---

[44] BHLUM, Stella B. Osborn Papers, Box 17, Walden Moore circular to AUC Board, March 7, 1952, with attachment: Clinton Gardner memorandum to Moore, February 26, 1952.
[45] LOC, CKS, Box II: 16, file 8, "Sixty-Eighth Meeting of the Executive Committee ... July 29, 1952."
[46] UOP, Sadie Alexander Papers, Box 56, file 24, AUC, "Twenty Third Meeting of the Board of Governors November 21, 1953 ..."
[47] LOC, AUC, Box 98, "Twentieth Meeting of the Board of Governors September 15, 1952 ..." and attached "Annual Report of the Executive Director for the Period September 1, 1951–September 1, 1952." Also see BHLUM, Stella B. Osborn Papers, Box 19, "1952 Strategy Conference of the Board of Governors and National Council of the Atlantic Union Committee," May 21–22, 1952.

renewed optimism could be detected, partly because any conflict in aims was latent and even more so because AUC leaders, prominent among them Streit, believed the incoming administration offered promising prospects. Eisenhower's victory in November 1952, Streit confided to an ally, may well "serve as the dramatic development you [and I] felt was necessary for us to reach the exploratory convention stage."[48]

LOBBYING THE EISENHOWER ADMINISTRATION

Eisenhower's presidency appeared to offer bright possibilities. Indeed, some AUC members had wanted to campaign openly for Eisenhower, a proposal ultimately rejected for fear of jeopardizing the committee's nonpartisan status. Streit, meanwhile, had been courting Eisenhower for several years, initially in the hope he could be convinced to lead Federal Union. Although Eisenhower declined the offer, Streit kept him regularly apprised of the AUC's activities.[49] Eisenhower's response to this courtship was noncommittal, especially after he became commander of allied forces in Europe in 1950. His advisors counseled caution when it came to Atlantic union, pointing to the uncertainty surrounding the extent of the AUC's political support in Congress. Aligning himself with the Truman administration priorities, Eisenhower informed the AUC that, while sympathizing with its "basic aims and aspirations," he leaned more toward European unity. "This does not mean that I may not arrive at a different conclusion," he added, "it merely signifies that, up to now, the step-by-step approach appeals to me strongly."[50]

Encouraged by Streit, the AUC placed even greater hopes in Dulles, Eisenhower's choice for secretary of state. Streit trumpeted his contacts with Dulles, pointing to their cooperation in 1939–40 on the text of an Atlantic federal constitution as well as their ongoing exchanges. Dulles himself confided in September 1950 that "I am working closely with the Streit-Roberts group."[51] Although Dulles, recently elected to the Senate,

---

[48] HTPL, William L. Clayton Papers, Box 96, file 1, Streit to Clayton, November 9, 1952.
[49] See EPL, Dwight D. Eisenhower Papers, Pre-Presidential, 1916–52, Box 112, file: Streit, Clarence K.
[50] Ibid., Box 112, file: Streit, Clarence K., MacArthur memorandum to General Eisenhower, December 11, 1951; and Box 126, file: Young, John Orr, Eisenhower to Young, September 26, 1950.
[51] SMLPU, John Foster Dulles Papers, Box 47, reel 15, Dulles to Lionel Curtis, September 7, 1950.

had refrained from joining the AUC's Council or from sponsoring its resolution in 1949, he did promise to vote for the latter. Even more auspicious, Dulles sent a message to the AUC's November 1952 convention praising the committee's "understanding of the nature of the infinite capabilities of the Federal System. It is important that this be understood in connection with the development of the NATO organization, because NATO can hardly succeed if it is merely a political alliance of temporary expediency." The message, which garnered considerable publicity, was understandably perceived by some observers as an endorsement of the AUC.[52]

Spurred on by Streit, the AUC wasted little time in approaching Dulles. As with Acheson, the committee's stature ensured its access: In the opening months of 1953, Streit and other members met several times with Dulles and State Department officials. Dulles, though, proved evasive, offering vague sympathy rather than meaningful support. In reality, Dulles harbored profound doubts about the AUC's resolution and, even more so, about Atlantic federal union. Writing to his brother (and future CIA director) in 1950, Dulles explained that, much like Eisenhower, he viewed European union as a priority – one that, while not precluding some vague form of Atlantic union, risked casting the AUC as a nuisance in the immediate future.[53]

Still, Dulles could not easily ignore the AUC: Its political clout required something else than outright opposition. In this context, Dulles opted to prevaricate, advising the AUC to hold off on its resolution while delicate negotiations were ongoing with the Europeans (particularly over the European Defense Community in 1952–54); at the same time, he urged endless revisions to the resolution, including having Congress rather than the president call a convention. All the while, Dulles worked behind the scenes with congressional allies on "delaying tactics," depicting Streit as "fanatical" and the AUC's resolution as "unrealistic." In a series of messages in July 1955 to Walter George, the chairman of the Senate's foreign relations committee, Dulles, pooh-poohed the resolution without

[52] For the message, see SMLPU, John Foster Dulles Papers, Box 63, reel 23, Dulles to Owen Roberts (AUC), November 13, 1952. For its reception, see "Atlantic Union Group Endorsed by Dulles," *Los Angeles Times*, November 23, 1952, 17; and "Choice of Dulles Hailed," *New York Times*, November 22, 1952, 12.

[53] SMLPU, John Foster Dulles Papers, Box 48, reel 16, Dulles to Allen W. Dulles, January 19, 1950.

however rejecting it by "point[ing] out certain difficulties which seem to me inherent ... [in it] as now drafted."[54]

Streit doggedly pursued his "confidential relationship" with Dulles on the AUC's behalf, convinced the secretary of state was a closet ally. The attempt to keep track of the resulting swirl of Streit missives left State Department officials "bewildered."[55] Yet despite Streit's pleas and the AUC's efforts to meet Dulles's series of objections and suggestions, the secretary of state held off from endorsing the AUC's resolution. Thus, in the summer of 1956, the State Department discreetly explained to senators that a resolution calling for a transatlantic convention of NATO countries would be counter-productive, cutting across the administration's more practical policies to strengthen transatlantic relations.[56] A bitterly disappointed Streit, who quickly learned of the State Department's letter, accused Dulles not only of sabotaging the resolution but also of being on the wrong side of History – and, he admonished, "it is with History that Presidents and Secretaries of State must stand or fall."[57]

LOBBYING CONGRESS

If Streit was frustrated with Dulles, by 1955 the AUC in general had abandoned the hope of convincing him.[58] The result was a reenergized focus on Congress. Here, the AUC benefited from several political developments. As mentioned in the book's introduction, one was the collective desire of Congress members to reaffirm the legislative branch's role in policy and in foreign relations in particular. Probably the most visible sign of this desire was the Bricker amendment seeking to check executive power to commit the United States through treaties with other

---

[54] EPL, John Foster Dulles Papers, Telephone Conversation Series, Box 3, "Telephone Conv. – General Jan. 3, 1955–February 18, 1955, "Telephone Call from Senator Ives," January 17, 1955; Box 4, Telephone Conv. – General May 2, 1955–Aug. 31, 1955, "Telephone Call to Senator Knowland," July 27, 1955; and CLA, RG 46, U.S. Senate, Box 47 B, Dulles to Walter George, July 11 and 28, 1955.

[55] SMLPU, John Foster Dulles Papers, Box 109, reel 43, Internal note, L. C. Mitchell, July 5, 1956.

[56] SMLPU, John Foster Dulles Papers, Box 109, reel 43, Streit to Dulles, May 23, 1956; and CLA, RG 46, U.S. Senate, Box 47 B, Robert Hill (State Department) to Senator James Murray, June 18, 1956.

[57] LOC, CKS, Box I: 7, file: Chronological correspondence, 1956–1957, Streit to Dulles, undated but June–July 1956.

[58] UCASC, Elmo Roper Papers, Box 9, file 521, Roper to William Clayton, July 27, 1955.

countries, and which just barely failed in the Senate in early 1954. Yet congressional demands for a larger voice did not simply reflect aspirations to curb the country's mounting international commitments. As the AUC recognized, these demands could also serve more activist projects such as Atlantic union. Just as importantly, the AUC could potentially benefit from partisan politics. While scholars have punctured the myth of bipartisanship on foreign policy during the 1950s, this does not mean that tacit cross-party coalitions were impossible.[59] Following Eisenhower's 1952 victory, the Democrats, in a minority in both houses, decided to attack the incoming administration on foreign policy, a realm in which the president was deemed vulnerable. While the Republicans enjoyed a majority from 1952, many congress members, most notably but not only among the "old guard" such as Robert Taft, were unwilling simply to follow the administration's lead. Streit and the AUC would seek to exploit these differences to forge cross-party support.[60]

Another and related development aiding the AUC was the rising importance of congressional committees. A 1946 reorganization had reduced the number of committees while giving the remaining ones, including the foreign relations committees, enhanced authority and resources (such as staff members) to "exercise continuous oversight of the executive departments and agencies having responsibility for carrying into effect policies determined or approved by Congress."[61] One result was a deepening interaction between government officials and the committees on foreign policy. Acheson described the committees as the "redoubt of congressional power," and recalled, in his four years as secretary of state, having met with congressional groups 214 times, well over half of which consisted of formal meetings lasting from one to three hours to half a day.[62] As Acheson's successor, Dulles felt equally compelled to cooperate with Congress and its committees. If Dulles sought to out-maneuver the AUC in Congress, Streit and his allies exploited the committee system to win publicity and political support for their project.

[59] Reichard, "Divisions and Dissent," 51–72; and Johnson, *Congress and the Cold War*, 1–68.
[60] Caro, *The Years of Lyndon Johnson*, 494; and William I. Hitchcock, *The Age of Eisenhower: America and the World in the 1950s* (New York: Simon & Schuster, 2018), 115–47.
[61] Peter H. Odegard, *The American Republic: Its Government and Politics* (New York: Harper & Row, 1964), 361–62.
[62] Dean Acheson, *A Citizen Looks at Congress* (New York: Harper & Brothers, 1957), 25, 65.

Still another helpful development was the growth of political lobbying. Although the phenomenon dates back to the Republic's early years, lobbying had become omnipresent by the mid-twentieth century. "Democratic government today," two students of Congress affirmed in 1952, "is unthinkable without lobbyists"; lobbying was "woven in our governmental fabric."[63] Earlier, a 1946 law had sought to impose some order on lobbying, requiring lobbyists to register with both houses of congress and to provide information on their spending. Although the AUC's initial spending on lobbying was impressive, ranking in 1950 between that of the National Coal Association and the American Federation of Labor, declining revenue prompted spending cuts. Yet despite its reduced means, the AUC's lobbying effort proved effective during the 1950s, principally because the Committee succeeded – with Congress' connivance – in framing Atlantic union as in the nation's interest and as popular with Americans.

In framing Atlantic union as in the national interest, the AUC exploited the reality of NATO. During 1953–54, the AUC had adopted a low political profile as the saga of the European Defense Community (EDC), which dominated headlines and constituted the cornerstone of the Administration's European policy, played itself out. But the EDC's demise in 1954 offered an opportunity to refocus attention on NATO. Accordingly, the AUC decided to re-introduce a resolution to Congress, which Kefauver duly did in the Senate in February 1955. Pointing to the "profound sense of shock" experienced by the American people due to the EDC's failure, he insisted that a new approach was needed to strengthen NATO and Western security more generally. The time had come to abandon "piecemeal methods" and "to explore on the broadest basis the possibility of a comprehensive, overall solution."[64]

Having re-introduced a resolution in early 1955, the AUC stepped up its lobbying campaign. Not surprisingly, Streit was active and even hyperactive in this effort. Swallowing his doubts, he pitched Atlantic union as the best means of strengthening NATO. In Senate Foreign Relations

---

[63] Stephen K. Bailey and Howard D. Samuel, *Congress at Work* (New York: Henry Holt, 1952), 268–69. Also see Donald R. Matthews, *U.S. Senators and Their World* (Chapel Hill: University of North Carolina Press, 1960), 182–93; and Emanuel Celler, "Pressure Groups in Congress," *Annals of the American Academy of Political Science and Social Science* 319 (1958), 1–9.

[64] BLCU, Declaration of Atlantic Unity, Box 4, Justin Blackwelder to AUC Board, October 11, 1954; and *Congressional Record*, Senate, February 9, 1955, Kefauver, 1366–70.

Committee hearings on the AUC's resolution in July 1955 and again in July 1956, Streit described NATO as "fearfully defective": Lacking the "machinery" to forge a united response to the mounting threat from the Soviet Union and the communist world, the alliance could not ensure peace. As always, he drew on US history, likening NATO to the 1,777 articles of confederation, which had proved inadequate to provide sufficient unity of purpose to the thirteen colonies. The message was clear: As with the thirteen colonies, NATO members needed to transform the alliance into a federal union. Although insisting any convention would be merely "exploratory," involving no commitment to a pre-set outcome, Streit clearly hoped the delegates would follow the example of the 1787 Philadelphia convention, which produced "the most astonishing and enduring success ever achieved in human history at a conference of States." What was needed, Streit wrote to one Senator in September 1955, was "a concrete plan for federal union – the United States Constitution ..."[65]

Other AUC members also focused on NATO in their testimony, though, tellingly, avoiding any mention of federal union. Elmo Roper, who took over as AUC director in 1955, thus deplored the lack of unity in the foreign and defense policies of NATO countries, labeling it a "dangerous disadvantage," compared to the Soviets who supposedly could dictate consensus within the communist bloc. Similarly, Senator Richard Neuberger, who cosponsored the resolution, explained to his senatorial colleagues that the Administration erred in treating NATO simply as a military alliance because various issues – foreign policy, the underdeveloped regions, transportation, and communication – were of "joint concern" to NATO members. "[E]vents," Neuberger elaborated, "are driving us [NATO states] to seek these common policies in any case. The question is only whether we shall seek them effectively ... or haltingly, through a dozen foreign offices individually responsive only to the divisive pressures of domestic politics."[66] Beyond congressional confines,

---

[65] LOC, CKS, Box I: 125, "Statement at the Hearing of the Senate Foreign Relations Committee in the Atlantic Exploratory Convention Resolution ...," Streit, July 25, 1955; and CKS, Box I: 15, file: Knowland, William, F., Streit to Knowland, September 12, 1957. Also see Clarence K. Streit, "The Diplomatic Potential of NATO," *Annals of the American Academy of Political and Social Science* 312 (July 1957), 116–26.

[66] *Hearings before the Committee on Foreign Relations, United States Senate ... on S. Con. Res. 12 ... July 25 and 26, 1955* (Washington, DC: GPO, 1955), Roper, 16–17, Neuberger, 65–70.

NATO dominated AUC's publicity material, which included a monthly newsletter entitled "Now in NATO."[67]

Framing Atlantic union in terms of NATO allowed the AUC to cast itself as a constructive critic of the Administration, endorsing the latter's proclaimed aim of strengthening the alliance while proposing more effective means. Such constructive criticism could appeal to Congress members from both parties, the Democrats in opposition (and then in the majority from 1954) and the Republicans unwilling simply to defer to Eisenhower and Dulles. Whatever Streit's private grumblings, effectively downplaying federalism and federal union promised to attract congressional votes for the resolution, while also answering the criticism, voiced by several participants in the 1955 and 1956 hearings, that Atlantic union threatened the nation's sovereignty and independence. Constructive criticism of this kind, it is worth adding, also resonated with several State Department officials who sympathized with the idea of Atlantic union but doubted the political viability of Streit's federal union project. These officials, as one of them recalled, envisaged "the progressive development of a true Atlantic Community (with a capital 'C') – that is, progressively closer unity in all fields."[68] For the AUC, such support from "below" could be useful in prodding Dulles to be more forthcoming.

Emphasizing NATO also allowed the AUC to frame Atlantic union in hard-headed realpolitik terms – terms consistent with what scholars have identified as a crystallizing "national security ideology" in the early Cold War years.[69] In a Cold War context, AUC speakers insisted, Atlantic union offered the most effective response to the communist threat. By amassing overwhelming power, a strengthened NATO would deter the Soviets from aggression in Europe and beyond. As Roper explained to one Republican senator, Atlantic union would "merge the great productive and cultural power" of NATO countries into "an unassailable block."

---

[67] "'Now in NATO' on Sale Today," *The Charlotte News* (Charlotte, NC), February 14, 1956, 19.

[68] Lawrence S. Kaplan and Sidney R. Snyder, eds., *"Fingerprints on History": The NATO Memoirs of Theodore C. Achilles* (Kent, OH: Kent State University, 1992), 24–25. For the State Department more generally, see Weisbrode, *The Atlantic Century*, 115–19; John Lamberton Harper, *American Visions of Europe: Franklin D. Roosevelt, George F. Kennan, and Dean G. Acheson* (New York: Cambridge University Press, 1996), 323–24; and Kaplan, *The United States and NATO*.

[69] Michael J. Hogan, *A Cross of Iron: Harry S. Truman and the Origins of the National Security State, 1945–1954* (New York: Cambridge University Press, 1998). Also see Michael S. Sherry, *In the Shadow of War: The United States since the 1930s* (New Haven, CT: Yale University Press, 1995).

Insisting the Soviets sought to fatally weaken NATO, Streit similarly assured the Senate's Foreign Relations Committee that Atlantic union "will cause consternation in the Kremlin," adding it might even "arouse explosive new hope behind the Iron Curtain" – an obvious appeal to Congress members enticed by the Administration's talk of "rolling back" the Soviet empire in Eastern Europe.[70] Atlantic union, the AUC repeatedly intoned, amounted to a powerful weapon with which to wage the Cold War.

Equally noteworthy, the AUC also sought to persuade Congress that Atlantic union enjoyed popular support. During the congressional hearings, Senators had asked about this, a question which reflected their understanding of themselves as representatives of the people – and of their constituents. The question posed an obvious challenge to the AUC, an elitist, Washington-based political lobby group. As we saw, early efforts to build a national organization, centered on local chapters, had largely failed. Afterward, the AUC continued to entertain hopes of attracting grass-roots support. The issue was periodically discussed, reports commissioned, and various plans concocted. But limited resources imposed their own reality. Tellingly, in April 1958, the AUC's chairman described the "chapter picture" as "obscure" due to the absence of information on AUC chapters, though he suspected many held no meetings and organized no activities. "Should these chapters be written off as inactive?" he queried.[71]

Not surprisingly, AUC leaders were tempted simply to abandon efforts to attract grass-roots support. If they chose not to do so, however, it was because of the need to provide Congress with some evidence of popular backing for Atlantic union. Consequently, the AUC pursued a multi-pronged strategy. One prong consisted of collecting endorsements of its resolution from existing organizations. Here, the AUC enjoyed some limited success, for example, receiving statements in 1956 from organized labor (AFL-CIO) and the National Farmers Union. Another prong was to recruit distinguished individuals to the AUC's Council. During the 1950s, the AUC signed up Harry Truman, George Marshall, and Adlai Stevenson as well as less prominent albeit influential figures such as

---

[70] UCASC, Elmo Roper Papers, Box 10, file 581, Roper to Senator John Sherman Cooper, June 14, 1957; and CLA, RG 46, U.S. Senate, Box 47 B, "Report of Proceedings," Senate, July 11, 1956, Streit, 102.

[71] For discussions, see LOC, AUC, Box: 97, "Thirty-First Meeting of the Board of Governors May 23, 1956 ..."; and BHLUM, Stella B. Osborn Papers, Box 19, "Report to the Atlantic Union Congress April 28, 1958," Gerald B. Henry.

Francis Biddle, Harold Ickes, Clare Boothe Luce, Harry Scherman, James Shotwell, and Cass Canfield. Council membership involved little direct responsibilities for the people concerned but the lengthening list (almost 800 by 1959) possessed publicity value, which the AUC worked to maximize. Public announcements accompanied the drafting of every big name, while pamphlets highlighted the breath of Council membership, breaking it down by state. Indeed, the AUC aimed to have at least one Council member from each congressional district, an achievement that would bolster claims of a nation-wide presence.[72]

But, while certainly welcome, an expanding Council membership did little to counter the AUC's image as an elitist organization. And so the Committee set about cultivating the plausible fiction of popular support by creating a Potemkin village of local chapters. And, here, appearances mattered far more than reality. Unable to pay professional field workers, the AUC relied on the herculean efforts of a few volunteers, almost all of them women. A striking case is that of Stellanova Osborn, the Canadian-born companion of a former governor of Michigan whose internationalist fervor initially expressed itself in a quixotic campaign to locate the United Nations' headquarters in Sugar Island, Michigan.[73] Soon afterward, Osborn re-directed her energies toward the AUC. Judging Streit a "genius" and Atlantic union the next "Magna Carta," Osborn during the 1950s crisscrossed several states (Michigan, Georgia, Kansas, Indiana, and Ohio), establishing "a string of chapters" along the way. Her "methods," she reported, consisted of organizing a speaking event and afterward persuading a handful of attendees, drawn mostly from the professional classes, to sign a petition for Atlantic union and to form a local chapter.[74]

The AUC was duly impressed. "The eruption of Osborn AUC Chapters," its membership director wrote to Osborn, "left everyone at Headquarters breathless. We are having a hard time keeping up with you!" To aid Osborn and others like her, the AUC printed how-to manuals for creating chapters for local distribution. At the same time,

---

[72] See the AUC's pamphlet, "Atlantic Committee Who?" in LOC, CKS, Box I: 38, file: Atlantic union resolution: general 1951–54; and "Truman Joins Council," *New York Times*, October 8, 1955, 10.

[73] Charlene Mires, "Sault Ste. Marie as the Capital of the World? Stellanova Osborn and the Pursuit of the United Nations, 1945," *Michigan Historical Review* 35 (2009), 61–82.

[74] BHLUM, Stella B. Osborn Papers, Box 4, Osborn to Hugh Moore, May 27, 1955. Also see "Mrs. Osborn Making Fifteen Talks Here," *The Manhattan Mercury*, March 19, 1952, 1; and "Classes Hear Mrs. Osborn," *Detroit Free Press*, May 26, 1953, 3.

the AUC fully understood that much of this was smoke and mirrors. As one official admitted to Osborn, the AUC's presence in Michigan, among other states, "will remain a paper organization."[75] Most of the chapters so formed exhibited little, if any, signs of subsequent life, compelling Osborn to work herself to the bone – to write chapter newsletters and to find people to serve as figurehead chapter chairs. The key point, once again, is that appearances trumped reality. "What I tell [local] people," Osborn reported, "is that what we want, primarily and most importantly, is that they shall GO ON RECORD, in a manner that we can report to Washington. If they cannot be active, they can at least contribute that all-important minimum." For the AUC, such fictions lent credibility to claims of national support. In re-introducing a resolution to Congress in February 1955, Kefauver thus boasted that the AUC possessed "more than a hundred local chapters in all parts of the country."[76]

Chapters mattered not simply in terms of numbers. Contemporary observers of lobbying emphasized the influence of letter writing – a point the AUC's congressional supporters confirmed.[77] Especially valued were letters from constituents, and here AUC chapters could play a useful role, forcefully supplementing the periodic flurries of letter writing by AUC Board and Council members as well as any well-known nonmembers who could be persuaded to do so, for example, the writer Walker Percy. All that was needed was letterhead with location (chapter address) and a name (chapter chair), requirements even the most insubstantial of chapters could fulfill. Accordingly, Streit, Osborn, and others urged local AUC members to write on behalf of their chapters to Congress members, particularly those on the foreign relations committees. In one such letter in 1956, Streit beseeched recipients "to phone, wire or write – better by air mail or special delivery – your Senators and Congressmen ..."[78]

To work, plausible fictions require a receptive partner. And, during the 1950s and into the 1960s, Congress proved willing to play along. Reflecting their self-defined role as servants of their constituents' wishes, Congress members asked the AUC for proof of popular support at the

[75] BHLUM, Stella B. Osborn Papers, Box 3, Don Dennis (AUC) to Osborn, July 17, 1951 and July 31, 1952.

[76] BHLUM, Stella B. Osborn Papers, Box 3, Osborn to Walden Moore, September 5, 1951; and *Congressional Record*, Senate, February 9, 1955, Kefauver, 1369.

[77] Celler, "Pressure Groups in Congress," 7–8; and BHLUM, Stella B. Osborn Papers, Box 6, Elmo Roper to Osborn, May 7, 1959.

[78] See LOC, CKS, Box I: 7, Streit to "Dear Friend," undated but 1956; and Box II: 17, file 6, Streit correspondence with AUC Kentucky branch, June 1960.

local level. Yet, just as importantly, they were not particularly demanding, accepting evidence that was anecdotal at best, if not fabricated. This complicity between Congress and the AUC raises the subject of public opinion – that elusive entity that so fascinated observers at the time and scholars afterward.[79] If it is clear that no consensus existed at the time on what constituted public opinion, it is also true that, in this context of uncertainty regarding public opinion, legislative success depended on the ability of interest groups to create plausible fictions of support.

The logic of plausible fictions also worked when it came to foreign support for Atlantic union. In the course of the AUC's lobbying campaign, the question of European interest in the project cropped up. Dulles openly queried claims the Europeans would simply defer to the United States – doubts Congress members echoed. The AUC, accordingly, found itself compelled to offer some evidence of Atlantic union's wider appeal. Several possibilities presented themselves. Early on, the AUC had created an Atlantic Affiliates sub-committee whose principal task was to encourage the creation of AUC-like committees in Canada and Europe. The AUC also cooperated closely with the Declaration of Atlantic Unity (DAU), a loose grouping of prominent people in the United States, Canada, and Europe formed in the mid-1950s to promote closer transatlantic ties. Streit, meanwhile, took it upon himself to provide more direct evidence. During the 1950s, he cultivated an array of foreign politicians, soliciting their public endorsement of the AUC's resolution. Streit, for example, maintained a regular correspondence with Lester Pearson, Canada's External Affairs minister for much of the 1950s and later Prime Minister, who sympathized with the idea of Atlantic union.[80] At times, the effort approached comedy. Looking to impress Congress, in 1951 the AUC, relying on Streit's list of contacts, circulated a letter signed by Senator Guy Gillette (Iowa) to several "European leaders" urging them to create national committees to promote Atlantic union. Many of the recipients responded in lukewarm fashion, but another problem, as Streit admitted, was that the list included too many politicians well past

---

[79] For public opinion, see Sarah Igo, *The Averaged American: Surveys, Citizens, and the Making of a Mass Public* (Cambridge, MA: Harvard University Press, 2007); and James N. Rosenau, *Public Opinion and Foreign Policy* (New York: Random House, 1961).

[80] See LAC, Wishart Robertson Papers, R 9206, Vol. 4, Streit – Pearson correspondence. For Pearson's interest in Atlantic union, see his "Canada and the North Atlantic Alliance," *Foreign Affairs* 27 (April 1949), 369–78. For one example of Streit's advocacy abroad, see RIIA, 8/1910, "Atlantic Union," anonymous (but Streit), February 19, 1951.

their prime – "merely nominal party leaders, men with no real political influence."[81]

Clearly something more was needed, and so Streit set about creating the plausible fiction of an international movement. In early 1953, he set up an "international working party" for Atlantic union in Paris under the auspices of his own organization (Federal Union) and under his son Pierre's direction.[82] When this initiative fizzled, Streit began working with Pierre Billotte, a retired French general with political ties to De Gaulle, to organize what became the International Movement for Atlantic Union (IMAU). Following a preliminary meeting in Bruges in September 1957, the IMAU was founded in Paris in July 1958 with Streit as president, Billotte as chairman, and Stellanova Osborn as North American secretary. Streit occasionally day-dreamed of using the IMAU to convince a European leader (De Gaulle) to take the lead on Atlantic union – a reverie that says much about Streit's peculiar understanding of French and European politics. In any case, the IMAU's more pressing purpose was to furnish Congress with evidence of Atlantic union's appeal abroad.[83]

Efforts to contrive plausible fictions reflected the tensions between two contending realities: the AUC as an elitist, Washington-based lobby group, and its need to demonstrate evidence of popular support at home and abroad. Intriguingly, these plausible fictions, despite their ill-disguised fragility, satisfied a growing number of Congress members, who generally refrained from subjecting the AUC's claims to critical scrutiny. In the end, the impression is one of play-acting: The AUC pretended to enjoy significant popular support, while Congress members, in backing the AUC's resolution, pretended to be responding to their constituents' wishes.

PROGRESS IN CONGRESS AND ITS PRICE

The AUC's lobbying campaign enjoyed growing momentum in the second half of the 1950s. One sign was a steadily growing list of congressional supporters. Other signs included the irritated reaction of opponents. The

---

[81] UIL, Guy M. Gillette Papers, Box 1, files: Atlantic Parliamentarians 1951, Streit to Gillette, March 1, 1951.

[82] LOC, CKS, Box I: 33, file: Board reports 1953 & undated, "Report to the Board of Federal Union, Inc. European Bureau, Paris, France," Pierre Streit, January 29, 1953.

[83] See LOC, CKS, Box I: 104, file: General 1958, and especially "Création du Mouvement international pour l'Union atlantique," July 15, 1958. For hopes in De Gaulle, see CKS, Box I: 33, file Roper, Elmo, 1956–1971, Streit to Roper, August 2, 1959.

Chicago Tribune, for example, warned in 1954 against dismissing Atlantic union as a "pipe dream," pointing to growing congressional support for its resolution. Over the next few years, its editorial page bemoaned the Eisenhower administration's seeming unwillingness to condemn the AUC and its project.[84] Writing in February 1958, another critical observer, Lyle Wilson, the United Press' Washington bureau chief, grumbled at the AUC's political rise. "There is more muscle than one might suspect in the movement for some kind of world federation in which the U.S. of America would become citizens of the U.S. of The Atlantic. Atlanticians, for short."[85]

AUC stalwarts were cautiously optimistic. Reporting to the executive committee in February 1957 on the situation in Washington, Roper "was glad to find increased interest in the Resolution, particularly from some unexpected quarters."[86] Despite the favorable news and after much discussion, the AUC decided against reintroducing a resolution during 1957–58, preferring instead to enlarge its congressional support through a stepped-up lobbying campaign. In particular, the campaign aimed at recruiting Republican supporters, who were less numerous than Democrats. As always, Streit threw himself into this campaign, distributing material and button-holing Congress members. By early 1959, the AUC was ready with a new resolution, which Hubert Humphrey (Senator from Minnesota and future vice president) and three others (Kefauver among them) introduced in the Senate in March 1959, calling for a convention of NATO countries to "explore possibilities for drawing even closer together."[87]

The AUC's political momentum, however, came at a price. Writing in the mid-1960s, the Committee's first historian identified a fundamental division within the Committee between radicals, grouped around Streit, and moderates who demanded "nothing less than a 'piecemeal' retreat from the original ideas."[88] The division is perhaps overly schematic, as

---

[84] "The Fever for Hands Across the Sea," December 5, 1954, 24; and "Four of a Kind," September 16, 1956, 24, both in the *Chicago Tribune*.

[85] Lyle C. Wilson, "Real Sentiment Exists in U.S. for Federal Union of Atlantic Nations," *The Evening Times* (Sayre, Penn), February 24, 1958, 5.

[86] BLCU, Declaration of Atlantic Unity, Box 1, AUC, "Ninety-Eight Meeting of the Executive Committee February 6, 1957 ..."

[87] *Congressional Record*, Senate, March 19, 1959, Humphrey, 4576; and UCASC, Elmo Roper Papers, Box 10, file 577, Roper to Senator John Sherman Cooper, January 15, 1957; and UM, Mike Mansfield Papers, Series 13, Box 17, file 12, Roper to Mansfield, May 23, 1958.

[88] Szent-Miklosy, *The Atlantic Union Movement*, 219.

almost all AUC members favored Atlantic federal union as an ideal. Disagreement, instead, revolved around tactics and timeframes, with moderates arguing for a gradual, step-by-step approach in which the ideal served as inspiration more than as guide. In practice, though, political lobbying, which enmeshed the AUC in a negotiating dynamic with Congress, would close off some outcomes – and Streit's federal union project in particular. As the overriding goal became the immediate one of getting a resolution passed, pressure mounted to be flexible in terms of its wording (and content). The risk, which even Streit did not fully grasp at the time, was that the pursuit of a congressional resolution would become an end in itself.

Ironically, it was under the direction of Elmo Roper, a genuine federalist but also a self-defined political pragmatist, that the AUC found itself ensnared in just such a negotiating dynamic. Soon after becoming director, Roper in early 1956 sounded several senators on the resolution's prospects. In doing so, he discovered "a surprising amount of feeling that the [AUC] had been guilty of a considerable amount of intransigence over the phraseology of our resolution," an intransigence all too-often interpreted as a refusal to accept anything other than "total and complete [Atlantic] federation." Equally troubling, several senators associated this intransience with "the old Clarence Streit 'union now' concept," viewing the AUC as a front for Streit's Federal Union – as "nothing more than getting the camel's nose under the tent."[89] Circulated widely within the AUC, Roper's report and its implicit assessment of policy resonated with committee members frustrated by what they viewed as a counterproductive attachment to old thinking. The AUC, one such member charged, suffered from "the rather long 'hangover' from the past."[90]

Moving quickly, Roper set up a policy committee to review the AUC's approach, whose report in August 1956 recommended greater flexibility without however spelling out what this meant.[91] Roper, meanwhile, moved ahead with forging what one ally described as "a more flexible and less dogmatic position" embodied in a "resolution that is capable of serious political consideration" – or what became known as the AUC's

[89] LOC, CKS, Box I: 38, file: Atlantic Union resolution, 1956, Roper to Senators John Sparkman and Hubert Humphrey, January 27, 1956.
[90] BHLUM, Stella B. Osborn Papers, Box 4, Sabra Holbrook to Ralph Epstein, undated but early 1956.
[91] BHLUM, Stella B. Osborn Papers, Box 4, Blackwelder (AUC) to Osborn, August 16, 1965 with attachment: "Report of Policy Committee," Thomas Burke.

"Fabian policy."[92] The first and least controversial element was to have Congress and not the president call a convention. Dulles had informally proposed this option in a talk with Streit, who embraced it in the hopes of winning over the secretary of state. A trickier element involved the question of which countries to invite to the convention: all NATO members or only those with democratic regimes? Roper favored the first approach, Streit the second. Consistent with his belief that democracies alone could form an effective federal union, Streit underscored the practical benefits of the more exclusive option. "When one aims to explore the possibility of uniting deeply, even federally, one should not risk overloading the boast and sinking it at the start," he contended. "To gain strength by depth of Union rather than by the number united requires starting with a few – those with the greatest existing community of interest."[93] Firmly in command of the AUC, Roper simply overrode Streit's opposition.

A bigger pill for Streit to swallow were Roper's efforts to disassociate the AUC and its resolution from all talk of federalism and federal union. The AUC, Roper assured a Republican senator in 1956, had removed "some inflammatory words and what were regarded as some political deficiencies." As he recounted to Adlai Stevenson soon afterward, this involved "carefully delet[ing] all references to 'federal union' as a possible solution ..."[94] Two years later, Livingston Hartley, a leading AUC lobbyist, informed Streit that supporters in Congress were advising the Committee itself to keep a low profile as it was too closely identified with federalism.[95] Streit, predictably, balked at such a self-effacing posture, insisting that the AUC should stand tall. Roper once again overrode Streit's objections, rallying the majority of Board members to his position by invoking the advice of the AUC's congressional allies, among them Kefauver with whom Streit had closely worked. Consequently, as Roper informed Streit, the AUC was "keeping a hands-off policy for a while" when it came to Congress. In reality, Roper sought to concentrate

[92] LOC, CKS, Box I: 38, file: Moore, Walden, 1954–59, W. Moore to Gerald B. Henry, February 22, 1956; and UPITT, Adolph William Schmidt Collection, Box 3, file 3, Justin Blackwelder to Gerald Henry, February 9, 1959.

[93] BHLUM, Stella B. Osborn Papers, Box 4, "How the U.S. Can Justify Inviting Only the Seven NATO Sponsors to the Proposed Atlantic Union Convention," Streit, January 25, 1956.

[94] LOC, AUC, Box 104, Roper to Senator Clifford Case, February 21, 1956; and SMLUP, Adlai E. Stevenson Papers, Box 69, file 5, Roper to Stevenson, May 24, 1956.

[95] LOC, CKS, Box I; 38, file: Atlantic Union resolution 1958, Hartley to Streit, April 25, 1958.

lobbying in his own hands and those of his closest allies. An unhappy Streit accused Roper of being "fuzzy-minded," but in the end he reluctantly endorsed the AUC's "Fabian policy," accepting the argument that the immediate priority must be on getting a resolution through Congress.[96]

More painful still, Roper worked to sideline Streit. There was a growing sense within the AUC of what Hartley called the "Clarence problem." Roper posed the question thus: "How Clarence can be persuaded not to do things that may cause damage?" Dick Wallace, Kefauver's personal assistant and the AUC's de facto legislative director, was blunter still: "Clarence in particular should keep out."[97] Streit, in some ways, was a victim of his publicity success, with many observers (friendly and unfriendly) identifying him with Atlantic federal union (and Federal Union). Yet at a time when Roper labored to undo the perception of the AUC as dogmatically committed to one single form of Atlantic union, this identity risked becoming a liability. Compounding the problem, Streit, despite promises to toe the AUC's more moderate line, did little to hide his belief in an Atlantic federal union whether in his magazine, *Freedom & Union*, in public speeches, or in conversations with congress members. Streit's persistent lobbying, in turn, alienated several senators. As Adolph Schmidt, an AUC activist and future US ambassador to Canada, privately recognized:

Clarence has become so wrapped up in his idea that he bores some people to death. The request for a fifteen minute interview turns into a one hour and a half lecture. Most busy and occupied men of affairs will take it only once. Then they begin to worry about him and what he is trying to do. Elmo [Roper] and I can name five key senators where this cycle occurred and they were vital to the passage of the Resolution.[98]

Side-lining Streit proved easier said than done. He enjoyed considerable sympathy within the AUC, many of whose members, Schmidt and Hartley among them, had been inspired by their wartime reading of *Union Now*. Everyone, moreover, admired Streit's personal sacrifices

[96] LOC, CKS, Box I: 33, file; Roper, Elmo, 1956–1971, Roper to Streit, March 11, 1958; and Streit to Roper, May 10, 1959. For "Fabian strategy," see UPITT, Adolph William Schmidt Collection, Box 3, file 3, Justin Blackwelder to Henry, February 4, 1959.

[97] BLCU, Declaration of Atlantic Unity, Box 21, Hartley to W. Moore, July 16, 1959; Hartley to Roper, July 15, 1959; and W. Moore to Hartley, July 23, 1959.

[98] UPITT, Adolph William Schmidt Collection, Box 7, file 5, Schmidt to Jane Elligett, July 14, 1960. Also see UCASC, Elmo Roper Papers, Box 10, file 580, Livingston Hartley to Roper, May 23, 1957.

and his tireless and disinterested commitment to the cause.[99] Streit, it is also worth mentioning, was an unrivaled fund-raiser, a skill not to be dismissed by an organization perpetually short of money. "Some of things he [Streit] does seem to against the grain with me, but there is no denying that he gets money," the AUC's executive secretary sighed in September 1958.[100] Multiple considerations, in any event, resulted in a tacit deal by which Streit would limit his lobbying activities to the House, leaving the Senate, judged to be the far more important chamber, to Roper and other AUC lobbyists. If anything, the deal affirmed and reinforced the AUC's attachment to a "Fabian policy."

A PYRRHIC VICTORY

Developments moved rapidly following the reintroduction of a resolution in March 1959, with favorable votes in the Senate and House in the summer of 1960. As expected, the AUC with Roper in charge lobbied actively, if also more discreetly than before. Shunted to the House, Streit once again threw himself into the effort, striking up a close working relationship with Thomas (Doc) Morgan, the Democratic chair of the House committee on foreign affairs, who agreed to sponsor the resolution.[101] Privately, Streit expressed his unhappiness with the resolution's final wording, which had been further watered down in the pursuit of congressional (Senate) support, warning, "[O]ne can win battles in such a way as to lose the war."[102] Nevertheless, Streit, as Hartley admitted, loyally followed the AUC's line with House members, assuring the latter, for example, that the resolution was anything but a version of "the old Streit proposal." Significantly, in overriding his own doubts about the resolution's value, Streit seized on Roper's assurances that the AUC would be able to steer an eventual Atlantic convention in a federalist direction.[103]

---

[99] See the comments on Streit in Livingston Hartley, *Atlantic Challenge* (Dobbs Ferry, NY: Oceana Publications, 1965), 52–64.

[100] UPITT, Adolph William Schmidt Collection, Box 3, file 3, Justin Blackwelder to Schmidt, September 9, 1958.

[101] See the Streit – Morgan exchange, March 1960, in LOC, CKS, Box II: 19, file 5, as well as "Present Attitudes of Members of House Foreign Affairs Committee on Atlantic Convention Resolution ...," Streit, March 11, 1960.

[102] HTPL, William L. Clayton Papers, Box 123, file 6, Streit to Clayton, February 4, 1960.

[103] BLCU, Declaration of Atlantic Unity, Box 10a, Hartley to William Clayton, May 16, 1960; and LOC, CKS, Box I: 23, "Notes on S.Con.Res. 17," undated.

Streit's loyal activism notwithstanding, the resolution's successful passage was principally the work of Roper and his allies. Well aware of the resolution's deficit in support among Republicans, Roper had made the recruitment of the latter a priority. Along with senators, he sedulously (and successfully) wooed vice president Richard Nixon, who wielded considerable influence among Republican congress members. With Nixon, Roper emphasized not only the AUC's flexibility, manifest in the resolution's nonbinding and open-ended nature, but also the project's Cold War aspects. Atlantic union, he insisted, "would provide a much surer bulwark against Russian imperialism or international Communism than we have now." Also important, Roper skillfully cultivated Christian Herter. A former diplomat and then congress member from Massachusetts, Herter, appointed under-secretary of state in 1957, kept the AUC abreast of State Department thinking, especially the Atlanticist sentiments among some officials, while also working to blunt Dulles's opposition.[104] Following Dulles's death from cancer in spring 1959, Herter became secretary of state, removing a major obstacle to the Department's endorsement of a resolution. In August 1959, a mere four months after Herter's appointment, the State Department signaled to the Senate foreign relations committee it "has no objection to the proposed resolution." A more formal "memorandum of consent" came in January 1960.[105]

Yet however important Nixon's support and Herter's appointment surely were, they need to be placed in the larger context of the growing concern in Washington policy circles regarding NATO's health and future. Here, Henry Kissinger provides a revealing barometer. Along with an academic position at Harvard, Kissinger worked as a paid advisor to Nelson Rockefeller during the 1950s, and in this role he had discussed Atlantic union with Streit. At the time, Kissinger was striving to make his name as a policy expert, someone who could aspire to high-appointed office. His strategy for attracting attention involved exploiting Cold War alarmism; still more to the point, NATO's deficiencies figured prominently in this strategy. The "goal of Western policy," Kissinger declared in a 1960 book, "must be to develop greater cohesion and a new sense of purpose" within the "Atlantic alliance" – a task, he suggested, that required the

---

[104] UCASC, Elmo Roper Papers, Box 10, file 578, Roper to Richard Nixon, February 4, 1957; and Box 10, file 586, Roper to Adolph Schmidt, December 12, 1957. Also see Weisbrode, *The Atlantic Century*, 147.

[105] CLA, RG 46, U.S. Senate, 86A-E8, Box 49, William Macomber (State Department) to Senator Fulbright, August 25, 1959.

United States "to examine carefully the possibility of creating federal institutions comprising the entire North Atlantic community ..."[106]

In making his case, Kissinger could draw on the work of leading scholars in his discipline of political science/IR. In the late 1950s, Karl Deutsch, a professor at MIT and then Yale, headed an interdisciplinary research project on "security communities." In a 1957 book, Deutsch and his collaborators examined what they identified as an ongoing process of North Atlantic political integration centered on NATO. This integration, they proposed, could take one of two forms: a "pluralist" arrangement without formal political structures or an "amalgamated" one along the lines of the AUC's (and Streit's) federalist-oriented project. Although questioning the political feasibility of the latter, they left no doubt that NATO's political status quo was unviable.[107]

Talk of North Atlantic political integration was not limited to Kissinger and his academic colleagues. An internal State Department report in 1960 on North Atlantic relations, for example, considered the possibility of an "Atlantic Confederation." Judging the option "premature at this stage," the report nevertheless remarked that "[i]t should not ... be foreclosed." Equally if not more promising for the AUC were the comments soon afterward of J. W. Fulbright, the chairman of the Senate foreign relations committee. NATO members, he insisted, must "press forward in the development of supranational institutions." "The time is now ripe overdue, for the vigorous developments of its [NATO's] non-military potentialities, for its development as an instrument of Atlantic community."[108]

Two points are worth making concerning the discussion of NATO's future. First, it was not simply a question of the nature of the military alliance.[109] From the outset, the subject of NATO was wrapped up in understandings of the North Atlantic as a distinct region, one defined in

---

[106] Henry A. Kissinger, *The Necessity of Choice: Prospects of American Foreign Policy* (New York: Harper & Brothers, 1960), 165–68.

[107] Karl W. Deutsch, Sidney A. Burrell, Robert A. Kann et al., *Political Community and the North Atlantic Area: International Organization in the Light of Historical Experience* (Princeton, NJ: Princeton University Press, 1957).

[108] "The North Atlantic Nations: Tasks for the 1960's," Bowie, August 1960, *FRUS, 1958–1960*, vol. VII, part 1, 637; and J. W. Fulbright, "For a Concert of Free Nations," *Foreign Affairs* 40 (October 1961), 14–16.

[109] Timothy Andrews Sayle, *Enduring Alliance: A History of NATO and the Postwar Global Order* (Ithaca, NY: Cornell University Press, 2019); and Paul Poast, *Arguing about Alliances: The Art of Agreement in Military-Pact Negotiations* (Ithaca, NY: Cornell University Press, 2019), 135–68.

historical and civilizational terms. The driving question was what political form this North Atlantic region required. Second, the budding sense of NATO's inadequacies cannot simply be explained as a response to De Gaulle's challenge to US leadership in the early 1960s.[110] Instead, it was also the product of a long-brewing debate in the United States – and one which the AUC had contributed greatly to nurturing. In this context, the AUC's proposal for a convention of NATO countries "to explore means by which greater cooperation and unity of purpose may be developed" possessed an obvious appeal. And it did all the more so because the AUC, as part of its Fabian policy, emphasized in its political lobbying the exploratory and thus open-ended nature of any convention in which the participants were not committed in advance to any specific outcome.

A combination of reasons, then, pushed the resolution through the Congress in the summer of 1960. For Streit, it was a moment of triumph and he undoubtedly savored the messages of praise he received, including one from Lyndon Baines Johnson, the Democratic leader in the Senate. "I was most happy to play a part in bringing this to the Floor," Johnson wrote Streit, adding, "I think you have some worthwhile ideas."[111] Yet any satisfaction proved fleeting. Eager to attend the upcoming Atlantic convention, Streit politicked hard to be chosen as a participant, enlisting several congress members among others in the effort. To no avail: Streit was not among the twenty people nominated to serve on what became the US Citizens' Commission on NATO. Tellingly, Roper and Kefauver appear to have conspired to exclude him. The resolution authorized the speaker of the House as well as Nixon as vice president to nominate members. In practice, the task fell to the chair of the Senate foreign relations committee (Fulbright). In drawing up a list of names, Fulbright turned to Roper and Kefauver for advice, both of whom omitted Streit from their list of recommended names.[112]

The maneuver to exclude Streit amounted to a continuation of the AUC's "Fabian policy." Once the resolution was passed and an Atlantic convention convoked for January 1962, Roper and his allies hoped to guide the US delegation in a generally federalist direction. To this end,

---

[110] For this view, see Jeffrey Glen Giauque, *Grand Designs and Visions of Unity: The Atlantic Powers and the Reorganization of Europe, 1955–1963* (Chapel Hill: University of North Carolina Press, Press, 2002); and Walter Lippmann, *Western Unity and the Common Market* (Boston: Little, Brown, 1962), 3–4.

[111] LOC, CKS, Box II: 19, file 3, Lyndon B. Johnson to Streit, June 6, 1960.

[112] See the Fulbright-Roper correspondence in the fall of 1960 in CLA, RG 46, US Senate, 86A – E8, Box 48.

Roper succeeded in getting several AUC people appointed to the citizens' commission, and a few in key positions (Clayton as cochair, Roper himself as vice-chair, and Dick Wallace as director). At the same time, as Roper understood, the commission had to include a broad spectrum of opinion on Atlantic unity, an implicit condition for congressional approval of a resolution – as well as a corollary of the AUC's lobbying strategy. Significantly, stiff resistance to federalist frameworks came from Herter, Roper's fellow cochair, who had been replaced as secretary of state when the Kennedy administration assumed office. During preparatory meetings, Herter consistently opposed efforts to forge a consensus within the commission, maintaining he "could not think of anything worse than for the co-chairmen to try to force a specific line of thought on anyone."[113]

From Roper's perspective, Streit as a commission member would complicate attempts to work out a consensus, as his proselytizing for Atlantic federal union risked alienating potential allies. No less worrying, Streit's identification with a hardline federalist approach to Atlantic union risked compromising any results a convention might achieve. Writing to Clayton in May 1961, Roper confided that Streit had "become our greatest liability":

I am sick at heart that the great prophet, Clarence Streit, can't be a delegate to the convention which he worked so hard for, but honesty compels me to say that if he were a delegate, I do not believe that recommendations of the convention – whatever they were – would have a ghost of passing the United States Senate.[114]

Streit had no choice but to watch from the sidelines.

THE DENOUEMENT: FROM ATLANTIC UNION TO ATLANTIC COMMUNITY

Roper arguably miscalculated. He failed to cajole the US citizens' commission to forge a consensus on Atlantic unity, with the result that the US delegates to the Paris convention in January 1962 voiced a myriad of positions, several of which opposed federalist frameworks. To be sure, there is little to suggest that a federal union found significant support among the other national delegations, which, like the US one, comprised

---

[113] HTPL, William L. Clayton Papers, Box 147, file 7, "Minutes of the Meeting of the U.S. Commissioners for NATO October 12, 1961."

[114] HTPL, William L. Clayton Papers, Box 151, file 4, Roper to Clayton, May 9, 1961.

an assortment of viewpoints. Tellingly, although a conference of NATO parliamentarians in November 1959 had endorsed the idea of a "special conference" of "representative citizens ... to recommend how greater co-operation and unity of purpose" could be developed, it studiously avoided mention of any concrete measures, least of all federal union.[115]

Not surprisingly, the Paris convention produced a "declaration" long on sentiments of Atlantic unity but short on meaningful recommenda-tions, aside from working to develop existing NATO institutions. Reporting on the convention, Roper explained that "[s]ome of us" worked for "the strongest declaration that could be made without pro-voking minority reports and of having any delegations pack up and go home." The imperative on compromise, though, meant avoiding "the use of any words which have proved inflammatory because their meanings are so widely misunderstood." Another delegate, Hugh Moore, was blunter still. In Paris, Moore conceded, "[W]e avoided like poison, and voted down any suggestion that such words as government, federation and union be used ..."[116]

At first glance, the Paris convention appears to have been something of a damp squib. It received little media attention at the time, a point Herter, who chaired the proceedings, inadvertently admitted in remarking that Streit's magazine, *Freedom & Union*, had provided the best coverage. A longer look, however, reveals the convention's importance: It helped to crystallize what soon became the dominant US approach to Atlanticism (transatlantic relations) – an approach reflected in the term "community" as opposed to "union." The US citizens' commission's report to Congress, likely drafted by Roper, encapsulated this emerging approach. The report presented NATO countries in Cold War civilizational terms, as a com-munity whose members were "united in a concept of government both modest and liberating, based on a faith in the possibilities of human lives lived in freedom." From this perspective, greater cohesion and coordin-ation of policies (political, economic, cultural) among Atlantic commu-nity member countries were certainly desirable, and even necessary both to combat Communism and to ensure the continuing flourishing of "our civilization." At the same time, more formal political structures were

[115] LOC, Percival F. Brundage Papers, Box 15, "Resolution Adopted Unanimously by the Fifth NATO Parliamentarians' Conference ... November 20, 1959: and ibid., LOC, CKS, Box II: 15, file, "Declaration of Paris," January 1962.
[116] HTPL, William L. Clayton Papers, Box 147, file 10, "Memorandum," Roper, February 5, 1962; and PUFL, Hugh Moore Fund Collection, Box 13, folder 6, Moore to William Clayton, February 12, 1960.

unnecessary, at least for the time being. Instead, like a living organism, the Atlantic community would be left to develop at its own pace and direction, without interference from governments. Community was very much a passive rather than active conception.[117]

That this conception of transatlantic relations left no room for federalist frameworks is evident from the emergence of the Atlantic Council, which would become the principal political vehicle of Atlanticism within the United States. The Atlantic Council's immediate origins lie in the wake of the congressional resolution in 1960, which triggered a debate within the AUC about its future. As early as November 1960, Adolph Schmidt informed Streit the AUC should be replaced with "something of a new and fresh nature" possessing "a new structure and new directions." Schmidt had in mind a well-funded and elitist organization of "men and women of genuine national stature" committed to propagating a Cold War-infused vision of the "Atlantic and free world nations" centered on NATO. The new organization would studiously steer clear of federalist talk. The Atlantic Council, a 1961 circular explained, "does not limit itself to a single solution" but will "support all responsible proposals designed to achieve greater Atlantic unity." Eschewing any intention of creating a "'grass-roots' organization," its founders envisaged "a smaller one whose membership guarantees that it will command attention and respect."[118]

The appeal of Schmidt's idea was soon apparent, as numerous AUC members signed up to the new organization, among them Roper, Hartley, and Clayton. Other prominent signees included Kissinger. Further evidence of the new organization's orientation came from the choice of its first chairman, none other than Herter. A small group hoped to keep the AUC going, but they lacked the numbers, resources, and convincing strategy to do so. Accordingly, in 1961 the AUC was quietly dissolved and the Atlantic Council moved into the former's office space in Washington.

Institutionally speaking, then, the Atlantic Council replaced the AUC. But there was more to it: The Atlantic Council's Atlanticism was defined largely in opposition to Streit-inspired federalist frameworks. Herter,

---

[117] For Herter, see HTPL, William L. Clayton Papers, Box 147, file 10, "Minutes of the Meeting of the U.S. Commissioners on NATO, March 8, 1962 ..."; and file 7, "Report to Congress on the Atlantic Convention of NATO Nations Paris, January 8–20, 1962."

[118] LOC, CKS, Box I: 33, file: Schmidt, Adolph W. 1949–1969, Schmidt to Streit, November 3, 1960; and ibid., Box 95, Justin Blackwelder to Elmo Rope, May 22, 1961.

himself, insisted on this point in a 1960 book published by Harper, whose editor, Cass Canfield, joined the Council. Invoking Cold War dangers to make the case for a "true Atlantic Community," Herter not only refrained from offering any framework, espousing instead a formless "process of evolution," but he also poured cold water on the aim of "political unity," describing it as "vaguely remote." Still more pertinently, he warned against a "dogmatic approach" by which he meant a "federal mechanism." In addition to downplaying the analogy between the thirteen colonies in the 1780s and the Atlantic countries today, a foundational pillar of Streit's vision, Herter rejected the latter's call for a "federated Atlantic union," concluding that "[f]rom a practical standpoint I do not believe it is possible to proceed in that way. I have felt that an evolutionary process – one, in fact, which is already under way – could alone bring us eventually to effective and lasting political commitments."[119] In private, Herter reassured State Department officials, with whom he remained in close contact, that his vision of Atlantic Community "differed from Clarence Streit's approach."[120]

Streit gracefully accepted an invitation to join the Atlantic Council, telling Herter he could hardly decline when it numbered "so many dear friends."[121] But his bitterness was palpable. Stung by the turn of events, Streit sought solace and renewed purpose in two organizations. One was the IMAU whose letterhead remained more impressive than its actual political presence but whose continued existence allowed Streit to convince himself (and a few others) that Atlantic federal union constituted an international movement. The other organization was Federal Union, whose federalist bona fides Streit carefully watched over. Under his guidance, Federal Union continued to lobby Congress to convoke a constitutional convention of Atlantic countries. In 1973, a Federal Union-backed resolution passed the Senate but failed to proceed in the House. Although stalwarts such as Paul Findley (Rep-Illinois) pledged to continue the struggle, the issue's political relevance quickly receded.[122]

In the end, the AUC contributed less to NATO's development than it did to promoting the conception of the Atlantic as a distinct and vital region. Indeed, the AUC became a prominent, if not the preeminent,

[119] Herter, *Toward an Atlantic Community*, 32, 55–56, 69–70, 76. Also see his "Atlantica," *Foreign Affairs* 41 (1963), 310–22.
[120] BLCU, Declaration of Atlantic Unity, Box 32, Herter to Schmidt, August 27, 1961 with attachment: "Memorandum for the Record," July 24, 1961.
[121] LOC, AUC, Box 95, Streit to Herter, July 18, 1961.
[122] ALPL, Paul Findley Papers, Box 126, Findley to Ray Morgan, April 17, 1973.

advocate of focusing US foreign relations on the Atlantic at a time when, it bears stressing, other regions competed fiercely for Washington's attention in the dual context of decolonization and global Cold War. Equally significant, the AUC's vision of the Atlantic was notably circumscribed. Although Roper rejected accusations that Atlantic union amounted to "a white man's club," the AUC throughout its life said little about the world beyond the north Atlantic while also carefully avoiding the subject of empire, whether European or American.[123] And, here, its talk of democracy as a common transatlantic heritage possessed a dual function, linking together the north Atlantic countries, even if some were non-democracies (hence the value of democracy as an abstraction), while distinguishing these countries from others in the second and third worlds.

This focus on a geographically circumscribed Atlantic had its domestic equivalent in the AUC's membership, which was almost exclusively white. Under Jim Crow, the rare African American member, such as the civil rights activist Sadie Alexander, found herself unable to attend AUC conventions in Memphis in 1951 and Louisville in 1956 because she would be denied entry to the hotels. For AUC leaders, Streit among them, the choice of cities amounted to an unfortunate oversight on their part, suggesting not only how little civil rights registered in their worldviews but also the limits of their approach to democracy at home, let alone abroad. The larger point, though, concerns the geographical and racial hierarchies deeply embedded in conceptions of Atlanticism. As the AUC's history makes clear, these hierarchies were not a given but required sustained if not always fully deliberate effort.[124]

---

[123] UCASC, Elmo Roper Papers, Box 9, file 519, Roper to Hubert Humphrey, January 19, 1955.
[124] UOP, Sadie Alexander Papers, Box 56, file 20, Alexander to Walden Moore, October 1, 1951.

Conclusion

Writing to a British acquaintance in March 1951, Walter Lippmann, then at the height of his fame as a foreign affairs commentator, described Clarence Streit as "an old friend" who "has built his whole crusade on an hysterical illusion" – that the federal union of the thirteen American states forged in Philadelphia in 1787 offered a model for the countries of the North Atlantic in the mid-twentieth century. "I regard the campaign as on the whole well-meaning," Lippmann explained in regard to Streit's activities, "but very misguided. Its effect is to miseducate rather than to educate American opinion, at least. But I never attack it or criticize it publicly because there are so many worse things abroad."[1]

Lippmann's letter encapsulates several themes of this book and which, taken together, illustrate Streit's significance for the history of twentieth-century US foreign relations. Lippmann called Streit a friend, and their relationship went back to the 1930s and to Streit's interwar career as a journalist. Early on, Streit had courted Lippmann, soliciting his opinion on – and support for – various ideas for resolving international problems. Lippmann, though, was just one of the many people whom Streit culti-vated as a journalist and then as an activist for Atlantic union. If nothing else, Streit was a determined and accomplished networker. Indeed, traces of his networking efforts can be found in the personal papers of numerous people, a remarkable number of which contain an entry for Streit in the correspondence files. Much more than a personality trait, networking

[1] John Morton Blum, ed., *Public Philosopher: Selected Letters of Walter Lippmann* (New York: Ticknor & Fields, 1985), Lippmann to Robert Brand, March 2, 1951, 561–62.

reflected Streit's understanding of how politics worked: through personal contacts with influential people and through discussion and persuasion.

Streit mobilized his considerable networking skills to publicize *Union Now*, his book-length proposal published in 1939 for a federation of the north Atlantic democracies. If his position as a *New York Times*' correspondent and recognized expert on the League of Nations garnered the book some attention, it was Streit, through his tireless promotional activities, who made *Union Now* into something of a cause célèbre. It is worth emphasizing that Streit had little money and no institutional backing. Relying largely on his own resources, he succeeded in creating a buzz around the book and its striking proposal. This buzz, evident in the extended wave of political commentary, was a notable achievement in itself. But Streit's publicity success also draws attention to the public dimension of politics in the foreign relations realm, and especially its vibrant and accessible nature at the time. This dimension offered possibilities to resourceful policy entrepreneurs such as Streit.

To be sure, Streit's book fell on fertile ground. Beginning in the wake of the Civil War, a veritable cult of the constitution flourished in the United States. One prominent expression of this cult during the interwar years was a celebration of the country's federal system, a phenomenon possessing both popular and more academic elements. In applying the US federal system to the North Atlantic region, Streit was not proposing something new so much as elaborating on a commonplace idea: that the United States offered a political model for export. If the proposal benefited from its familiarity, it also arrived at a propitious moment. In 1939, the nature of the international order and the United States' role in it were becoming urgent questions. With war looming in Europe, with liberal democracy seemingly under siege, and with the League of Nations conspicuously ineffective, many Americans searched for proposals that might prevent war or, if not, could guide the construction of a more durable and peaceful postwar order than the one after 1919. In presenting Atlantic federal union as just such a proposal – and one with the added benefit of being home-grown – Streit's *Union Now* was very much a product of its time.

Yet however important this larger context, Streit's contribution remained vital. His ability to package several disparate elements (federalism, democracy, peaceful international order) into a seemingly coherent whole, as well as his success in publicizing the result, were critical to *Union Now*'s success. The proposal for Atlantic federal union would not have gained the visibility it did without those qualities Lippmann deemed "hysterical": Streit's missionary zeal, his relentless energy, and his unwavering belief in the value and feasibility of his project.

If networking is one theme highlighted in Lippmann's letter, another is Streit's political activities – his "campaign." In writing *Union Now*, Streit's ultimate goal was not to create a buzz. That constituted merely a means to the end of achieving an Atlantic federal union. And this posed challenges. "[T]o get any idea before the public" was hard enough, Streit later acknowledged, but "it is much harder to translate political thought into action."[2] Streit's status as a policy outsider rendered the challenge all the more difficult. Scholars in recent years have explored the influence on US foreign and defense policies of policy insiders such as Hans Speier, Shepard Stone, or Roberta and Albert Wohlstetter, people who quietly labored in think tanks, foundations, and other sites. Unlike them, Streit operated in front of rather than behind the scenes.

In his campaign to achieve Atlantic federal union, Streit adopted several sometimes overlapping but nevertheless distinct approaches. One approach, a product of his penchant for networking, was to woo an influential elite, the political figures, businessmen, financiers, editors, and journalists among others who shaped the contours of public debate on foreign relations in the United States. Another approach was to build a national movement with local chapters across the country, an approach pursued by numerous organizations including America First before December 1941 and the Foreign Policy Association before, during, and after World War II. A third approach consisted of direct political lobbying, both of the executive branch and, after 1945, more and more of Congress.

Each approach had its advantages and its limits. A focus on influence-makers helped Streit to gain visibility and even legitimacy for his project, especially during the wartime years when federalism entered into public debates on the postwar international order. Yet visibility in particular was difficult to sustain, and Streit and his project receded from public view during the second half of the war, though without ever disappearing. Efforts to develop a vibrant national organization ended in disappointment as it proved far easier to create chapters than to keep them active. Despite the claims of several historians and social scientists, the experience of Streit's Federal Union suggests that grass-roots mobilization resembled an ideal far more than a practical reality both during and after

---

[2] LOC, CKS, Box III: 9, file 2, "Political Statement," Streit, July 16, 1953.

World War II. If political lobbying in Washington, DC, had the advantage over the other two approaches of offering a direct entry into the policymaking process, access came at a price. Streit's Atlantic Union project became entangled in the dynamic of congressional political give-and-take, from which it emerged as a pale version of its original form.

Obviously, Streit never managed to craft a winning approach as Atlantic federal union went unrealized. In this sense, his "campaign" was a failure. And this failure undoubtedly goes far in explaining why Streit is now all but forgotten, his public visibility and political activities over several decades unknown. To dismiss Streit as a failure, though, is to misjudge his influence, which was far from fleeting. Admittedly, his project had little, if any, chance of becoming a reality. An Atlantic federal union required far-reaching transformations of constitutional and practical politics in the United States, to say nothing of its implications for other member countries. The obstacles were simply overwhelming. This is not another story of a missed opportunity, of a plausible might-have-been if events had only unfolded in slightly different fashion.

That said, the political impracticality of Streit's project renders it all the more intriguing. After all, most proposals for far-reaching political change of various kinds enjoy a short shelf-life; in the best-case scenario, they momentarily attract some attention in the public and even policy worlds before disappearing from view. The remainder bins of bookstores provide plenty of examples. Yet Streit's project possessed considerable staying power, a reality that is ill-captured by the inverted U-shaped curve of *Union Now*'s sales or references to it. What needs to be explained is why – or, better yet, how – Streit and his Atlantic union project remained in the public eye for several decades. For this question holds the key to understanding Streit's influence. In his March 1951 letter, Lippmann lamented that Atlantic federal union had the effect of miseducating the US public – in itself a grudging recognition of Streit's political visibility. A closer look, however, suggests that there is more to Streit's influence than Lippmann's negative assessment suggests.

Streit's influence is most clearly evident in two major debates in twentieth-century US foreign relations. The first debate occurred during World War II and concerned the nature of the postwar international order and the United States' role in it. Thanks in good measure to his promotional efforts, Streit managed to insert federalist frameworks into this wartime debate. Federalism provided a familiar language as well as conceptual lens to many Americans seeking to understand international politics. In so doing, it worked to domesticate the latter. More precisely, talk of federalism assuaged fears of a loss of national sovereignty as the price for greater US involvement in the world – a price opponents of membership in the League of Nations had harped on since 1919. As Streit repeatedly contended, the situation facing the United States could be likened to that of the thirteen colonies/states in the 1780s. Much like the articles of confederation, the League of Nations had failed to ensure sufficient unity among its members, prompting the conclusion that federal union was the answer now as it had been then. No less importantly, the domestic analogy at the heart of Streit's federalist project also tempered the stakes involved in federal union: Rather than a zero-sum proposition (the maintenance or loss of sovereignty), the issue became the more mundane one of jurisdiction between different levels of government.

At the same time, once federalist frameworks entered into the public dimension of politics, they became vulnerable to appropriation by other actors for other ends. And this is precisely what happened during World War II. Faced with the challenge of overcoming opposition to a renewal of the interwar League of Nations, widely judged by 1939 to have been a dismal failure, proponents of a postwar United Nations Organization (UNO) seized on federalism as means to rehabilitate international organizations in general and to promote their project in particular. James Shotwell, Clark Eichelberger, and Quincy Wright among others deftly labored to separate federalism from Streit's Atlantic federal union. In a bitter irony for Streit, his success in publicizing federation contributed to precisely the outcome his project was designed to prevent – an international order centered on interstate organizations and especially on a revamped League of Nations. Although the UNO's emergence was arguably over-factored, Streit's allergy to compromise – evident in the refusal to collaborate with the Commission to Study the Organization of the Peace – not only denied him an influential forum for advocacy but also left others free to exploit federalism's popularity. But faulty calculations aside, a crucial point is that the development of wartime internationalism in the United States cannot be understood without including federalist frameworks – and thus Streit.

The second debate highlighting Streit's influence concerns postwar Atlanticism. During the 1950s and well into the 1960s, the nature of transatlantic relations figured prominently on the political agenda. Much of the debate centered on the question of NATO's future: Should NATO remain a military alliance or should it be broadened to encompass some element of political collaboration and even integration? Within Washington political and policy circles, no group did more to emphasize the urgency of this question than the Atlantic Union Committee (AUC), a lobby group founded in 1949. From the beginning, Streit was hyperactive within the AUC as a fund-raiser and lobbyist but also as a political actor who strove to mobilize the committee behind his Atlantic federal union project.

If the AUC led the charge within Washington for a more developed political structure for NATO, within the committee itself Streit's version of Atlanticism faced mounting competition. Indeed, by the early 1960s an alternative version of Atlanticism had emerged, one largely defined in opposition to Streit's federal union. Rejecting the latter, its proponents envisaged the Atlantic countries as a community whose informal political structures would be the exclusive preserve of a coterie of like-minded political and economic elites centered in and on Washington. The embodiment of this alternative Atlanticism would be the Atlantic Council, which emerged as a successor organization to the AUC, literally taking over its offices in Washington. Well-funded and politically connected, the Atlantic Council today is the preeminent advocate for transatlantic relations within the United States. In what amounted to another bitter irony for Streit, in the end Atlantic federal union functioned as a foil for the articulation of an Atlanticism that effectively precluded his own project.

Whether it was wartime internationalism or postwar Atlanticism, Streit did exert a notable influence on US foreign relations. It was just not in the way he had hoped. What for Streit amounted to bitter ironies point to some of the hazards of political activism. Like several of Streit's journalist colleagues during the 1930s, Lippmann for the most part eschewed the political fray, preferring to influence policymaking indirectly by way of political commentary aimed at orienting policy in a general sense rather than promoting a definite program. Streit, by contrast, sought to achieve just such a program, a goal that pushed him toward political activism. Yet, as Streit discovered, the politics of political activism could be treacherous. There was the reality of unequal resources, and Streit's ambitions perennially outran his means. But there was another and arguably under-appreciated reality: the risk of losing ownership of one's project. In the heat of political battle, Streit could not prevent federalist frameworks, which he had done so much to publicize, from being appropriated by other actors pursuing different goals. Politics is a messy business, and political activism can lead to perverse outcomes, at least from the perspective of the activist.

Whatever their differences, Lippmann refrained from publicly criticizing Streit's Atlantic federal union project, remarking in his March

1951 letter that "there are so many worse things abroad." If friendship likely had something to do with this restraint, the two men also shared a larger purpose. Throughout their lengthy careers, Lippmann and Streit, each in his own way, promoted the idea of the North Atlantic as a distinct region whose states and peoples possessed a common historical, cultural, and political heritage. For both men, it followed that the Atlantic region deserved a privileged place in US foreign relations. Like so many others, Lippmann and Streit endeavored to naturalize this conception, rooting it in geographical, demographical, historical, political, and economic factors. Yet the idea of the North Atlantic as a distinct region did not simply spring from past and present "realities." It was always a construct, one that required – and continues to require – political work. This is all the truer in the twentieth century when, in a context of globalizing international politics, other regions and continents vied for the attention of the US public and policy-makers. If the conception of the Atlantic region as a distinct and privileged region continues to resonate in the United States, it is because of the sustained efforts of its promoters. In this way, as in others, Streit and his Atlantic federal union project were far from marginal to the history of twentieth-century US foreign relations.

List of Archives

Abraham Lincoln Presidential Library (Springfield, IL)
    Paul Findley Papers
British Library of Political and Economic Science (London, UK)
    Federal Trust Papers
Center for Legislative Archives (Washington, DC)
    Senate and House files
Columbia University, Butler Library (New York, NY)
    Carnegie Corporation of New York Records, 1872–2000
    Carnegie Endowment for International Peace. New York and Washington
        Office Records, 1910–54
    Declaration of Atlantic Unity Records
    Harper & Row, Publishers Records
    James Shotwell Papers
    Harry Scherman Papers
Dartmouth University, Archives and Manuscripts (Hanover, NH)
    Grenville Clark Papers
Eisenhower Presidential Library (Abilene, KS)
    Dwight D. Eisenhower Papers
    John Foster Dulles Papers
George Washington University, Special Collections Research Center
    (Washington, DC)
    Carnegie Peace Pamphlet and Microfilm Collection
Harry S. Truman Presidential Library (Independence, MO)
    William L. Clayton Papers
    Harry S. Truman Papers
Harvard Business School, Special Collections (Cambridge, MA)
    Thomas W. Lamont Papers
Harvard Law School Library, Historical and Special Collections
    (Cambridge, MA)
    Manley O. Hudson Papers

Harvard University, Houghton Library (Cambridge, MA)
    Jay Pierrepont Moffat Papers
League of Nations Archives (Geneva)
    Association internationale des journalistes accrédités auprès de la Société des Nations
    League of Nations files
Library and Archives Canada (Ottawa)
    Wishart Robertson Papers
Library of Congress (Washington, DC)
    Carl W. Ackerman Papers
    Atlantic Union Committee Papers
    Percival F. Brundage Papers
    Leslie Raymond Buell Papers
    Russell Davenport Papers
    Norman H. Davis Papers
    Philip Jessup Papers
    Clarence Kirschman Streit Papers
    Clare Boothe Luce Papers
    Henry Robinson Luce Papers
    Arthur Sweetser Papers
McMaster University Library (Hamilton, ON)
    George Catlin Fonds
New York Historical Society (New York, NY)
    Henry Luce Papers
    Time Inc. Archives
New York Public Library (New York, NY)
    Campaign for World Government. Records of the Chicago Office
    Campaign for World Government. Records of the New York Office
    Clark Eichelberger Papers
    New York Times Company Records. Adolph S. Ochs Papers
    New York Times Company Records. Arthur Hays Sulzberger Papers
    Schwimmer-Lloyd Collection
    Student Federalists Records
Princeton University, Firestone Library (Princeton, NJ)
    John Foster Dulles Papers
    Selected Papers of Harper & Bros
Princeton University, Seely G. Mudd Manuscript Library (Princeton, NJ)
    Hamilton Fish Armstrong Papers
    Hugh Moore Fund Collection
Rhodes Trust Archives (Oxford, UK)
    Clarence Streit file
Rockefeller Archive Center (Sleepy Hollow, NY)
    Nelson A. Rockefeller gubernatorial records
    Nelson A. Rockefeller Personal Papers
Swarthmore College, Friends Historical Library (Swarthmore, PA)
    Frank Aydelotte Papers

University of Chicago, Hanno Holborn Gray Special Collections Research Center (Chicago, IL)
    Quincy Wright Papers
University of Connecticut, Archives and Special Collections (Storrs, CT)
    Elmo Roper Papers
University of Indiana, Lilly Library (Bloomington, IN)
    United World Federalist Papers
University of Iowa Libraries (Iowa City, IO)
    Guy M. Gillette Papers
University of Michigan, Bentley Historical Library (Ann Arbor, MI)
    Clare E. Hoffman Papers
    Stellanova Osborn Papers
University of Montana, Mansfield Library, Archives and Special Collections (Missoula, MT)
    Mike Mansfield Papers
    Clarence Streit Papers
University of Oregon, University Archives Collections (Eugene, OR)
    Atlantic Union Committee Records, 1949–54
University of Pennsylvania, University Archives and Records Center (Philadelphia, PA)
    Sadie Tanner Mossell Alexander Papers
University of Pittsburgh (Pittsburgh, PA)
    Adolph William Schmidt Collection
University of Tennessee, Betsey B. Creekmore Special Collections and University Archives (Knoxville, TN)
    Estes Kefauver Papers
Williams College, Archives and Special Collections (Williamstown, MA)
    Frederick Lewis Schuman Papers
Yale University Library, Manuscripts and Archives (New Haven, CT)
    Chester Bowles Papers
    William C. Bullitt Papers
    Elizabeth Page Harris Papers
    Chase Kimball Papers
    Walter Lippmann Papers

Index

Printed in the USA
CPSIA information can be obtained
at www.ICGtesting.com
LVHW010807030124
767616LV00031B/74